QUEER INTENTIONS

Amelia Abraham

QUEER INTENTIONS

A (personal) journey through LGBTQ+ culture

PICADOR

First published 2019 by Picador
an imprint of Pan Macmillan
20 New Wharf Road, London N1 9RR
Associated companies throughout the world
www.panmacmillan.com

ISBN 978-1-5098-6616-8 HB

1 3 5 7 9 8 6 4 2

A CIP catalogue record for this book is available from the British Library.

Typeset in Dante MT Std by Palimpsest Book Production Limited, Falkirk, Stirlingshire
Printed and bound by CPI Group (UK) Ltd, Croydon, CR0 4YY

For Emily, and my grandmother, Doreen

A NOTE FROM THE AUTHOR

From LGBT to LGBTQIA+, there are lots of ways of referring to our community. I have decided to use LGBTQ+ throughout this book as an inclusive shorthand for 'lesbian', 'gay', 'bisexual', 'transgender', 'queer' and other identity categories like intersex and asexual. That said, mainly in the Istanbul chapter, I have used the term LGBTI because this is what is generally used locally. Elsewhere, I have stayed true to my interviewees' acronyms of choice within their quotes. When I am speaking about a specific subsection of the LGBTQ+ community I have named this subsection. Similarly, I have used the word 'queer' where relevant, either as an umbrella term for the identities that fall under LGBTQ+, or to refer to a more radically politicized sector of the LGBTQ+ community. I hope this usage becomes obvious in context.

A note on pronouns: I have used the pronouns that my interviewees asked me to use at the time of writing. I acknowledge that these may have changed, or might still.

And finally, on a couple of occasions names or other minor details have been changed to protect privacy.

A (NOT SO) QUEER TIME AND PLACE

There's something acutely embarrassing about crying on an easyJet flight. I could tell I was making everyone feel uncomfortable, but I couldn't stop. I was blinkered by the unparalleled narcissism of break-up misery. The kind of cloying break-up misery that will evolve from *Will I make it from my bed to the shower ever again?* to *Why won't this bottle of wine fit into the pint glass?* to *Am I going to die from this?* The kind of break-up misery you experience when you're not just mourning the loss of an individual, but also the grand narrative of a life together. I was crying because one version of the future had slipped away again, and I was back to an uncertain one.

The easyJet flight landed at Luton airport, which is the least welcoming place imaginable to herald tourists into the UK. There are no posters, no bad patriotic artwork on the walls, just rows of people queuing for security and transfers, like cattle filing into an abattoir. Outside, the area directly through the building's sliding doors is always crowded with men sucking on rolled-up cigarettes, bagless, so you can't tell if they're arriving, departing, or even catching a flight at all. I stood with them and puffed on a cigarette of my own. The crying had stopped, and I enjoyed the mundanity of watching tourists wheeling suitcases across the car park as a burst of sunshine hit my face. I realized I hadn't seen the sun for almost two weeks.

My journey had carried me home from a remote part of Iceland called Ísafjörður, where there had been only a few hours of daylight, the sky had been a constant shade of grey and the wind had felt like a chemical peel. I'd moved there to be with my girlfriend, Salka. It was a Wednesday evening, earlier that year, when we matched on Tinder. I was the last person in my office and I had nowhere to be, so I started chatting with the smiling headshot in my hand. By the time the conversation had outrun my commute home, it became clear that this person on my phone wasn't interested in small talk. Maybe it was an Icelandic thing. Maybe while British people want to make banal conversation about their hangovers, weekends and mutual friends, Icelandic people want to know your hopes and fears for the future, what you look for in a partner, and whether this conversation is going anywhere. My mum told me this is how the over-fifties behave on dating apps – an age bracket, she said, in typically morbid fashion, with no time to waste 'because we are all going to die soon'. I wasn't expecting this brilliant level of directness from a beautiful twenty-six-year-old redhead, and it charmed me almost instantly.

'Do you want to go for a drink?' I asked before I went to bed that night, assuming she lived in London.

'I was in London last week,' she typed. 'Now I'm back home.'

I absolutely cannot tell you what inspired me to book a

flight to Iceland three weeks later. But I can tell you that it was out of character. Maybe it was because I was dating a few people in London that flying for two and a half hours to meet a pure stranger didn't have the air of desperation that it might otherwise have had. Besides, we'd FaceTimed to make sure she wasn't a catfish.

'This is how all good Nordic crime dramas start,' my flatmate said as I packed my bag. 'She's going to murder you with an ice pick.'

Other friends thought it was romantic: 'Maybe you'll fall in love and start behaving like an adult.'

I was unprepared for both eventualities, so I pretended I was writing a travel article and blagged a free hotel room as a backup in case something went drastically wrong. Only, I never checked into the hotel room. When we first met, in a sun-drenched bus station car park not unlike the one at Luton airport, she walked right up to me and kissed me. For the next few hours, our bodies were in constant contact; making out, lying in one another's laps, holding hands. It felt like the first time you fall in love, when you're naive and fearless because you don't know what a broken heart can do to you yet. It was like every bad romcom, except this time, both of the protagonists were girls.

Conversation with Salka wasn't all that different from talking on the phone – only now the words fell out faster. We told the usual pretentious stories that you tell when you're trying to impress someone new: how she'd once moved to South America alone; how I cried after I inter-viewed my heroes. But neither of us really listened to the other showing off because we were too distracted by the mounting question of when we were going to sleep together. It happened early evening. Immediately after, lying in bed together, she asked me if I wanted to go and have dinner at her parents' house. I felt relieved, almost, as though if she hadn't done something so psycho that first day it would have all felt like a giant prank – like I'd landed someone too 'normal' for me. I think it was the relief that compelled me to agree, coupled with the fact that I wanted to see more of her life, and I had only two days in which to do so.

We drove out West, to her family's weatherboard house in the middle of nowhere and when we got there, she showed me around. In their lounge, a huge reindeer head was mounted on the wall. Salka explained that her dad had shot and killed it, and I suddenly got a strange feeling in my stomach. It seemed to be telling me that, if anything went wrong, my head would end up next to that reindeer's. And yet, at the same time, I felt like I wanted to stay there forever. It was all very exciting.

Over the next six months, the excitement between Salka and me turned out to be very expensive. We would fly back and forth to visit one another, and if we couldn't be together physically, we would talk constantly in between.

This wasn't my first relationship – I'd had several – but this time, things were different: I'd never been so sure about someone so quickly, and a wedding, kids and old age played out in my mind like a tightly edited trailer for a film. Before we'd met, looking into a child's eyes had still felt like staring down the barrel of a gun, but over the course of six months, Salka slowly began to desensitize me to the idea of having children by talking about them constantly. When I was hanging out with her, it felt as though everywhere we went together – the supermarket, the public baths (as popular in Iceland as, say, pubs are in England) or restaurants – we ran into friends of Salka's who had babies, and faster than I would have expected, their lives became the blueprint for our own.

When we realized a long-distance relationship was no longer sustainable, we agreed that I should move to Iceland, and I found that I was willing to give up my job, flat and friends in London to pursue a semblance of what 'forever' looks like – moving in together, pooling our funds, arguing over baby names. So I put the wheels in motion, quitting my job and giving notice on my flat. But I never mentioned that I was sacrificing anything, because for Salka it meant too much responsibility. 'Tell me you're not doing this all for me,' she'd say dramatically. And so I just pretended I'd woken up one day as a child and realized it was my dream to live in Iceland.

Back in London, I didn't know any children, but I had definitely not been acting like a grown-up: going out constantly, exhibiting a general disregard for financial planning, failing at monogamy with most of the people I had been dating. My friends, even those in long-term relationships or in their thirties, didn't seem interested in kids. Many were gay men who had casual sex and casual relationships by choice, and would stare at me blankly if I asked them whether they'd considered the idea of starting a family, some because they had been brutally rejected by their own. In my immediate friendship group, we'd

occasionally discuss which of the gay men would impreg-
nate which of the lesbians and where we should base our
queer commune. But we hadn't turned it into a reality
yet, preoccupied as we were with existences that centred
on underpaid creative jobs, social media, clubbing,
chemsex, drinking all of the free wine at art openings,
fucking our way through dating apps, dealing with mental-
health problems, throwing ad hoc drag pageants, and
incessantly talking about ourselves.

To us, the idea that everyone ought to fall into distinct
categories of 'hetero' or 'home' was a ridiculous one. But
at the same time, what these categories meant beyond sex
itself felt real. 'Hetero' didn't necessarily mean being in a
straight relationship or even having straight sex, it meant
heteronormativity: having your shit together in the boring,
traditional sense of the term. It meant falling into comple-
mentary gender roles, marrying someone of the opposite
sex, and staying faithful till death do you part. Our very
existence as people – as gender variant, same-sex attracted
and potentially likely to cheat with a stranger in a club at
4 a.m. – meant that this wasn't really an option for us. So
did our economic situations (as one friend told me: 'Maybe
you could buy a flat if you stopped buying trainers,' to
which I couldn't help but think, I wish I had six thousand
pairs of trainers). Instead, we opted for what we saw as
queerer ways of living: rejecting conformity, making irre-
sponsible decisions, attempting to be more free. Or at least,
that was my life . . . until I met Salka and she told me she
wanted to marry me someday, which wasn't the first time
I realized I might be able to settle down – that happened

when same-sex marriage was legalized – just the first time I thought I might want to.

I prepared for my new normative lifestyle as if I was preparing for the apocalypse; I purchased thermals, said goodbye to my friends and put all my belongings into storage. Meanwhile, as my moving date grew closer, Salka grew more distant. She reassured me – work had been busy – but I could feel the gulf between us for the first time. 'You're moving there in three weeks. She should be buying you a double gym membership, not ignoring your calls,' my best friend told me. I didn't know what to say. Things were getting so bad between us that I had gone into a state of denial, and still hadn't booked my flight. When Salka did bother to contact me, we laughed less and argued more, the pressure of the decision we'd made, and the speed at which we'd made it, creating a palpable tension. Still, 'We've come this far,' we both reasoned, 'maybe things will be better when we're together.'

They weren't. When I got to Iceland, Salka didn't pick me up from the airport, she hadn't cleared out a drawer for me, and she had made a lot of plans that didn't involve me. These should, in hindsight, have been tell-tale signs that things weren't as they should be – especially for me as a journalist, who gets paid, albeit not very much, to notice things – but out of her mouth came all the words you want the person you're in love with to say to you: 'I love you,' for example. It was just that her behaviour didn't match up.

In the end, my move to Iceland lasted just ten days.

Yes, ten days.

And we spent the last five breaking up.

If you've ever seen the French film *Blue Is the Warmest Colour*, you'll know what a long, drawn-out lesbian break-up looks like. If you haven't, it's a lot of sex, arguing and crying – like straight people's break-ups; only with lesbians, all three happen at the same time.

The decision I made to come home was one of the hardest I'd ever made – we didn't leave one another on bad terms, just very confused terms. She was confused about how you can love someone so much and still not feel 100 per cent sure that they're right for you. I was confused about why we couldn't just 'be', but always had to be deep in love or deep in an argument, with no middle ground in between. I think maybe Salka didn't trust that I was a forever type of person, and no grand gesture from me – not even moving to another country – was going to be enough to prove otherwise. Maybe, deep down, I didn't believe I was a forever type of person either. In that sense, we both got catfished in the end, in the same way a lot of people in relationships do; you hope for one thing and you get another. It's not the other person's fault, it's just that your particular dynamic makes you act like strange versions of yourselves, until you can no longer control, or even recognize, who you are any more.

However we would come to see that break-up in the future, one thing was clear: I didn't want to be back in the UK, standing outside Luton airport. I still desperately wished I was with Salka, in whichever country she was living in.

★

A few weeks after my return from Iceland, I called my friend Amrou Al-Kadhi. I first met Amrou in 2015, at a performance event where our mutual friend was doing drag. Amrou – pronoun 'they' – was also a drag queen, in a drag troupe called Denim, whom I'd seen perform on stage at Glastonbury Festival one year when I was there for work. Denim met at the University of Cambridge in 2008 and had a reputation for being quite political – they didn't just lip-sync, but sang live covers (they all have great voices), and wrote original shows that covered topics like racism and homophobia, always with trash and hilarity. If the film-maker John Waters did the Spice Girls, you'd get something like Denim: a girl band made up of five people in drag performing ludicrous characters like soccer mom Aphrodite Green. Amrou's character was called Glamrou La Denim, a Middle Eastern goddess inspired by their mother's glamorous brand of Iraqi femininity – which was fitting given that Glamrou played the mother of the group too, bossing all the other queens about.

When I first saw Amrou perform as Glamrou, I immediately developed a friendship crush. So I did what I usually do in that situation: asked if we could do an interview. 'My autobiography would be called *Hijabs to Hollywood*,' was the first thing they said to me, sitting on a faded avocado-green sofa in their living room, in full drag, wearing a pink wig and silver stilettos. 'The sequel would be *From Burkas to Bikinis*,' Amrou continued, 'and then *From Quran to Queen*.' I said I probably couldn't publish the last one because it might annoy people too much.

Undeterred, Amrou went on to explain how their parents

are from Baghdad, and how they grew up between Britain, Jordan, Bahrain and Dubai. They were encouraged from a young age to behave as a Muslim boy is expected to: masculine, straight and observant of Islam. But for Amrou, this was impossible. When their parents found gay porn in their bedroom at sixteen, they ordered Amrou to step back into the closet. 'This is a phase,' they said. 'You have to get over it.' Then, when Amrou was twenty-one, their parents spotted a G-A-Y club stamp on their wrist and realized the phase wasn't over. They reacted by throwing away anything Amrou owned that was pink, as though this would magically cure them of their gayness. It didn't, and now, with their parents living in the Middle East and Amrou based in the UK, the two parties just 'agree to disagree'. There's a whole terrain of conversation that they don't cover and when Amrou saw their mum recently, she urged them to marry a girl.

Whenever a relationship ends, I dread talking to certain friends because, as you tell them about your break-up, you can see the cogs turning in their minds: *Another one bites the dust*, they think, working out that the common factor in all the failure is in fact you. But I knew Amrou wouldn't make me feel like that – not because I hadn't known them long enough for them to have seen all the others come and go, but because they weren't judgemental.

'This is just the end of a relationship, not the end of your entire life,' Amrou told me as we sat in Dalston Superstore, a gay bar where we'd both, separately, spent most of our early twenties, single and trying to chat people up. It was a stupid place to meet; it just emphasized that we were *still* single but now even older.

'Look, you've gotten over a relationship before and you will again,' they continued.

I protested that it wasn't the same before, that I had never actually expected to spend the rest of my life with someone. Which was true, but part of me was also sick of hearing these kinds of post-break-up platitudes.

'Settling down with someone is just one way of doing things,' Amrou reminded me.

We ordered a drink and Amrou started telling me the story of an Arab wedding they had gone to over the summer, and how it stood for everything that bothered them about hetero-normative institutions like marriage. 'It was my cousin's wedding in Mykonos. It was incredibly lavish. Everyone was in couples. I remember a moment when my cousin took me to one side and said, "Don't *you* want all this, Amrou?"'

They mimed a sympathetic head tilt and outstretched their arm as though they were offering me the scene of a beautiful wedding in front of us. 'I was like: "Umm, no, not really, but I'm happy for you."' Amrou said the cousin seemed annoyed at this response.

'I don't know,' Amrou continued. 'I think it's unfair. Why are we expected to celebrate straight people's choices and to want to make the choices they make, but when it comes to ours they don't get celebrated? I mean, where are the hallmarks for us? No one sent me a bunch of flowers after the last time I sucked off a stranger in a dark room.'

I told Amrou I still felt ambivalent; I agreed, obviously, but I was worried that Salka had shown me an ugly truth: that I just wanted to have a lavish wedding in Mykonos.

'Don't you ever feel like that?' I asked.

'I get what you're saying,' Amrou said. 'I definitely experience it at work.'

Amrou explained that, while Denim perform in gay bars and stage fundraisers for queer organizations all the time, personally they had become near fixated on the need to transgress straight spaces, which basically meant seeking out gigs at brand parties or big festivals or kids' birthday parties and bar mitzvahs.

'Do you feel weird about it?' I said.

'All the time,' they said quietly. 'But I think it's just about wanting to be accepted or feel legitimate, isn't it?'

Amrou told me to stop talking to Salka, so I took their advice. There was one weak moment when I screen-grabbed a photo of her with someone else on Instagram and texted it to her with the question: 'WHO THE FUCK IS THIS?' But other than that, I remained composed. Mostly I just wrote her letters that I never sent. I cried at dinner parties. I went on a break-up speaking tour, boring all of my friends while I shaped what had happened into a neat narrative with a beginning, middle and end, until it began to sound more remote each time I rehashed it. Privately, I would go through our messages to one another, as though I was in a Netflix crime documentary where combing over old evidence was going to bring to light something new. Instead it just made me feel empty inside. I oscillated between being grateful that she was in another country, so that I wouldn't have to run into her, and missing her small Icelandic town deeply: the imposing mountains, the long open roads, the weatherboard houses, and of course, her.

By day, I started to go for meetings to try to get some freelance work. But I walked into my old office and quickly found myself surrounded by dozens of ex-colleagues asking why I wasn't in Iceland – the emotional equivalent of having a beehive thrown at you. I deflected, turning the whole story into a joke, with 'ten days!' as the punchline. By night, I began to rejoin the same dinner party circuit, went back to the same gay bars. I even started sleeping with someone I knew – a lawyer called Emily who seemed to be the opposite of Salka in every conceivable way. I moved between Emily's flat and friends' sofas in order to get out of my sister's old bedroom, where I had been staying, and before I fell asleep, I would often cry into my pillow (sometimes, while this new strange person was sleeping next to me), not only because I missed Salka, but because my life had no structure. I would, at particularly low points, fixate on how she owned a house, had a good job as a doctor, and would probably meet someone new any day now. And when I would cry about the relationship, I would also cry about how heteronormative I sounded, as if our invisible children had been the be-all and end-all, the only road to happiness.

It was around this time that my friend Zoe lent me a book that she said might help. It was called *The Queer Art of Failure*, by the brilliant transgender writer Jack Halberstam. It was about 'finding alternatives to conventional understandings of success in a heteronormative, capitalist society', and asking why we value certain types of success and not others. I'd read one of Halberstam's books before, I told Zoe: *In a Queer Time and Place*, which talked about 'heteronormative time and space' – marriage, kids, domesticity – versus what he called 'queer' time and space, defined as an alternative way of living, more transient and erratic. While some people grow up to do what's expected of them, Halberstam wrote, others never grow up at all – some might see this as selfish, others might see it as a political choice. In *The Queer Art of Failure*, Halberstam goes one step further and asks us to deconstruct conventional life markers, such as settling down and baby making, and consider a life 'unscripted by family, inheritance and child rearing': a queerer way of living.

Zoe told me she found both books after the end of a seven-year relationship with a man, at a time when she was feeling anxious about not being with anyone, about her work, and about being in her thirties and childless. She said it helped her see that she could be radical or queer or refuse the pressures of expectation, particularly as a bisexual woman living in a world that constantly reminds you of what she described as her 'so-called ticking biological clock': 'It made me look around and appreciate the fact that I have a cross-generational group of friends who refuse to conform to the social ideals of an ordered and sensible adult life,' she said. 'It helped me realize that over something structured, I'd rather have anarchy. Or spontaneity.'

Zoe's outlook was exactly what I needed, so I tried to start doing what you might call 'checking my heteronormativity' – stopping myself when I was having self-indulgent thoughts about how I'd never own a home or get another job or find 'the one', and starting to ask myself why I viewed these as markers of success to begin with, why there were right and wrong ways of living that we all subscribed to, why we felt we were meant to jump through certain hoops to be happy. But it wouldn't work; something in me, I realized, had changed.

Eventually, I called my friend Paris Lees and confided in her about how I was feeling. A well-known transgender activist in the UK, she confessed she'd been having similar thoughts.

'Five years ago it was all, "I'm queer, I don't give a fuck, I'm a strong woman, don't care about taboos. Fuck marriage! I'll wear what I like – a suit one day then a dress the next! I'll lick a pussy, and suck a cock, don't slut-shame me . . . I'm Madonna, I'm Kim Cattrall!"' She suddenly inhaled (I hate talking on the phone, but you can never get Paris off it). 'It's like, yeah, that's fun for a bit, isn't it? And then you realize you're left with this big gaping hole – and no, I don't mean what you're thinking! An emotional one.' She paused so I could absorb the poetry of what she had just said, then continued: 'These days I just want to be a middle-class mum who stays at home and bakes for their kids.'

'Really?' I said, surprised to be hearing this from the closest living person I had met to Samantha Jones from *Sex and the City*.

'Yeah. I used to think I didn't want all of this – so maybe I'm just going from one extreme to the other, and maybe I'm never satisfied? But I think we all feel like that, don't we, whether we're straight or gay or trans or whatever? Maybe "I want a husband" is just another fucked-up, perverted fantasy.'

*

Talking to Paris had made me feel less alone, but it hadn't made me any less confused. She was right that most people feel torn over their life options at some point or another – not least after a break-up, which tends to throw even the most resilient person into an existential crisis – but the more people I talked to and the more I thought about it, the clearer it became that this ambivalence is more pronounced for queer people. On the one hand, we have a desire to live differently, to say 'fuck you' to tradition, to mainstream visibility, to the institutions that have rejected us for so long; and on the other, we long to feel accepted, to find legitimacy in the mainstream, even if just for our own safety or happiness. It is this tension that causes us internal conflict, that so often divides our LGBTQ+ community on political issues, like what we should be fighting for, and that left me with countless questions: Was increased acceptance always a good thing? What would happen to queer culture if we *did* all suddenly decide to live like straight people? And, perhaps most importantly, who would get left behind, especially in the places where LGBTQ+ rights aren't so advanced?

My personal choices felt connected to these big questions, so before I could make up my mind about how to live my own life, I needed to go in search of answers. I needed to explore this strange moment that we were living in, when it suddenly felt like we were expected to emerge from clubs and bedrooms, blinking into the daylight, and find someone to spend the rest of our lives with. I needed to talk to more queer people about what was happening to our culture.

*

On Boxing Day, six weeks after I came back from Iceland, I got drunk, broke my promise to Amrou and called Salka. She told me that she still loved me, and that she still wanted to marry me some day.

Finally, it seemed wise to cut contact.

Why is everyone so obsessed with marriage? I thought, for at least the fiftieth time since we broke up.

That seemed like a good place to start.

chapter one

COOKING DINNER FOREVER

On 29 March 2014, forty-seven years after homosexuality was partially decriminalized in Britain, same-sex marriage was legalized, making England and Wales the sixteenth and seventeenth countries in the world to adopt the law. The night before, I was sent on my second proper reporting job. I had to go to one of the UK's first gay weddings and write about what it meant for the LGBTQ+ community.

For many people, marriage was a watershed moment in gay rights: the final frontier in gaining equality, the ultimate public symbol that gay people were recognized as being just like everyone else. I also knew the counter-arguments. That it was too little too late. That marriage was a trivial pit stop on the way to actual equality, which should improve the lives of all LGBTQ+ people, whether they wanted to get married or not. That queerness is supposed to be radical, whereas marriage is in many ways the ultimate institution, something to submit or conform to. The queer theorist Lisa Duggan famously described it as a 'political sedative', sarcastically suggesting that first we 'get marriage and the military, and then we go home and cook dinner, forever.'

Personally, I wanted to have the choice to get married as an LGBTQ+ person, but I didn't want to take it. My reservations were a combination of Duggan's ideas and the fact that I thought of marriage as a horribly sexist institution. Until the late nineteenth century in Britain, a man marrying a woman meant she was his property under the legal doctrine of coverture. But while I didn't necessarily believe in marriage, I did believe in weddings. Weddings are great. They're a positive affirmation of our ability to love one another, a place where you can start drinking before midday, and an opportunity to eat a delicious meal that has been pre-paid for. The couple whose wedding I was being sent to, Sean Adl-Tabatabai and Sinclair Treadway, were extremely accommodating on this front; they invited me to watch them get ready at home, then to attend the ceremony and the after party too. The exchanging of vows was to take place at midnight because that was when the law would formally come into effect; Sean and Sinclair would be racing a few other couples around the UK to get there first.

Sean and Sinclair had met on the gay hook-up app Grindr in 2013. They were both in Los Angeles at the time, and arranged to meet at Sean's hotel for drinks – the Beverly Wilshire, which, coincidentally, is the one from *Pretty Woman*. Sean, a thirty-two-year-old TV producer from the UK, was on a business trip to LA, where Sinclair, then twenty, was living as a student. Sinclair was downtown for his aunt and uncle's wedding anniversary dinner, but when he saw Sean's profile picture, and learned that he was from London (Sinclair had always found the British accent sexy), he knew he had to skip out early. He knocked on Sean's door late at night and they ordered room service, 'fooled around' and talked until daylight. They told me it wasn't like other Grindr hook-ups, where you usually just fuck the person and leave. It was romantic.

Two nights later, they met up again, and things were the same, only more intense and this time there was more sex. In the morning, Sean had to fly back to the UK and their relationship moved from Grindr over to Facebook, Skype and iMessage. Sinclair booked a flight to London, but Sean went quiet. Sinclair started to panic; the same panic I would later experience with Salka. He wondered whether he should even make the trip. Was he going to get rejected on the other side of an ocean?

Sean told Sinclair to come, and when they reunited in London, the two weeks flew by and Sinclair just didn't – or couldn't – leave. By this point, they were too in love.

That was the end of summer 2013. A few months later, around New Year, marriage came up in conversation and the feeling was mutual; neither Sean nor Sinclair proposed per se, but they both felt certain that they wanted to get married as soon as possible. It would allow them to live in the States as a couple, and it also 'felt right'. Long distance had been too hard and they didn't want to go through it again. They knew the bill had been passed allowing same-sex marriage in England and Wales, but they also knew that it hadn't quite come into motion yet, so they emailed their local council in Camden to request when it might be possible. The response they got surprised them. It asked if they wanted to be the very first same-sex couple to marry in the borough. It wasn't something they'd had in mind, but they thought, why not? Wouldn't it be a bonus that they would be making British history while declaring their love for one another?

As befitting a serious historic event, the dress code for the ceremony was 'hot, sexy and camera-ready'. For Sinclair, this meant a shiny blue velvet suit jacket, while Sean wore a smart navy blue suit. I watched the couple get dressed together at their house in Kentish Town, as they did away with the tradition of staying separate before the ceremony. When I got there, they seemed quiet, nervous perhaps, and sipped on champagne as I asked them intrusive questions. My being there, and them playing the role of public figures for the night, had created a kind of forced intimacy that I was not yet familiar with, and I didn't quite know how to punctuate it.

Sean explained why he thought some gay people would oppose same-sex marriage: 'A lot of gay people feel like they've been excluded from heterosexual society, so they think, "We'll keep our culture separate,"' he said. I asked if he'd ever felt the same. 'I was a bit anti-marriage and anti-establishment,' he acknowledged. But now he thought the fact that the law was changing was 'positive and progressive', and by getting married, he hoped to show his support. Besides, he loved Sinclair, and wasn't marriage something that two people who are in love are entitled to?

After the couple had fixed their outfits, we all jumped into taxis to Camden Town Hall, where the wedding was to take place, and were greeted by Jonathan Simpson, Camden's first openly gay mayor. Jonathan resembled a heavyweight boxer more than he did an elected official.

He explained that he wrote his speech quickly. 'I was speaking from the heart, but I am nervous,' he told me. 'I think I'll struggle not to cry, what with the music and the importance of the occasion.' Jonathan explained that, for him, the wedding could not be viewed in isolation. 'It's a political act,' he said. 'Around the world kids are living in fear every day because their families won't accept that they're gay. They will see this, and it will give them hope.' I asked him whether he thought gay weddings should adhere to the normal traditions, and he said he thought it was up to the individuals: 'If someone wants to get married in an underground sex club, that's up to them.' Then I asked if he would ever get married. 'If I found the right person,' he said, smiling.

When we entered the hall to take our seats I chatted to Stephen, the registrar (who was also gay), and he explained to me the deeply unromantic process of ensuring that Sean and Sinclair were the first couple to get hitched. A document had to be printed out at midnight, as soon as it became available, then Sean, Sinclair and Stephen had to sign it before the couple would officially be wed. I downed my champagne. The room, all polished wood and green leather chairs, looked a bit like the House of Commons. It contrasted nicely with Sean and Sinclair's pre-made playlist, which was blasting 'Fantasy' by Mariah Carey as guests shuffled into their seats.

Sean's friend Natalie took her place as best man, and the grooms' mothers led the boys down the aisle to give them away. Despite these details, the ceremony itself was much like any other wedding, including that awkward moment of silence when the registrar asks if anyone objects. I had half expected something bad to happen at that moment, like an angry mob of fascists bursting through the doors with pitchforks, but everything went smoothly. At about six minutes after midnight, Stephen uttered the words, 'I now declare you husband and husband.'

I cried. Jonathan cried. Few people who actually knew the two grooms seemed to cry. The band came in with strings, but those words, 'husband and husband', hung in the air.

Outside the hall, the women of the Camden Council PR team were scanning Twitter on their iPhones, disputing whether Sean and Sinclair had in fact been the first gay couple in the UK to marry. The grooms didn't seem to care, making out in front of the camera crews on the street like a pair of horny teenagers. Then we piled into one of those tacky old London buses and headed to the reception. When I walked in, Kylie Minogue's 'Can't Get You Out of My Head' was playing, and the room was shrouded with red silk. The evening had officially reached peak camp. I sat in the corner with a mustachioed gay man in an all-white suit and we discussed the 'fag hag' stereotype while necking drinks from the bar. After a few drinks I drunkenly cornered Mayor Jonathan and asked him everything I'd desperately wanted to ask him up to that point, like, 'Are you allowed to go to gay clubs if you are Mayor?' He cryptically described himself as a 'naughty mayor' before slipping off to give an impromptu speech: 'Tonight we made fucking history in Camden. Islington might have beat us, but we had the sexiest couple!'

At about four in the morning, after hours of being asked whether I should be drinking on the job, I surveyed the room. Sean's co-workers were dad-dancing in circles, forty-something men were sneaking off for a joint, and Natalie the best man was drunkenly telling Sean and Sinclair to 'never be the one who's scared to show their love more'.

All in all, it really did seem like every other wedding I'd been to, except I wasn't looking like Nigella Lawson because I didn't have to wear a wrap dress and my mum wasn't there telling me the bride looked fat. I danced with Mayor Jonathan to Kylie. I told him that I didn't believe in marriage, but I was starting to think I could get on board with the gay kind. The next day at 9 a.m. I filed my copy, with a terrible, terrible hangover.

I didn't think about Sean and Sinclair's wedding much after that day in 2014; at least, not until after my phone call with Salka, when the pair popped into my mind and I looked Sinclair up on Facebook. I suppose I wanted to see if he and Sean were still together, and I felt genuinely pleased when I saw their small, smiling faces in a selfie dated just weeks earlier. In my lingering misery it gave me the vaguest feeling of hope. From their tagged locations, they appeared to be living in LA. So I messaged Sinclair.

'I'm coming to LA,' I lied. 'I'd love to meet up with you guys and talk to you about your marriage again.' This last part was true at least; when I had gone to their wedding, marriage wasn't very high up on my agenda, whereas now, after my relationship with Salka, I suddenly felt differently, it suddenly seemed important to find out if marriage was all it was cracked up to be, and what was at stake. I was also curious about what Sean had told me: that he'd felt reticent about marriage, until he'd met Sinclair. Did his 360 mean that decrying marriage was a stance people only took until they found 'the one'? Was this what had happened to me?

Sinclair replied the next day saying I was more than welcome to visit, which surprised me given how much I had freeloaded at their wedding. Then I did what felt like the right thing to do post-break-up: I asked my only friend in the city if I could crash on her sofa and spent all my worldly money on a flight to Los Angeles.

LA was just like the pictures and the films: palm trees, congestion and people who are either too friendly or not friendly at all. My friend Alix picked me up from the airport in a Mini convertible that we struggled to get my suitcase into. I hadn't seen her in four years. She had been in my classes at university, the daughter of a wealthy Texan, which was convenient now because it meant she could take a week off work to 'assist' me in my investigation by driving me round LA. Alix was a loyal friend, generous with her time and hilarious. She was also straight. Which meant she might ask my interviewees the questions I wouldn't, and that I wouldn't try to sleep with her in a post-break-up meltdown. Her apartment, when we eventually made it through the evening traffic, was in a spacious, modernist building in the sleepy family neighbourhood of Mount Washington, overlooking LA, where a fiery sun was dropping behind the mountains.

Two days later, I found out that Sean and Sinclair had a pretty good view too. They lived in a village-like neighbour-hood called Larchmont, and when Alix dropped me off with them, we went up to their rooftop, looking out over the city. Their apartment wasn't fancy; it was under-decorated except for lavish red carpets in the shared cor-ridors. But Sean and Sinclair looked good, more tanned than when I'd last seen them. They'd both been working from home that Wednesday afternoon, and seemed pleased to clock off early when I arrived. They offered me a glass of wine and I tried to better justify why I was there. 'I want to know a bit more about you,' I said, explaining that their wedding was a watershed moment for me – which was of course true, but around my head whirled the other, more private reasons I'd come. Like my break-up. Or that there were now too many married gay couples in the world to have chosen one to talk to at random. Or that I had wanted a reason to go on holiday to LA.

'Sure, ask away,' said Sinclair obligingly, and with an unexpected jerk of my hand I accidentally spilled my wine all over their white sofa.

Sinclair was born in the Los Angeles Valleys. His mom was an air traffic controller; his biological father was mostly absent. He 'always knew' he was gay, but was in denial about it for most of his adolescence. His earliest memory of having a same-sex attraction was seeing Bill Clinton on TV when he was four or five, during the Monica Lewinsky scandal. 'We were talking about the president in kinder-garten and I told my mom that I liked Bill Clinton for the way he looks. She said that was strange and that's when I realized it wasn't normal for guys to like the way other guys looked.'

Increasingly guilt-ridden about his sexuality, Sinclair didn't come out until he was twenty, when he got engaged to Sean. In the interim, he pretended he was straight to his friends and family, and convinced himself he was bisexual. Though he never slept with girls – usually saying something about waiting for marriage – he was a 'big slut' when it came to men. His first experiences were with male classmates and friends, until he went online and pretended to be of age to meet guys on the Web. This was pre-Grindr, so he'd use craigslist (the mention of which made Sean cringe for Sinclair's safety). Sinclair remembers this period as an unhappy one. He felt as if he was hiding. He was convincing himself, in his own words, that it was all just a phase, that he was straight, would marry a woman and have a nice house in the suburbs with kids.

'I was frustrated and angry. I hadn't seen my dad since I was really little, but I thought that if he knew he would probably beat me up. I was worried that my mom might not accept it; she never came off as homophobic or anything, but a lot of gay kids are afraid our families won't love us the same. When she found out, she was surprised but she didn't care at all, she just said, "I wish you would have told me."'

Sean grew up in a different world entirely, on a council estate in North London. His parents were together – his mum British, a housewife; his dad Iranian, an accountant. His dad's side of the family were non-practising Muslims, and Sean was sent to a Catholic school. Like Sinclair's mom, Sean's parents didn't really know, or at least weren't informed, that he was gay until the marriage, although he remembers run-ins with boys as a child – hugging his male best friend in bed until the friend's mum caught them in the act and they weren't allowed to play together any more. 'My parents will have seen that sort of behaviour because I was very expressive. I was also obsessed with Wham! and the Pet Shop Boys.' In other words, all the signs were there. 'I think they must have known something . . . but once I knew what it was, what being gay actually meant, I never told them or said anything about how I really felt.'

Instead, in his teenage years, he got a girlfriend – which wasn't too laborious, since at the time, he said, he did feel genuinely attracted to her. Whether that was because she'd gone out with his best friend, whom he also fancied, he wasn't sure, but he got 'stuck' in the relationship for two years. They broke up at eighteen, but that was it – he was put off relationships and spent university and most of his twenties single – a mixture of fear, laziness and not meeting the right person until Sinclair came along. He didn't formally come out either: 'I think the idea of coming out annoyed me because I wasn't uncomfortable with being gay and I knew deep down my mum wouldn't be either. And even if I was straight, I wouldn't be telling them the gory details anyway.'

I nodded and Sinclair poured us another glass of wine. Despite their twelve-year age gap, they didn't look to be of starkly different ages – or really seem that way – maybe because they were so in sync. I was starting to remember things about the last time I'd met them; they were what

the gay community might call 'straight-acting' – not just
as individuals, in the sense that they weren't at all camp,
but also with each other, keeping contact to a minimum.
Until the moment they kissed and said 'I do', they could
have been just friends. Now it was the same.

Over the next two hours, we went over their marriage
with a fine-tooth comb – three years in, they still argued,
but less; they still had great sex, but less of that too; they
planned to live between LA and London, even though they
had significantly fewer friends in LA; they didn't currently
plan on having children – Sinclair still thought 'kids are
gross' – but if they did, they'd want to raise them in London
for the school system. The main thing that had changed
in their relationship was the level of respect. Their love,
they said, had only grown deeper.

When we returned to the question of *why* they got
married, Sean seemed to hold the same opinion as before:
that falling in love made him want to make a public commitment.

'Why did you want to marry Sean?' I asked Sinclair.

'I've just never been any more obsessed with any other
guy. If I could create my dream man it would actually be
Sean. When he first took off his shirt, his hairy chest and
his beautiful eyes . . . it was like he was just perfect and I
couldn't fuck this up. I remember when he invited me to
London I was like, OK, I'm gonna win him over, he's going
to be mine, I'm going to look better than when he met
me.'

Sean laughed, a little embarrassed. 'You didn't need to
do that.'

Sinclair carried on: 'I wanted to go to London and I wanted him to see me and be like, "Wow, you're better than I remembered," so I got a gym membership, I got a personal trainer and I got a chin implant.'

Is that what true love is? I thought, unsure of what to say. I was also trying extremely hard not to look at his chin. Luckily, Sinclair broke the silence, telling me something even more personal.

'I'd always wanted a serious relationship but I thought that I wouldn't be able to have that as a gay man,' Sinclair said. 'There's a lot of hooking up in the gay community and not a lot of relationship-oriented people. That had a huge impact on me. That made me scared to have feelings for a guy.'

'Where do you think that pressure comes from?' I asked.

'I think the media, definitely. I remember watching *Queer as Folk* when I was really young and they're very promiscuous. Then, when I went online looking for guys, I realized, wow, this is all about sex, what position they like, how big their dick is. I met guys and I realized after a few encounters that to them sex was just sex and there were no emotions in it. I thought if I were an out gay man that would be my life. I felt that whole experience was really lonely, which was why I was probably so angry when I was younger, before I met Sean, because I felt like I could never meet anyone like him. It made me so, so depressed – I considered suicide many times. I didn't want to live my life like that but I thought it was my only choice.'

Sean agreed: 'I think there are gay people out there who want relationships, proper, serious, boring relationships that could lead to marriage, whereas before, that option wasn't really there. People like me weren't really getting into relationships because they thought they couldn't.'

'I guess when you put it like that, gay marriage would have been pretty important for you to see as a teenager,' I said.

Sinclair told me that, after they got married, they received emails from gay people around the world explaining that seeing their marriage in the press gave them hope. Sean and Sinclair saw marriage as a 'turning point' for the gay community; whether it would take a few years or a few decades, it was going to change things for everyone.

Sean and Sinclair's wedding was the first time I'd seen two gay men brazenly kiss in front of a crowd and be met with a round of applause. It wasn't the kind of kiss you see in gay clubs, where two sweaty men or women embrace in the darkness, strobe lights bringing them in and out of view. It wasn't like the kisses you see at Gay Pride events either, which basically go unnoticed because everyone in the crowd is gay, and more interested in who they can kiss than who is already kissing. This was different; it was above ground and under bright lights. Everyone was watching. It was the first time I saw a gay kiss that felt formally condoned by the straight establishment, and as I looked at the pictures in the press of all the other same-sex couples to get married over the next few days – the lesbians, other gay men, young and old – I couldn't help finding the images odd, as though something was out of place. I guess my eyes just needed time to adjust to seeing gay couples in this new context, surrounded by flowers, wearing pastel colours, leaning over one another to sign the documents. It was gay as I'd never seen it before: palatable and public.

While talking to Sean and Sinclair made it clear to me that same-sex marriage had the power to change the way the world viewed gay relationships, obviously not everyone agreed with them. One of the reasons it had seemed like a good idea to travel to California was that the state's gay residents had lived through an experience I found difficult to fathom. In 2008, they had been granted the ability to marry; later that same year, the option was taken away after a public vote in favour of Proposition 8, which moved to ban same-sex marriage. America's most liberal state took a big step forwards, and then a big step back again, and during this small window of time, thousands of same-sex couples got married. Their marriages were still recognized by the state after the ban, but socially and psychologically, the legitimacy of the unions was thrown into question. If I could talk to someone who had experienced this, I wouldn't just get an account of why we need the right to marry, but what it feels like to lose it.

Now I was in California, it occurred to me that I vaguely knew someone this had happened to: Patty, a musician I had interviewed years before. I dropped her an email and waited. In the meantime, I realized I hadn't planned what else I was going to do in LA. I lazily put up a Facebook status asking if anyone knew somebody who might be relevant to speak to about what marriage might mean for LGBTQ+ people, and went to the beach. Responses were few and far between. Alix told me to relax, that people were inherently self-aggrandizing and would want to talk to a journalist, especially about themselves. The next day, still nothing. Then a contact introduced me to someone I hadn't heard of before: a guy called Steve Deline at the LA LGBT Center.

Steve was well known, it turned out, as an activist who'd campaigned against the passage of Proposition 8 with a special method called 'deep canvassing'. He was also in no way self-aggrandizing. When I emailed him he kindly invited me down to the centre. I got there on a Thursday afternoon and found a tall, sandy-haired man with glasses waiting for me. He led me out into the leafy courtyard of the building, which had the air of a hospital or mental-health facility – maybe because I could see a counsellor sitting on some steps having a sympathetic conversation with someone who looked very upset. In a way it *was* like a hospital; they offered one-on-one support to LGBTQ+ people experiencing discrimination at home or in the work-place, as well as STD testing on site. But they also had a programme of comedy, events and talks.

Steve's gig was 'The Leadership LAB' – a core team that helped to organize people to fight homophobia in their communities. Steve explained that, of the eleven years he'd lived in LA, he'd been working at the LA LGBT Center for almost six. He grew up on the East Coast, in the suburbs of Baltimore, with fairly liberal parents, and came out at nineteen. He could have done it sooner, he said, but was conscious that he'd have no control over the outcome – how it would make people feel about him. In college, he learned about queer theory, but 'was not at all political';

he didn't go near the LGBTQ+ scene – social or activist – because he was, he confessed, privileged enough not to have to think about it. Being gay didn't have to be a big part of his life. As he put it: 'Even when I came out, I didn't have to step out of my socioeconomic bubble.'

When Steve moved to LA in 2005, that thinking began to change. He started working at a record store up on Sunset, and doing social documentary stuff on the side. 'I was literally out front on my break one day and a volunteer from the campaign against Prop 8 said: "Hey, we really have to fight this! Do you want to come to the phone bank to call voters?" I'd never done anything like that before in my life but I said, "OK, I care about this, it seems important, I'll try it." So I came to a few phone banks.' By this time, Steve had met his first boyfriend, who also happened to be the first person he ever kissed and his manager at the record store. Living together, they were what he called 'marriage-minded gays'. He didn't remember when they first talked about it but remembered thinking it was an obvious option: 'Like a hetero couple, that was always my internal narrative.'

As much as Steve wanted to get married, soon that possibility would evaporate. On 5 November 2008, Proposition 8 came into effect, approved with a close-cut 52.2 per cent majority at the ballot. Steve found out it had been passed the same night that Barack Obama was elected. Gaining a president he'd voted for and losing the right to marry on the same evening was a surreal experience. He'd been campaigning against Prop 8 for more than six months at that point. He called his sister who lived in Washington

DC, and she said everyone was celebrating in the streets, but he couldn't share her happiness about Obama's win when he felt so devastated that all he'd been working for at the phone banks was lost.

'The thing is, we just didn't expect to lose that vote,' he said gravely, wind blowing the leaves across the courtyard. 'I mean, most of the polling data said that we were gonna win by a sixty–forty margin.'

'Do you think that's why you weren't *super* passionate about it – because you didn't think you would lose?' I asked.

'Well, part of it was that, but . . .' He paused. 'It took me a while after we lost to really realize what an impact it was having on me. Almost immediately that night I could see that it was the first time in my life I was experiencing animus in the diffuse sense, because I was so privileged. That feeling of, "People around me have cast judgement on me and have limited my life options based on some arbitrary feeling they have about who I am." A lot of people experience that every day, for a number of reasons, but I had never experienced that before. My first taste of it was enough to totally freak me out. I was moody, I was picking fights with my boyfriend, I just was not a happy person, and it took me a while to realize, "Oh shit, that's what this is about."'

After Prop 8 was passed, protesters took to the streets across California in their thousands. Steve joined a march two nights after the election in LA, which was made up of straight and gay people. He said he'd never experienced a crowd so angry. 'It wasn't like a violent sort of atmosphere but there was a lot of screaming and yelling, people leading chants, trying to draw as much attention, just needing to be heard, needing the media, fellow citizens in Los Angeles, or people who were just trying to drive home, to stop and take notice of this hurt and the enormity of what we were all collectively feeling.'

At another march, Steve met someone with a clipboard who invited him to a meeting about how to try to fight Prop 8. It felt like a way to take back agency and power. First it was rewarding, he said, but pretty quickly it wasn't: 'It was a lot of people who were feeling upset in a room venting to each other without really doing anything.' Steve felt that most of the blame seemed to fall on communities of people of colour. 'They'd say it was black or Latino people who voted against us. They'd say, "They're so conservative, if their communities weren't so backwards we could have won." Then people of colour were turning around and rightly saying, "Well, excuse us, the campaign put no resources in our neighbourhoods," or, "You're painting us with an incredibly broad brush and saying we're backwards, it's disgusting.' They were just at each other's throats, and it was not a very satisfying environment to be in.'

'So what happened next?'

Steve heard about a new project that involved knocking on doors, talking to voters who voted against same-sex marriage in Prop 8. He thought it sounded like something he definitely didn't want to do, but people kept asking him, so in January 2009 he signed up. Until then, canvassing had traditionally focused on getting your supporters out to vote. This, by contrast, was about targeting neighbourhoods where the majority were against you. I asked him to show me what he did.

'Whaddayawant?' I asked Steve, putting on a man's voice.

'Hey, are you Amelia?' He had missed that I was in character.

'I am, that's right.'

'Hey Amelia, my name's Steve, I'm a volunteer with Vote to Equality. We're talking to people in your neighbourhood about that gay marriage ballot we had a few months ago, the probate, do you remember that vote?'

'Kind of.'

'OK, yeah, do you remember how you voted?'

'I didn't vote.'

'Oh, really?'

'Should I pretend I voted? Sorry. OK, I voted against same-sex marriage.'

'What you just did is . . . a lot of people say they didn't vote but we know from ballot drop boxing that very few people didn't vote.'

'So that was actually quite accurate acting?'

'OK, so you voted so that gay couples would not be able to get married. Why was that the right decision for you?'

'I just think it's perverse.'

'OK, yeah. So on a zero to ten scale, if you were gonna vote on this tomorrow, would you vote the same again? Zero meaning that you totally think gay couples should not get married – and ten means that you think gay couples should be able to get married.'

'One.'

'One, got it. And why is that the right number for you?'

'I feel like I think it's wrong but maybe if it wasn't in a church then it would be OK.' I was losing my footing. (Usually, for reasons half to do with self-preservation and half to do with privilege, I try not to think about what goes on in a homophobic person's mind.)

'Are you religious yourself?'

'I'm a Christian.'

'I'm curious, what's on the other side of it? Because you're a one, you're not a zero. So what's that little bit that keeps you from being a zero?' Then he whispered: 'It's because you know someone who's gay.'

'Oh right, because my neighbour's gay.'

'OK, got it. So you probably remember during the campaign, people on both sides ran a lot of TV ads – do you remember seeing some of those?'

I nodded and Steve got out his phone to show me a YouTube video of a TV advert that was shown to Californians before the Prop 8 ballot. It featured a little girl saying to her mom, 'Today I learned how a prince married a prince and I can marry a princess.' Then a deep voiceover said: 'Think it can't happen? It's already happened. When Massachusetts legalized gay marriage, schools began teaching second-graders that boys can marry boys. The courts ruled parents have no right to object.' Then a second voice: 'Under California law, public schools instruct about marriage. Teaching children about gay marriage will happen here unless we pass Proposition 8. Yes on 8.'

I wasn't surprised by the advert. A similar, if not more extreme, campaign popped up in Australia in the lead-up to the 2017 vote on same-sex marriage (which was passed).

Photos of homophobic posters in Melbourne went viral. They read: '92 per cent of children raised by gay parents are abused, 51 per cent have depression, 72 per cent are obese.' These stats were based on a bogus study. A review of seventy-nine studies published by the Public Policy Research Portal at Columbia Law School, and referenced in a *Medical Journal of Australia* article, found 'an overwhelming scholarly consensus . . . that having a gay or lesbian parent does not harm children'. If anything, they found, discrimination does.

Data showed that the average Californian saw the Prop 8 ad twenty to forty times before they passed their vote, and following the polling data from before it aired to after, you can see support for gay marriage drop off a cliff. 'Our side completely failed to come up with a successful counteractive message,' Steve said. 'The reason for showing the video is to learn who was impacted by this and how, but also to unveil people's true feelings when they were in the ballot box, so to recreate the environment when they have seen that ad and it's on their minds. When we're facing future votes, that's the environment we're going to be in.'

Steve said that the most interesting thing they found from canvassing people was that their reasons for voting against same-sex marriage generally fell into three categories: religion – they would say, 'My church believes . . .' or tradition – 'This is what the word marriage has always meant, can't you just find a different word?' and then kids – 'What's gonna happen to my kids?'

The conversations Steve was having with people weren't just about these factors, though; they were about homophobia more broadly. Is it OK to be gay? How do people come to be gay: is it a choice, is it not a choice? Is it healthy, is it not healthy? Steve and his team recorded the conversations by filming them – more than three thousand – and then analysing them. They found the most effective way to change people's minds was talking to them about their own lives and feelings. It was about sharing their own experiences and being personable, partly because they hoped it would affect voters, but also because it created a two-way street of vulnerability and honesty. A lot of people had never had the opportunity to talk about the issue; they couldn't tell their Republican friends they were unsure about gay marriage, just as they couldn't tell their lesbian cousin. But they had questions. Some people asked Steve if he'd been abused as a child, how many people he'd slept with, whether he was in a relationship. One door he knocked on even led him to meet an older guy who was a zero on the scale, but after inviting Steve in, he broke down in tears and started talking about his son who'd committed suicide and whom people suspected had been gay. 'They were almost giving themselves therapy, like they're talking through their own experiences and re-evaluating the conclusions they've drawn, and kind of changing their own minds,' said Steve.

In late 2012, Steve's team of eleven people relocated to Minnesota for three months in the lead-up to a vote on gay marriage there. They taught their findings to local campaigners, as well as deploying them in neighbourhoods themselves. They took the idea of visibility – allowing people to see or meet a gay person – and applied it to their media-messaging too. They put gay people on TV, talking about being gay, and refuting the message about schools (until this point, pro-gay marriage organizers had pretty much kept gay people off-screen and avoided the word 'gay' altogether). The campaign in Minnesota was successful – the gay marriage bill was passed in May 2013, making it the twelfth state to legalize same-sex marriage in America.

Steve told me that, through his work, one of the biggest things he learned is just how important the right to marriage is for LGBTQ+ people's mental health. According to social scientists, banning gay marriage or losing a vote on passing it has a catastrophic psychological impact on members of the LGBTQ+ community. In an analysis published in 2010 by the *American Journal of Public Health*, researchers studied data on mental health recorded before and after state bans on same-sex marriage in 2004–5. For people who identified themselves as gay, lesbian or bisexual living in states that had experienced the bans, there was a 37 per cent increase in mood disorders, a 42 per cent increase in alcohol-use disorders and a 248 per cent increase in generalized anxiety disorders.

California never went back to the ballot (or hasn't yet) on same-sex marriage – but when it was reinstated through a judicial hearing in 2013, experts were brought in to testify on the psychological damage that legal discrimination inflicts on LGBTQ+ people, and the chief economist for San Francisco even testified that the state of California would save money by allowing same-sex couples to marry because it would reduce costs to mental-health services.

As for Steve, he was just pleased that neither he, nor the

LGBTQ+ community, had to go through the trauma of people voting on their rights again and that the issue was resolved in court, even if it did mean the door-knocking technique wouldn't be put to the test in his home state. In February 2014, Steve's boyfriend proposed to him by a campfire during a holiday in Hawaii. Steve said yes and they were married in a botanical garden in LA that summer. Like Sean and Sinclair, Steve said it wasn't a political statement but that it just 'felt right' – a personal choice, but one he conceded probably isn't for everybody. Steve had never slept with or even kissed anyone else, so monogamy didn't feel like a big change. 'Plus we didn't have to hash through it a lot because it exists out there in the world and we could just take it off the shelf and apply it to our lives.'

'So you kind of just did it because it was an easy option?'

'Yeah. It didn't feel radical, or like I was making a big statement to society. Going door to door on the campaign asking people if they had a problem with gay people, *that* felt radical or transgressive. But getting married itself – with all the people there that wanted to see me get married? That just felt normal.'

The day after I met Steve, and not long before I was set to return to the UK, Patty emailed me back. She was in Palm Springs with her wife and daughter, she said, but I could come over for dinner the next day. I didn't know any lesbians with kids in London, and as I replied to her it dawned on me that this would be the first time I could see the template of what my life might look like in the future – a crazy thought. But when I got to Patty's house

– a big, Gothic, gated property in the neighbourhood of Silver Lake – she told me she used to be in the same position.

I knew Patty *very* tenuously; like Sean and Sinclair, we had met once. She had been in a successful grunge band called Hole, with the notorious Courtney Love. She joined in 1992, when the band had enjoyed some underground or industry acclaim, but had yet to break into the mainstream. Two years later, their 1994 album *Live Through This* went platinum, and they enjoyed much of the same global success as other grunge bands like Nirvana or Sonic Youth. But being in the band contributed to severe addiction problems for Patty, and when heroin got her too addled to do her job, she was kicked out. She later made a brilliant film about the experience, which pieced together all her archive Super 8 tour footage to tell the story of the band's rise to fame and of her recovery.

I interviewed her when I was twenty-one, after her film came out, and we'd been social media friends since. I felt like we had something in common after that first conversation; not only the feeling of growing up with a lack of lesbian role models, but also a desire to talk about it. The difference was, Patty was actually in a position to do so. She came out publicly in *Rolling Stone* magazine in 1995. 'It's important,' she told them at the time. 'I'm not out there with that fucking pink flag or anything, but it's good for other people who live somewhere else in some small town who feel freaky about being gay to know that there's other people who are and that it's OK.'

We went through to Patty's garden, and sat in the exact

spot where she and her wife Christina got married nine years before. I recognized Christina and their daughter Bea from Patty's Instagram photos. Christina had a young, round face, and tattoos; Bea was brilliantly blonde and tanned, the picture of a Californian child. They were making dinner together, and Bea kept glancing shyly at me the way all six-year-olds do when there's a stranger on their turf. On the other side of the yard, I asked Patty about her marriage.

Patty told me that, growing up in Marysville in the State of Washington, she didn't know anyone gay. When she started to realize she was, in the 1980s, as a teenager, she says she looked around and 'felt ripped off' that she didn't get to have the same experiences as everyone else. 'When I was attracted to a girl I couldn't do what the other kids would do and ask her to the dance. And I knew then, I'm not gonna have that marriage like I see all these straight people have. Part of me could, maybe, but it would have to be a secret. I would stare out the window in class and have fantasy thoughts of a pretend world where I would be married with a girl.'

When Patty came out to her friends and family and herself, she was nineteen. She moved to Seattle, where there were 'maybe three places for women to go'.

'I guess they didn't have Tinder back then,' I said.

'Right,' she said, smiling, as if to say, that didn't stop me.

As a young lesbian, Patty said she was a 'serial monog-amist', making up for lost time. She used to partake in activism – going to gay rights marches, attending meetings with the AIDS activism group ACT UP – and threw herself into queer culture in San Francisco for a while. That was where she first met Christina, but they didn't hook up until later. In the meantime, Patty bought the property in Silver Lake and turned it into a party house that I very much wish I had been around to visit. Christina later told me that every lesbian over forty in LA had been to a party there in the nineties, which I solemnly believed.

In 2005, Patty and Christina met again in a gay bar called Shotgun, and started dating. Then they moved in together, and then they got married in 2008, during the short period when gay marriage was legalized. 'We were planning to get married anyway and just have a commitment ceremony,' said Patty. 'And then I got a text from my mom that said, "Congratulations, they legalized gay marriage".'

'Why did you decide to do it?' I asked.

Patty paused. 'Well, we fell in love. It felt like the right thing to do.' That phrase I kept hearing. 'I felt like I wanted to have that life with a partner.'

'What about you, Christina?' I called over to where Christina was standing by the barbecue. 'Why did you want to get married?'

'What, versus a commitment ceremony? I got married because I fell in love with Patty and we were committed to each other. But in terms of . . .' Christina had sounded slightly defensive; now she fell silent for a minute to think. 'I don't know, it just seemed to legitimize it.'

'How?'

I expected her to say something about how marriage legitimized them socially, but Christina surprised me: the decision was as much legal and financial as anything else, she explained. She told me that she had read an article in the *New York Times* comparing a straight married couple and a gay unmarried couple over the course of their lives. Although there were a lot of variables on income, location and the like, they found that in the end the gay couple lost out on things like partner health insurance (not available to same-sex couples before marriage), social security benefits and being able to transfer pension payments to a non-working spouse. And this was all before estate tax. 'In our worst case, the couple's lifetime cost of being gay was $467,562,' wrote the *Times* in 2009, although 'the number fell to $41,196 in the best case for a couple with significantly better health insurance, plus lower taxes and other costs.'

Either way, it was a lot of money, said Christina, at which point she told me they still hadn't paid the $3,000 for Patty's second parent adoption, which they still had to pay even though they were married and Patty was named on Bea's birth certificate.

'That's the kind of stuff where I was like, "We should get married to have all those benefits,"' Christina continued. 'They needed like ten documents for me to add Patty to the insurance before we were married, showing that we were on the lease together, that we had a joint bank account. Part of it was just the bureaucracy.'

It wasn't the first time I'd heard these arguments for same-sex marriage, just the first time I'd seen for myself how they might work practically. During the 1980s and 1990s, if AIDS-related illness claimed the life of one half of a long-term same-sex couple, the other half would be left with no inheritance or property rights. Christina's argument also recalled that famous case of United States v. Windsor. A lady named Edith Windsor had lost her spouse, Thea Spyer (whom she'd married in Canada in 2007) in 2009. Spyer left her entire estate to Windsor, but Windsor was not given spousal tax exemption since the US Defense of Marriage Act (DOMA) stated that marriage must be between a man and a woman to qualify. Windsor took the case to court and won, setting in motion the Supreme Court's challenge to DOMA, which would eventually lead to the legalization of same-sex marriage across all fifty states of America in 2015.

We sat down for dinner. Bea placed herself between Christina and Patty, jumping around in her chair. Patty later told me that Bea had been conceived with Christina's egg and her brother Larry's sperm through insemination (saving them money they might have otherwise spent on donated sperm and IVF), so she was related to them both. You could see the likeness: Christina's nose; Patty's ginger hair, strawberry blonde on Bea.

'Are many of your friends married?' I asked Christina.

'Most,' said Christina, explaining that the ones who weren't had been actively taking a stance against hetero-normativity, but when Trump had been elected they'd started expressing more of an interest in marriage.

'I suppose a lot of people want to have the choice, but don't want to actually take it,' I said, thinking of myself. 'But when the choice might be taken away from you, you suddenly want to take it.'

Then I asked about what it was like when Prop 8 was

passed, and they said they didn't feel upset, or take it too personally, they just felt enraged. They boycotted businesses with signs that said 'Yes on 8' and they went out to protest.

'There were a whole bunch of us at this one protest and on the other side they kept saying, "We just don't want our children to know about this,"' remembered Christina. I thought about the advert Steve had shown me. 'I just kept saying over and over again, "But I still love you, even though you don't love me!" And this woman was so mad at me!' Christina laughed. 'That whole fear of the gay agenda . . . it's just two gay guys sat at a table reading newspapers with their breakfast. It's so boring . . . you know what I mean? We're literally eating our dinner at 6 p.m. What is so scary?'

We were indeed eating our dinner at 6 p.m. The sun was still shining, Bea was playing with her food. It was all quite idyllic, as far as my only first-hand experience of what married lesbian family life looked like.

'Do you ever face discrimination here?' I asked.

'I think the only time I ever did was in that Prop 8 rally. I don't feel like I ever have,' Christina responded.

'We talk about it, Christina and I,' said Patty. 'How we couldn't really move to Bozeman, Montana. We still think about how we can't really go and live in some suburb like straight people do, because it would be a little bit scary to move there. For Bea too. She's never had a day when people are like, hmm' – she mimed craning her head to stare – 'because here we hang with people that are like-minded.'

'But isn't that a bubble?' I asked.

'Yes. Totally. When Trump was elected I was like: my God, I've been stuck in a vegan, lesbian, preschool bubble.

It's crazy. But you relax into it, you stay where it's safe. I feel like I have to do more now – now that Trump is president and there's all this hatred for minorities, lesbian and gay men. I just want to say, "Fuck you! This is my family, you can't tell me I'm not allowed to be married, you can't do that."'

'How would you feel if your right to marriage got taken away again?'

'Shit would go down. I'm fifty, I'm married, I'm middle-aged, but I think the threat of something like that would make me get the fuck up off the couch and get back to the roots of being that ACT UP punk rock activist, but this time it's gonna be with my wife and my child.'

'It sounds like you used to do a lot of activism and you don't any more. Is that cause you've got what you want?'

Patty seemed startled by my question, so I backtracked before she could answer. 'I just mean, oppression is what makes people go and protest, so if you're not experiencing any, why would you? I don't think that makes you a bad person.'

'Maybe it is that bubble. It's scary . . . I don't wanna just sit around and be like, "Well, it's not totally at my front door yet!" But then what does it take? The threat of . . . I don't know . . .' Patty looked slightly wounded.

I apologized for coming to her house and asking such serious questions. She graciously told me they were the right ones. We finished dinner, and then I left.

As I walked down Patty's street back towards the main drag in Silver Lake, I figured that Sean and Sinclair, Steve, and Patty and Christina, they were all what I thought of as heteronormative, but talking to them had highlighted the bottom line for me: that to ban same-sex marriage was to discriminate against us. I'd never been so sure of why same-sex marriage was fair as in that moment, especially as all the couples I'd met looked so happy. But on the way back to Alix's house, I thought about something Steve had said before I left the LA LGBT Center: while marriage had meant a lot to him personally (not least changing his tax status) and had gone some way to putting an end to the public lie that a lot of being gay was just about sex (as Sean and Sinclair had hoped it would), it had also created a problem. Donor money for LGBTQ+ activist work had dried up, even though the work wasn't yet done, even though the political climate was precarious. This of course spoke to the difficult dilemma that Patty's situation presented: were LGBTQ+ people allowed to sit back and actually enjoy the rights they'd been granted? Or was same-sex marriage the opiate of the gay masses?

On a personal level, it occurred to me that maybe if I'd ever been exposed to a life like Patty's sooner, it might not have taken until I met Salka to ask myself if marriage was something I wanted. At Alix's, I told her I was still on the fence about whether getting married was a choice I would make. She kindly pointed out that it probably didn't matter anyway, since people weren't exactly queuing up to marry me.

My trip was coming to an end, and I was meant to go back to London in a couple of days. Then something much more pressing happened: we found out DragCon was in town, and I decided to stick around.

chapter two

THE BUSINESS OF DRAG

For the past five years, a drag queen convention has descended on the 720,000 square foot halls of the LA Convention Center. It started off with 13,000 guests, and has now surpassed 50,000. As Comic-Con does for comic book fans, the two-day event brings together drag enthusiasts from all over America and the rest of the world to dress up in platform shoes and flammable wigs, spend a load of money on merchandise, and attend talks or panel debates hosted by their heroes.

The biggest festival on the planet celebrating drag culture, DragCon is based around a cult TV series called *RuPaul's Drag Race*, which is a lot like *America's Next Top Model*, only the contestants are drag queens. On the show, host and drag expert RuPaul dishes out critiques and mottoes of empowerment to a cast of 'young hopefuls', who must compete in weekly challenges that involve everything from glamorous photo shoots to creating costumes out of debris found in a dumpster. The contestants 'throw shade' (catty but hilarious comments) at one another, and those who aren't tough enough inevitably crack – heightening their chances of getting sentenced to 'lip-sync for their life', a battle between the week's two lowest-ranking contestants, resulting in one getting thrown off the show. It's extravagant, it's tacky, and at the end of the series, there's a winner – America's Next Drag Superstar, who lands fame and a great big make-up sponsorship deal.

The convention is ostensibly for fans of the show, but anyone looking for a novel way to spend a weekend could go. Alix and I first heard about it from an American drag queen I'm friends with on Facebook, and immediately logged onto the website to find out more. A quick browse promised us a weekend of acceptance and celebrity. 'At RuPaul's DragCon, we celebrate all the colors of the rainbow. We have an orange president that wraps himself in red, white and blue. How are you going to make America great again if you can't love all the colors of the rainbow?'

There was also a list of drag queens from the show that would be in attendance – seventy-eight in total, including names like Alaska Thunderfuck, Bob the Drag Queen, Jinkx Monsoon and Kim Chi. Day tickets to the convention cost $30, or $50 for the whole weekend, and $100 for VIP tickets that let you cut the queues. Kids, I noticed, were admitted for free. Suddenly it wasn't the idea that seventy-eight drag queens would be there that made me want to go to DragCon, it was the idea of meeting families with drag-loving children.

In recent years, drag has moved from being a staple of seedy gay bars – an art form littered with rude jokes and niche nods to queer culture – to something arguably much more palatable and commercial, but its history goes back further. Men have been performing on stage as women for thousands of years: in Ancient Greek tragedies, Shakespeare plays and baroque operas. In seventeenth-century Britain, women started to play men on stage, but the phrase 'drag queen' was first used to describe men appearing in women's clothing in the nineteenth and twentieth centuries, in a type of British slang called Polari, used by gay men in London's theatre community. In the seventies and eighties, drag permeated club culture in London, New York and LA – still the drag capitals of the world today – with figures like Leigh Bowery and Lady Bunny straddling the roles of performance artist and drag queen. In 1984 Lady Bunny invented Wigstock, a drag festival that took place in New York's East Village. RuPaul, originally from Atlanta but newly relocated to New York, used to perform at Wigstock as well as the nearby Pyramid Club, which was famous for nurturing drag culture in all its glory; raw, garish, and definitively camp.

RuPaul's CV made him the perfect person to package drag and sell it as prime time TV, and although that wouldn't happen until decades after Wigstock, it was in the Pyramid Club era that he had befriended Randy Barbato and Fenton Bailey, whose company World of Wonder produces the show. Before *Drag Race* they produced a series that followed Pamela Anderson around her daily life, another where Perez Hilton dished out gossip, and the documentary film and ensuing TV show *Becoming Chaz*, which followed Cher's son, Chaz Bono, through transition. Between 1996 and 1998, they also produced RuPaul's hugely successful VH1 talk show with co-host Michele Visage, which featured guests from Cher to Debbie Harry to the

Backstreet Boys. Despite all this, when they took the idea for a reality show about finding the next big drag queen to the newly launched LGBTQ+ channel Logo TV in the mid-2000s, it was initially rejected. 'Early Logo TV did not want to frighten the neighbours. It wanted to present the idea of gays as the guys next door. Regular suburban folk,' wrote Bailey and Barbato in their book, *The World According to Wonder*. These were the George Bush Jr years, which might have had something to do with it, they added. 'Every Gay Pride you hear the same complaints that the drag queens and fisters just ruin it for everyone. So in the end we just gave up pitching them.' However, as the West became more accepting of LGBTQ+ people more generally, so did it become more accepting to drag queens.

After *Drag Race* was eventually greenlit by Logo in 2008, it became an overnight success. Now in its eleventh season, it has moved to the bigger US channel VH1, and is shown around the world from Australia to Latin America. The audience is varied; it's watched by straight and gay people alike, and as all good camp does, seems to straddle high and low culture. In 2017, perhaps surprisingly to a lot of people, the show's dedication to helping people 'foster a true you' was named as the key influence in the curation of the Whitney Biennial art fair. But its reach and influence do not stop there.

The queens on the show each have hundreds of thousands of Instagram followers, even millions. Some make appearances on *Drag Race* spin-off shows, such as *Drag U*, in which drag queens make over regular American women, or *Untucked*, which is a behind-the-scenes look at *Drag Race*. And massively successful *Drag Race* viewing parties have sprung up everywhere, bringing together fans to watch the show en masse in gay bars and clubs. The single time I went to one, I felt as if I'd stepped onto another planet. Being in a club to watch something on TV at 8 p.m. was bizarre, not to mention the fact that everyone was screaming at the screen and cheering. It was like watching a football match in a British pub, except the noises were totally different – everyone was shouting 'yass' while clicking their fingers in the air. *Finally, a sport for gay people*, I thought. And yet drag clearly wasn't just for gay people any more: straight people around the world were watching from their living rooms.

If marriage offered gay people a slice of straight culture, then *Drag Race*, DragCon and RuPaul were surely doing the opposite: giving straight people a gateway into gay culture, by taking the individuality and creativity of LGBTQ+ people and encouraging it to be celebrated within the mainstream. Yes, in many ways marriage and drag couldn't be more different – drag was a subversive practice that mocked and transgressed the boundaries of gender, while marriage was institutional and traditionally based around gender-certain roles – and yet, if marriage was a site of our institutional assimilation, wasn't the popularity of drag where this was happening culturally?

I thought of Amrou, and their desire for legitimacy and acceptance through success in drag. I understood why Amrou wanted – even needed – it. But when I considered what was happening to drag more broadly, its commercialization, its corporatization, its moment in the spotlight, I wasn't totally sure that it was a positive thing.

Every night of the week leading up to DragCon there is an event at which queens hawk their talents. A friend suggested we go to a spot in Downtown LA called Redline, where some queens they knew would be performing. It was a dingy corner bar, half full, and as we walked in the compère, Heklina, a San Francisco drag legend, was yelling 'FUCK ART, I WANT MONEY' into the crowd, as people padded up to her with their dollar bills. To find out more about the changing face of drag I wanted to meet someone who was on the outside looking in, a drag purist, someone who would be objective about how RuPaul's show had changed the industry first-hand. A queen who yelled 'fuck art, I want money' didn't seem the right choice.

I chatted to two queens outside and it turned out one of them had been on *Drag Race*. After so many seasons, it was as though I couldn't avoid its stars; I figured she'd be no good to me because she'd have her *Drag Race* PR patter down. About an hour later, it turned out I was wrong: I caught the pair going into the toilet together and asked them what they were up to. 'COCAINE!' one of them yelled at me. 'Put THAT in your book,' screamed the other, letting the bathroom door slam behind them.

Alix and I stood at the back of the room while other queens performed. A trans woman in a green-sequined pantsuit did a Whitney Houston mash-up; a big guy in a leather jacket and high-rise thong did an energetic rendition of Cher. I felt like RuPaul, waiting for my own Drag Superstar to present herself to me, lip-syncing for her life. And then it happened. Miss Barbie-Q walked on stage wearing a cute paisley dress, red stockings and a demure brown wig that could have been her real hair. The music started playing and she began to lip-sync to a soul song that I recognized from a film called *Hidden Figures*, the untold story of three black female engineers working for NASA during the Cold War. She got the audience to clap along. It felt like a classic performance; Barbie had a Dionne Warwick or Shirley Bassey kind of class to her. She wasn't like the other girls. Or actually any other drag act I'd seen.

After she'd finished, we went outside for a cigarette and I told Barbie that I liked her red shoes and matching red stockings.

'Are you going to DragCon this year?' I asked. She looked cynical.

'No. I only went one time. And I only went because I didn't wanna shit-talk something I hadn't seen.'

'I'm going this weekend,' I said. 'What should I expect?'

'You pay for everything,' she said, putting her cigarette out. 'People come with their families and buy cotton candy and take pictures with us? This is what we've allowed it to become? We've allowed a corporation – World of Wonder, gay owned – to sweep in, take who we are and make it into a commodity.'

'I see your point,' I said. 'That's what I'm interested in, though. What it's done to drag, and why it's so popular. Would you talk to me more about it? Somewhere quieter?'

She thought about it for a second before getting her

phone out. Her calendar was blocked out for different activities in different colours. Meditation had a ten-minute slot, a colonoscopy another. 'You wanna come for breakfast at my house tomorrow?' she said. 'I have to go to the DMV at two.'

I asked what I could bring.

'Hmmm. Meat,' she said. 'Bring sausages.'

The next morning I arrived at MJ's small, cream-coloured house downtown. There was no answer when I rang the bell. I hovered awkwardly on the porch, holding my sausages in the sun. Eventually MJ answered; he'd overslept. I didn't recognize him in what he called his 'boy clothes', or daywear. 'Boy clothes' didn't seem the right term. He explained that he thought of himself as gender non-conforming – or 'GNC', he said, pronouncing it like 'G&T'. He alternated between the pronouns 'they', 'he' and 'she'; he said he doesn't mind which people use.

'I'll wear perfume and women's jeans with combat boots and a baseball hat,' he told me, unpacking a clothing delivery we'd picked up off his porch.

'Like a lesbian?' I suggested.

MJ laughed. 'Uh huh. That's me. Queen Latifah.'

As MJ started making us eggs, he told me his story. He was born in 1971 in Toledo, a small town on a lake near Ohio. The oldest of six kids, MJ grew up 'poor, but happy'; it was a 'we're all in this together kind of deal', he said. 'I read books like crazy, that was my escape,' he remembered, putting the sausages in a pan on the hob. 'I used to read Danielle Steel,' he laughed. 'Y'all would hear all this "riding a horse to a villa in Tuscany". I had to look it up in my encyclopedia! "Where the hell's Tuscany!"' I liked the way MJ's voice got more high-pitched when he was excited, like a stand-up comic reaching the punchline. 'They'd go to the French Riviera and be tanning in Monte Carlo – I thought, "Someone buy *me* a drink at a bar in Monte Carlo!"'

MJ said this was when he first knew he was gay, when he was fantasizing about that man at the bar in Monte Carlo.

In high school, MJ gravitated towards drama, and later musical theatre. When he started doing these activities outside school, it allowed him to be louder, more confident, better at expressing himself. MJ thought these interests defined what he went on to do later: radio, producing plays and musicals. The first time MJ did drag he was twenty-three. It happened by accident. 'One of my drag sisters, Raja, dressed me up for Halloween one year and I loved it. "Drag is just like musical theatre," she said. Then after she'd done my make-up: "You look really pretty."' MJ liked feeling pretty. His first paid performance was later that year at a club called Ozz in Buena Park. His natural look recreated the 'female illusion', as he put it – but not to mock or caricature women, like a lot of other queens did. He didn't have any particular aspirations about turning drag into a full-on career back then: 'It's funny, performing on stage, I didn't think, "I'm here to fill a gap in the market," I just love performing. And one of my things was that I loved seeing the audience smile. Especially when the kids knew the song and would sing it with me.'

Politically, it felt freeing. Drag was in your face, a way of defying everything MJ had been taught about being male. 'It's this notion of going against the grain, doing something that people tell you no, you shouldn't do,' said MJ. 'Because we are told no all the time. Gay boys are always chastised for being feminine. But the drag has taken that to another level. You think I'm feminine? I'm gonna put on a dress, I'm gonna put on a wig, I'm gonna put on boots. Drag queens are like' – he paused – 'the personification of gay oppression.' He stopped again: 'Ooh! That was good!' he cackled. 'Write that down!'

From the minute I had walked in the door at MJ's house, I'd felt instantly at home, because MJ was so accommodating. The house itself was a hoarder's paradise, with belongings stacked floor to ceiling. It was one room wide, with first a reception room leading open plan into a small kitchen, and then behind that a small bathroom and a bedroom. Dotted about the front room were at least ten mannequin heads with wigs on top; long black hair, styled reddish-brown updos, and even a blonde bob.

'It's like *Silence of the Lambs* in here,' I told MJ, and he pretended to stroke my head.

'What nice hair you have . . . it's so long.' On his dressing table was a jewellery box with tiny cut-out pictures of Madonna glued onto it, and a little sign emblazoned with the mantra: BE BOLD – BE KIND – BE TRUE – BE YOU.

Over breakfast, I talked to MJ about my own life. When I told him I was gay he let out a gasp. 'Did you think I'd be writing a whole book about queer culture if I was straight?' I asked incredulously. We laughed and went back to our eggs and sausages.

After we'd finished eating, MJ led me into the bedroom to show me something. It was a dirty zebra-print suitcase, stashed at the back of his wardrobe. As he stood looking at it, he told me he'd used it when he was homeless.

At first, doing drag on the club circuit felt as though it was giving him a voice, and saved him from isolation, allowing him to express himself. He was getting booked, and he wasn't like the other drag queens – he was more authentically feminine, he was black, and he was what he called 'hefty'. But the line between representing a minority and being a minority felt thin. MJ would see all these groups of friends – he called them 'tribes' – laughing, and he felt disposable. 'They'd come to you and say, "You're so great," but one of them of course has to put me in my place, so they'd say something catty or racist, then they'd all laugh and walk away. That's when I started becoming very isolated, very lonely.'

Hurtful too was the fact that drag was a turn-off to a lot of gay men. It wasn't accepted or attractive to be feminine or trans. MJ didn't yet know whether or not he was trans (the term 'gender non-conforming' didn't come along until a few years later), but he knew he didn't fit in. 'I guess I'm like a natural femme. A lot of the queens think you have to put on all the make-up, contour . . . I don't want to do any of that stuff. My drag was different, but a lot of guys were like: "You're not like the other ones, so what's wrong with you?"'

This story wasn't unfamiliar. My friends who do drag told me it was acceptable to dress as a woman, to look 'fishy' (a questionable word meaning convincingly feminine), but only if you took the make-up off afterwards, and had a beard and muscles underneath. RuPaul had made headlines for being what some considered transphobic or misogynistic. He had been called out for using the term 'tranny', and in an interview with the *Guardian* he claimed that drag is most effective when men are doing it, because that's when 'it's a real fuck-you to male-dominated culture', a statement that seemed to ignore all female and non-binary drag queens' ability to subvert gender stereotypes. In the same interview, he also talked about the 'dichotomy of the trans movement versus the drag movement', as though there could be no overlap.

Feeling isolated by the femmephobia in the industry, MJ began drinking, not for the confidence to perform ('because I *am* a performer'), but for the confidence to perform to a bunch of drunk gay people who heckled and shit-talked him. 'It takes balls. Even if we're not meant to have any on stage. You know how catty the gay scene can be – get them drunk in a group, they feel they can say and touch and do whatever. I'm not gonna blame them cause it's not their fault. They've been told that they're nothing, they're gonna die of AIDS or something. The oppressed always end up being the oppressors, even if they don't mean to.' It was about having a sense of entitlement, said MJ. '"I went through being in the closet, I went through whatever else, so I have the right to say and do what I want to now," which is bullshit.' But complaining wasn't allowed: 'It was always this weird thing of like, "Oh, I guess I have to put up with it because I'm a drag queen."'

The drag scene MJ had found himself a part of didn't take this seriously, because it didn't take much seriously: 'You're there to look pretty, perform and do a death drop, and you can't talk about your politics because you're not that smart.' Still, he empathized: 'Gay people have to struggle to come out, and they finally accept who they are, then get into the party scene, then there comes a moment when we become mature, we start realizing we need to be activists, and we start going through gay power and rainbow rings. But drag queens, we seem to be stuck in the party time.'

Looking back – right from those Danielle Steel books and wanting a man to buy him a drink, through to the drag bars and clubs – he realized now that every situation he'd put himself in, imaginary or otherwise, had involved a bar. But it was always like that for LGBTQ+ communities, wasn't it, he said. 'Take away the bar and what do we have?'

Addicted to substances like alcohol, meth and cocaine, as well as dabbling with ecstasy, MJ slept in bathhouses and parks, and rode the bus up and down Santa Monica Boulevard. There was one bus that went to the beach, then downtown, then back again. That was the one he'd ride. He'd also party and hang out at people's houses, go to his dealer's and stay there, sleep on people's couches. He was sexually assaulted, held at knifepoint and gunpoint. He stared down at the zebra-print suitcase, which served as his drag bag and his entire life at that time. 'Drag was the only thing I had to hold on to. I would ask people, "Hey, I have a show tonight, I need a place to get dressed at." Because if a drag queen asks you if they can put on make-up and get glamorous at your house then people are like, "Yeah, that sounds awesome!"'

He'd stay in people's houses and smoke meth out of their bathroom window secretly, or overstay his welcome. I found it hard to imagine MJ this way, not just because he was so together now but also because he was so caring towards me that it seemed strange he wouldn't have shown himself the same sort of affection. 'There's a saying in the homeless community – when you stay at someone's house you can only stay three days before it starts to go bad,' he told me solemnly.

The final straw came when MJ was staying with a friend, Zackary Drucker, one of the producers of the TV show *Transparent*. It was 2014 and Drucker had an exhibit at the Whitney biennial. 'I was like, "Wow, yeah, I wanna do something at the Whitney, that sounds amazing,"' remembered MJ. 'She looked at me and said: "No girl, you won't be doing anything like that. You can't be an addict and an artist." It was the first time someone ever called me an artist. Not a drag queen. Not a clown. She said: "You're a performance artist, you know that, right? You're an artist and you're squandering your talent."'

After that MJ enrolled in rehab, where he was told to put his drag away. It was an all-male facility, but that wasn't why. The doctor said: 'Your recovery comes first . . . if you don't stay sober you're not going to be able to do your drag.' MJ was affronted. He'd fought long and hard to be Miss Barbie-Q. But he had no choice. 'I put my wigs in a bag under my bed. I'd take it out once in a while just to brush them.' After the first year, when he did occasionally check out of rehab for a night to do a gig, drugs were always put under his nose within the first five minutes. And so he'd do his number, get on a bus and go right back to rehab again, where things felt safe for the first time in a long time.

Eventually, MJ was discharged, but when he went back to the clubs he got scared. Things were different now. It had been almost four years since he was on the circuit and he could visibly see how drag had changed: 'I don't do ass jokes, I don't do too much flesh, I don't do a lot of dirty stuff. Sure, I can laugh about it but I don't do vulgarity. The LGBT community expects drag queens to be vulgar. I'm like, actually, the bathhouses are the place to be vulgar. I want my drag to have a certain level of integrity and class.'

Suddenly, MJ found himself chastised for that. People would say, you're not pushing yourself, you're not rolling with the times, you're stuck in the old-school way of thinking. 'I do sometimes feel that, especially when I see the younger girls. Every song they're performing is a mix – mash-ups – and it's nice but I realized, "Wow, I stand out even more. Am I relevant? Are people gonna like me still?" Drag queens are seen as youthful, just like models, or any profession in entertainment . . . but I was older.' He was also three and a half years sober, meaning the armour was off; he'd have to deal with the world of drag without drugs

and alcohol, or leave it behind forever. He decided to perse-
vere. And because of that, I'd wound up in his home,
asking him his life story, and questioning him about the
threat *RuPaul's Drag Race* presented to the queens that came
before it.

The way MJ talked about *RuPaul's Drag Race* reminded me
of the testimonies of defectors from Scientology. He was
angry, like the cult of RuPaul had taken something from
him; yet he seemed cautious, edgy even, when he criticized
it. When *Drag Race* started, MJ watched it with pride – a
lot of his friends were on the show, and he could see how
it was going to take their drag to the next level – but then
he noticed the editing, and he noticed that his friends didn't
seem the same as they did in person. 'Think of any reality
TV show,' he said. We were sitting on the front steps of
his porch now, smoking cigarettes in the midday sun. I was
getting sunburned but I didn't want to interrupt him. 'Like
The Real World, *Survivor*, *Top Chef* – you need a bitch, you
need a slut, you need a this, you need a that, you always
need these characters. It's funny, you're asking drag queens,
who are already characters, to be characters.'

MJ was honest about the fact he once auditioned for
Drag Race, something he felt conflicted about. He did it
because his friends encouraged him: 'People would ask me
all the time if I wanna be on the show and I'm like, hmm,
it's good business sense.'

He recalled a conversation he'd had with a *Drag Race*
casting person. They asked him, 'What character would
you be? Would you be the nice one, the bitch or the mama?'

MJ said: 'Well, I'd just be me,' and the casting person said, 'That doesn't make good TV.'

Drag Race billed itself as a show about authenticity and individuality and giving marginalized people a voice – or at least, this was the dialogue that had been constructed around it. But MJ believed it was all fake. 'You know when they do that mass casting, "we got ten thousand entries" thing?' said MJ. 'You know damn well they can't go through ten thousand entries, so they cast it. Yeah, they pluck girls from Dallas, Miami, New York, London, and for good TV they cast people who will have conflicts. It's taking it, packaging it, putting it in front of our faces, and telling us we have to accept it because if we don't, we're assholes and we're not being inclusive.'

MJ presented this information to me as a big conspiracy. But I wasn't surprised. *Isn't that how all reality TV works?* I thought. Besides, I knew that after queens come off the show, they also sign the next two years of their life away doing promo tours and events like DragCon – it's part of the Faustian pact of being a 'drag success'. I put this to MJ and he nodded furiously: 'They pay them well, but after the show you should be able to do whatever you want,' he said, sceptical that it was all worth it. 'I hate to say it, but on *RuPaul's Drag Race*, have you seen any winner do anything really big after? No. It's like: "You're the Drag Queen Superstar! OK, next season!"'

And then there was the content of the show itself: like on *America's Next Top Model*, the contestants have to do ridiculous challenges to prove their worth. 'If you want to have a show about drag queens, have a challenge where her song skips or her wig falls off or her heel breaks on stage, and then what does she do? That's happened. Don't make me jump into a vat of water or have wind blown on me or fuckin' make me jump on a trampoline. I don't know any queen in any country who does that as part of their act. And personally it feels like it's RuPaul and the people that run *Drag Race* going: "I'm gonna make you do some monkey-ass challenge to show you you're on my show."' He put on a voice: "'How bad do you want this?"' Then, in his own: 'Not that bad!'

The way MJ saw it, the whole circus represented a kind of cannibalization. 'We're once again capitalizing on our own culture, making money out of it and not giving back. You can do *Drag Race* all day but they should have an HIV fundraiser, they should be in the forefront of HIV research or whatever it is, homeless LGBT charities. I tell every queen coming out that you should do a benefit for free once a year, if not more. I do it at least once a quarter.'

Instead, *Drag Race*, said MJ, is trying so hard to be everything to everybody that being political doesn't always end up being a priority. 'They don't touch enough on misogyny, ageism, racism.' Drag queens had been there fighting for LGBTQ+ rights for decades, he said. 'We were visible, with the big hair, standing up for our rights, but it's moved so far into the Disneyland area being political is not cool. *Drag Race* tells us to go buy wigs, earrings, heels. They say, "Well, drag's expensive!" I'm like, drag was never that expensive! You'd get a dress, glue some rhinestones on it and call it a day. $1,500 for a fucking silicone breast plate? Are you out of your mind? It's capitalism.'

'Does it make you want to stop doing drag?' I asked tentatively.

MJ shook his head. 'I keep doing my drag to keep showing other queens you don't need *RuPaul's Drag Race* to be "successful" – you can create, you can sing, you can dance, you can act, you can write, you can produce, you can direct, you can do radio, you can host a big event, you can do spoken word, you can be in charge. I've asked other queens, "What's your goal in doing drag?" and a lot of them are like, "I just wanna do a show at a club." I say, "OK, well I wanna own the club that does the show. I wanna own many clubs in other cities and countries."'

'Like Monte Carlo?' I asked.

'Exactly. That's where my mind goes. My whole thing is, if you think drag queens want attention, I'd turn it on the queen and say if you want attention, what do you have to say? What do you represent? What do you stand for?'

'What do you think you stand for?' I asked.

'I stand for integrity, understanding and encouragement to be whoever you wanna be. I stand for bringing back the dignity into the LGBT community.'

On Saturday morning, Alix and I woke up early and set off for DragCon. We arrived at a massive, corporate, glass-walled conference centre to find drag queens of all varieties queuing to enter in the LA heat, towering over their non-dragged-up mates. The staff didn't bat an eyelid, nor did the guests seem to find this a spectacle. In the cafe, a beautiful older drag queen dressed as a Miss World winner was scoffing fries in a full face of make-up. Drag queens whizzed up and down elevators in saris and leather. There seemed to be an accidental irony to the situation. Alix and I stood in the foyer, agape. Alix went to the bathroom. 'There's no gender-neutral toilet,' she said when she came back.

The main room was carpeted with soft pink runways, and stalls were stacked as far as the eye could see, selling wigs and T-shirts and bondage gear. Around us there was a cornucopia of brightly coloured synthetic materials, but if we looked up there was nothing but a grey ceiling with bright strip lighting. I thought of what MJ had told me about when he went to DragCon: that it was like Disneyland. He was right – drag queens milled around waiting for someone to ask for their photo, people were cramming candy and hot dogs into their mouths, and there was a queue for literally everything except the toilet. 'Welcome to America,' said Alix, deadpan, for the first forty minutes, each time we saw something of this nature. I wanted to chat to some guests, but a tannoy sounded, RuPaul's voice announcing the arrival of someone I couldn't make out – the sound was muffled in the commotion that ensued.

The crowd parted to reveal a sea of pink, and down the main stretch in a golden carriage came a performer I recognized as Bob the Drag Queen. Everyone had their phones out, thousands of people snapping photos for Instagram and Facebook. It was like the gayest red carpet event of the century. Or the queerest. The crowd was wildly varied: young people, old people, people of all races, people with disabilities, people in drag, not in drag, in half drag, or just wearing drag-related merchandise. The only conspicuous absence was drag kings – I must have seen only two. Maybe that was because they had their own conventions, like Austin International Drag Festival's Kingfest and King Con in Ohio. Or maybe it was because drag kings had not been represented or supported by *RuPaul's Drag Race*, so they felt no desire to come along and support the show back.

I approached a family called the Smiths from Fairfax, California. The mom, Erica, dad, David, and nineteen-year-old son, Miles, were all in drag. Miles told me they'd been watching *Drag Race* as a family since it started, and this was their second DragCon together. Miles was fifteen when he started dressing like a woman, with the inspiration coming from *Drag Race* along with a couple of his parents' friends who were part of the gay community of San Francisco. 'He's been wearing dresses since he was one and a half years old,' said Erica of her son proudly. 'We've always been theatre people too, so I taught him how to sew and do make-up. He learned a lot from YouTube tutorials. Now he's styling his own wigs and making his own costumes. He made everything he's wearing.' Miles was too young to do drag in bars or clubs, and therefore too young to make money from it, he explained. It was really just a hobby. He had done it at the local town parade though, and in 'school drag shows' at his college up in Oregon. But DragCon was something else entirely: 'It's super hectic and super amazing,' he gushed. 'It's such a love fest, really, people complimenting each other – "I love your earrings" or "I love your wig".'

Alix interrupted: 'No one has complimented me yet.'

Not only was this a family affair, it was also as kid-friendly
as the website had promised. I saw a child dressed as Baby
Jane within ten minutes of being there. There was a children's area with a bouncy castle and face painting, where
they were holding Drag Queen Story Hour, which involved
drag queens such as fourteen-year-old Amber Jacobs, Panda
Dulce, Lil Miss Hot Mess and Pickle reading to the kids.
It reminded me of Amrou saying they loved performing
at kids' birthday parties and bar mitzvahs. The Kid Zone
was included to 'publicly advocate the importance of
instilling acceptance for all at a very early age, especially
in our nation's most current political climate'. Drag Queen
Story Hour was part of a wider initiative started by LA
author Michelle Tea, whereby drag queens read to kids at
local bookstores and libraries across America.

Elsewhere at the event was a stage for young people
to perform in drag. It was covered in branding for Gilead,
a global pharmaceutical company that produces HIV-
prevention drugs and hepatitis C medication, but price-
hikes them to the extent that they aren't actually affordable
to the UK healthcare system. MJ's words about 'not giving
back' and capitalism rang in my ears.

The publicist for DragCon, the cheerful Kelli, later
explained that the Gilead branding was on the Men's Health
Foundation stage, and that the Men's Health Foundation
was one of the sponsors, but Gilead wasn't. The other
official sponsors were World of Wonder, VH1 and Jeffree
Star Cosmetics. The brands and companies that could have
a stand were also carefully selected; some were for
non-profit organizations like the Human Rights Campaign,

others were vendors like Boy Butter Lubricants or the offensively titled Obsessive Compulsive Cosmetics, which has since shut down. In 2016, $2.3 million was spent on the floor of DragCon, via the two hundred vendors and exhibitors selling 'DragCon exclusive merchandise'. One drag queen I talked to – Alma Bitches, thirty-six, from Seattle, who'd been doing drag for seven years and was wearing a T-shirt that said 'Pizza and Anal' on it – said that, besides coming to see the queens from the show, she came for the shopping opportunities: 'I bought some one-of-a-kind shoulder pads – they're like $400 but silver-studded and fierce as hell.' She also bought some shirts, and some make-up. All in all, she spent about $700.

I wandered the hall and met Ronaldo, a sweet, earnest guy running a stall for his online kink store Torso and Trunks. Formally a dog walker, he'd had the idea for the brand to promote safe sex at gay men's underwear parties, by making underwear with pockets so you could carry lube and condoms with you. Then he branched out to what he called everyday kink wear. 'You can't always wear your leather harness, puppy mask or tail in public, so we're building a brand so that community can stand out and see each other,' he explained, reaching for one of the products. 'Like this pup hat – you could wear this in the street and only other pups would recognize it. Anyone else would think you're just a guy that loves dogs!' I pointed to a trucker hat that said 'Help: bottoms wanted' and suggested that maybe it wasn't as subtle. 'That actually sells a lot in New York because there are no "bottoms" there,' said Ronaldo enthusiastically. 'Everyone in New York is a "top"

and everyone in LA is a "bottom".' Ronaldo told me that
if you booked early as a vendor, it cost $800 for the stall,
and later $1,000, which he found reasonable. He wasn't just
here for the business opportunity, though. 'I love *Drag Race*.
Drag is a fun way to express yourself – and that thing
where RuPaul says we're born naked and the rest is drag,
well, I really believe that. Businessmen are wearing drag
– those are their power suits. For the gay community, the
wigs, the dress, that's a power suit for them as well.'

You didn't have to be a vendor at DragCon to be there
for the business opportunity. Vivien Gabor, a tall drag queen
from Seattle, told me that the first year she came as a fan,
but this year she meant business – she was primarily here
for 'hardcore networking' and to get new ideas and inspir-
ations. At twenty-six years old, and with two years in the
business, she considered herself semi-professional. She still
had a day job, working in the back room at a Goodwill
thrift store, but by night and on weekends she hosted and
produced drag shows. While Seattle has a pretty eclectic
drag scene made up of activists, people with musical theatre
backgrounds and queens that are more punk rock, Vivien
placed herself at the 'pretty girl' end of the spectrum. This
surprised me, since she was dressed in leather with an
executioner-style hooded headpiece. 'I like to make people
laugh, give people a break from having to think about bad
things, but at the same time use it to raise money for
charities,' she said.

She told me that a lot of her drag work came about
from personal connections, and since she was a producer
as well as a performer, she was there looking for sponsors

– underwear, make-up or alcohol companies that would financially back her events in return for dressing dancers in branded underwear or promoting their alcohol. Vivien wanted to make drag her full-time job, but said for now that seemed pretty difficult to accomplish without going on *Drag Race*. 'It's what I like to call a side art,' she said. 'It's not a typical visual art; it's not mainstream at this point, mostly in bars or concert halls rather than big venues. That makes it harder for people to see us. To get your name out you have to work real hard.'

Alma Bitches told me that she thought *Drag Race* was catapulting drag from a side art to a mainstream art and that this was a good thing. 'I'm of a mind where I want it to get big because I love doing my shows, but I need people to come to them. The more people that love drag, the better it is for all of us,' she said. For her it was about getting bums on seats. Vivien thought the popularity of drag was pushing drag queens further – a positive, yes – but explained that it also led to what she called a backlash. 'We're shown a lot of perfection and so now we're getting comments from fans saying, "You don't look the same as you do on Instagram," or you're not what they know of. It changes the game. It is a lot about pleasing ourselves, but now it's also about remembering that we have audiences who know what drag is to them and we're having to tailor it more towards that audience.' I asked for an example. 'Well, I can't really do a song because it's something that really touched my heart recently; or I can do that number but if I do it I have to do two more numbers that are on Top 40 lists . . . like Lady Gaga or Katy Perry.

As soon as one of their songs drops, you're learning it so that two nights later you're performing it. The audience is gonna be expecting you to know it already.'

'That sounds stressful,' I said.

'It isn't necessarily bad,' said Vivien. 'It's just a change in the game. And a lot of queens don't know how to make that change.'

I thought of MJ, and how he'd been told he was at risk of getting 'left behind', an anachronism in a world of overly made-up, Barbie-pink young drag stars who learned everything they knew from YouTube and *Drag Race*. That first night we met he stood out to me because he didn't dress like the other queens, because he sang a song that meant something to him – it was what made his show feel personal, touching, authentic.

As I walked around talking to people – the two lesbian teenagers who'd saved up money from working extra jobs to come from New York, the older Israeli woman who had brought her gay son all the way from Tel Aviv to show that she supported him doing drag – the more it felt like a melting pot. And one that everyone I spoke to agreed felt safe. So what if it was hyper-capitalist? People can spend their money on what they want, within reason. Why shouldn't they spend it on a plane ticket to America to buy merchandise with a man dressed as a woman on it? Going back to their hometowns wearing that was bound to raise eyebrows in precisely the right ways.

For all the money spent at DragCon, the event wasn't only about shopping. Throughout the course of the weekend there was a tight programme of panels. Forty-seven, to be precise. Alix and I scanned the schedule. Some were more political than others. Some were political without seeming it. 'Tucking 101', for example, dedicated an hour to discussing how and why drag queens tuck their genitals. We opted for 'The Art of Resistance', a panel about drag as a political art form. Admittedly the event happening in the conference room next door – a meet and greet with *Drag Race* contestants Trixie Mattel and Katya – was much busier, and admittedly it was jarring to hear a compère read out a list of the brand sponsors at the beginning of a talk on political resistance, but the panel was touching. Sasha Velour, a drag queen on Season 9 of *Drag Race*, explained what the political importance of drag was to her. It was about redefining beauty (she shaved her head bald when her mother was diagnosed with cancer and had to undergo chemotherapy) and it was about how being unafraid to gather and celebrate your value was a form of resistance in a climate of politics that doesn't value you. In her eyes, drag was the ultimate queer form of activism because it melded tears and pathos with extravagant drama and the challenging of norms.

Next, Alix and I went to a similar talk on 'Drag in Trump's America', hosted by the magazine *Teen Vogue*. The panel featured three queens from *Drag Race* – Bob the Drag Queen (who'd entered on the chariot), Alaska Thunderfuck and Eureka O'Hara. The room was full. 'Fuck yeah, it's fucking good that drag has gone mainstream,' said Bob – or gone from 'being referential to being referenced', as she put it. She believed that, paradoxically, drag was something real in a world of fakeness, a world that tried to erase certain identities. '*Drag Race*,' she said, 'is the most important show on television because it shows trans women and trans women of colour, and it's not *CSI* or *I Am Cait*.' And with that, the whole room booed Caitlyn Jenner. Whenever Donald Trump was mentioned, he got a good heckling too. 'Trump is just a symptom of the problem,' said Bob the Drag Queen solemnly. 'It's not the first time we've had people like Trump against us, it's just white, straight people's first taste of discrimination.'

I was surprised at the directness of the panel. Perhaps because of what MJ had said, or because the various series of *Drag Race* I'd seen seemed to keep things politically non-partisan – possibly so as not to offend viewers, possibly because the show just didn't feel like the place for such discussions. But DragCon was the place; here were three drag queens from three different parts of America with three different experiences mouthing off about the Trumps and the Jenners on stage. The atmosphere in the room was one of defiance and solidarity. Suddenly paying $50 for a weekend ticket felt like it might have been worth it. Changing my flight to attend definitely felt worth it. Even Alix was having a good time. She had stopped saying 'Welcome to America' because in this throbbing mass of silicone breast plates and skinny-jeaned homosexuals, there was clearly no one homogeneous America to joke about.

At the end of DragCon each year, ringleader RuPaul gives a keynote speech to the lucky VIPs and traders from the conference who are given access. That year, he took to the stage in a turquoise suit and lilac shirt, and kicked off by announcing there would soon be a New York version of DragCon. I suddenly felt bad for the young lesbians from New York who'd saved up to travel all the way to LA, though I had an inkling that they would probably save up to go to the New York version too. Ru told the crowd that DragCon had once again captured the ethos he wanted it to – it was all about showing young people how to live their lives without worrying about being judged. He walked the crowd through his life as a queen in Atlanta and New York, explaining that experiences good and bad had come to be his currency. His speech was packed with self-help jargon like 'say that you love yourself all the time' and 'clear out blockages in your life' and 'deactivate the ego'. Despite this, it felt surprisingly ad-libbed, unrehearsed. I guess it needed to be, in a room of LGBTQ+ people feeling precarious about their future in Trump's America. When Ru brought up the US President, he was adamant: 'We're not going back in time,' he said. 'A problem cannot be solved on the same conscious level it was created on.' The whole thing was like a church sermon crossed with a group therapy session. I felt a long way from home, but I didn't feel altogether cynical; after all, the adoration for Ru was palpable. He might have been very wealthy, and at times transphobic, but the levels of acceptance that he preached now seemed to match those in the room; I'd never seen so many people who'd otherwise be outcasts smiling together in one place.

As we shuffled out of the LA Convention Center that Sunday evening, Alix went to make a phone call, so I sat

on the carpeted floor of DragCon, bedraggled queens
pushing past me to their respective homes, some in faraway
cities and countries. There was a man sitting next to me
and we got talking. He was white, in his thirties, wearing
an orange polo shirt and cargo trousers. His name was
Eric. I assumed he was a gay man but just as I asked
whether I could interview him, a neat, Waspy woman came
over and joined him. 'This is my wife, Susan,' he said. They
were lawyers, newly married – Eric from Wisconsin, Susan
from Mississippi. Now they lived together in Las Vegas,
and had come to LA specifically for DragCon because they
adored RuPaul and the show. They had met at a drag night
by accident in St Louis, so watching the show felt like a
way of keeping that alive – then they fell in love with it.
'We found it a very positive concept, hilarious and beautiful,
affirming on so many levels,' said Susan earnestly. 'It's not
hard to be excited about something like that when you
hear the opposite messages so much more.' For her, RuPaul
embodied a political statement that said 'everyone is
welcome', but exerted his power subtly, using laughter to
turn the world onto drag. Eric agreed. Ten years earlier
he had represented a high-school student who was charged
with disorderly conduct and cited quasi-criminally for
wearing a dress to the prom. He'd been thinking about it
a lot at DragCon: 'There's still hate and bigotry to fight
and probably always will be, but this atmosphere is beautiful because it's so body positive and positive to wherever
one is on the sexual spectrum,' he said.

When I'd asked the teenage lesbians from New York
why they thought DragCon was a good thing, they said it

was not just because it fostered a community and culture for queer people, but also because it allowed straight people into that community. Their answer bowled me over. It wasn't what I'd expected to be a priority for gay nineteen-year-olds, but like DragCon, they existed in a time and place where apparently gay culture no longer needed to stay separate. I figured now I was face to face with the straight people that they were talking about. Eric and Susan might not have been Republicans, but they were Anglican Christians who went to church every week. I found this pretty amazing. Especially when they told me that their two weekly rituals were church service and watching *RuPaul's Drag Race* when a season was on. 'We're not so lucky to get DragCon every week of the year,' joked Susan. Eric looked pensive. 'For me . . . well, I identify as straight so it's kind of easy street for me. But for a lot of people in a lot of parts of America and parts of the world, it's a constant fight. They're dealing with bullying that doesn't end in junior high or high school. I was thinking, there's people flying back to parts of the United States to places that aren't nearly as welcoming as the West Coast. The US Supreme Court can move when the public allows them to move; LGBTQ+ rights in this country are very fragile. So when DragCon helps say, "We're not gonna go back in time"? It's very cool.'

chapter three

IN THE BEGINNING,
THERE WERE GAY BARS

A few weeks after I returned from LA, I found myself sitting in a circle of people in a draughty London warehouse. We started by going around the group, sharing our name, our pronouns, and why we were there. Some were first-timers who had read about the campaign online and explained that they were 'looking to do more activism'. Then there were the core members, who'd been going to the meetings for three years. I was there as a journalist, I said, who was thinking of writing an article to raise awareness about the campaign. Which was true, but I was also short on work.

Things had been looking up for me in my personal life since Iceland and LA; I was still dating Emily the lawyer, crying less while she was asleep next to me, and although I wasn't totally sure that I was ready for anything as serious as what I'd had with Salka, we'd continued hanging out. Something about the relationship just felt promising. But work-wise, I was listless, and still out of a full-time job, so I had decided to throw myself into writing about LGBTQ+ issues again. Only now I was regretting it: sitting across from me was someone I'd ended things with on the third date four years ago, her eyes boring into my soul.

We were at the meeting to talk about resurrecting my favourite gay bar: The Joiners Arms, a now defunct but legendary place – a grimy, one-storey, one-room bar-cum-club with a pool table in the centre that had made it look like a depraved youth club. It opened in 1997 and had been going for twelve years when I first arrived; although I knew people like the designer Alexander McQueen and photographer Wolfgang Tillmans had long since partied within its four walls, I never felt I'd missed the zeitgeist. Not even when it was near empty on karaoke Tuesdays. I remember Beth Ditto from the Gossip turning up at The Joiners and singing at karaoke, my friends trying to chat up the gay members of The xx – which isn't to emphasize its celebrity cachet, but to illustrate the fact that it put everyone on an equal playing field. It was famously cheap, welcoming and uninhibited. The air always felt thick with possibility, as well as the odour of sweat and testosterone. It was a male-dominated space, although transgender matriarch Stephanie always propped up the bar and Sunday nights were full of women.

Between the pub itself and the local all-hours after parties, you could spend most of your weekend in or around The Joiners, emerging wide-eyed on Monday morning in an outfit that had somehow seemed like a good idea on Friday night. And I did: between 2009 and 2012, I went to The Joiners Arms (along with one or two other gay bars) pretty much every weekend. The blueprint was always the same. I would arrive, already drunk, probably with one gay male friend and one straight girlfriend who was pissed off that she'd lost by majority rule and been dragged along. We'd swiftly get drunker, to acclimatize. Then, as these were the days before dating apps, we would survey the room, our cruising ground – or even circle it, depending on the floor plan that evening – looking for people we might be attracted to. Sometimes I'd ask my straight friend to flirt with me to 'drum up attention'. Over the course of the evening, we would work up the courage to hit on people. Four out of five times the attempt would fail and I'd leave with my gay male friend, the straight one having left out of boredom hours ago. On the night bus, or on the walk home, we'd lament the fact that no one but each other wanted to accompany us – a ritual that brought us closer together. Sometimes, we'd go on to another club to continue the party, like East Bloc, an underground techno and house club near Old Street with Keith Haring-esque paintings on its black walls and a labyrinth of corridors and rooms, the only place I've ever taken drugs that I found on the floor.

The Joiners closed in January 2015, after property developers snapped up the land. A lot like Brooklyn in New York, Hackney was an area of London that had become increasingly expensive since artists, gallerists and fashion designers took advantage of the comparatively cheap rent there in the 1990s and 2000s. The bar wasn't struggling for customers – it was full every weekend until its dying day – it just got priced out. The elderly landlord, David Pollard, had rented the building from a brewery, and when the brewery sold the land to property developers, he was informed that his lease was not going to be renewed. It turned out that the developers had also purchased the adjacent buildings on the street and planned to turn the site into a block of luxury flats. These flats would contribute to the shiny new gentrified facade of Hackney, a process that saw locally owned businesses replaced with chain restaurants and hip coffee shops while low-income families living in the surrounding council houses were also priced out.

In the years between 2006 and 2016, London became a gay bar graveyard. In this decade, 58 per cent of London's gay bars closed their doors, compared with 44 per cent of non-LGBTQ+ nightlife venues. I didn't really care so much about Candy Bar, one of the first I noticed go, a gay bar for women in Soho that closed in January 2014 after a 50 per cent rent increase. Although it did look like a brilliant caricature of a lesbian bar – all glittery interiors and a clientele in fedora hats – like something off the TV show *The L Word*. Personally, I preferred mixed spaces and cared more about the closures of Escape and Madame Jojo's, two fun clubs next door to one another in Soho – the former a generic gay bar that could have been in any city in the UK with its rainbow neon lights and pop chart playlist, the latter an iconic drag and cabaret club that had been hosting more and more straight nights over the last few years for economic reasons. Soho, London's foremost gay neighbourhood, was the area suffering hardest, but there were closures all over the city: The Black Cap, a beloved drag pub in Camden; The George and Dragon, a gay pub in Shoreditch; Hoist, an S&M club in Vauxhall.

So many closed that it felt as though we lost another every couple of weeks; my gay friends grieved, while many of my straight friends failed to notice.

Other cities were undergoing a similar transformation. In Manchester, the *Queer as Folk* heyday of the late 1990s and early 2000s gave way to a spate of closures, including the popular bars Taurus and Eden. New York's Chelsea lost a number of its gay bars to drugstores and bank chains during the 2010s, and a similar thing happened in San Francisco, due in part to the invasion of the tech industry: 'The tale is familiar in a city that is becoming ever wealthier with the arrival of newcomers taking high-paying technology jobs downtown or in nearby Silicon Valley,' said the *Los Angeles Times* in 2016. 'In 1992, nearly 1,300 businesses closed or changed locations, according to a 2014 report by the city's budget and legislative analyst. By 2011, that number had grown to nearly 12,800.' Like San Francisco, the reason London seemed to be hit particularly hard was due to its high land value. In 2016, it became the city with the most expensive rents in Europe. Yes, many gay bars couldn't afford to hold ground, but with these high rents and a high cost of living, a lot of my friends couldn't afford to go to them quite so often either.

However, the closure of London gay bars wasn't just down to the economic situation; many argued that they were a casualty of the cultural climate for LGBTQ+ people. Shortly after The Joiners shut up shop, I decided to start writing about the club closures for work, which, perhaps ironically, caused me to sober up and ask myself the bigger questions about what was happening to these places. In talking to LGBTQ+ people for the articles I wrote, a new idea emerged: that the physical gentrification of the city wasn't the full story; that our desire to go to gay clubs itself might be on the wane. If marriage rights and parenting rights were an upshot of our acceptance, the closure of gay bars might be the downside. After all, why would you need to go to gay bars if your sexuality no longer had to define you? Or if you were at home looking after a baby?

One of the founders of a drag party called Sink the Pink put it well when I interviewed them in 2014: 'We didn't feel like either of us belonged in a gay club or a straight club, so we just wanted a club where you bond on what you're into and what you're wearing, as opposed to who you fancy. This is what works for us and seems to fit how people want to club at the moment,' they told me, their words affirmed by the fact that this night was quickly becoming one of the most popular in London. The lesbian writer Eleanor Margolis echoed their sentiment when she suggested, in the *Guardian*, that the closure of Candy Bar was due to 'the gradual acceptance of queer women into the mainstream'. Others told me it was no coincidence that most of the closures peaked around 2014, the exact same year same-sex marriage was legalized. In early 2015 I found a quote in a book by Sarah Schulman that summed it up perfectly. It was by the legendary New York performance artist Penny Arcade, and it was about the homogenization and gentrification of New York's Lower East Side after AIDS first hit: 'There is a gentrification that happens to buildings and neighbourhoods, and there is a gentrification that happens to ideas,' she said.

Amidst the closures, I found myself wondering whether Penny Arcade's words applied to me. At some point, I had stopped going to gay bars as frequently as in those early days at The Joiners and East Bloc. I had found my people, come to terms with my sexuality, got a girlfriend and decided to stay in more. Much like a lesbian Carrie Bradshaw, I came to think: 'Am I no longer going to gay bars because they're closing, or are they closing because people like me are no longer going to them?' But then, also like Carrie, I got consumed by another relationship and forgot that I'd even asked the question to begin with.

Routinely throughout my adult life, I had frequented gay bars when I was single, but not when I was in a relationship. It was the same after I came back from Iceland; if the upshot of my break-up had temporarily been an excuse to punish my body with alcohol and cruise strangers in clubs, or at least to drown my sorrow in them like I had with Amrou, that plan had quickly been foiled by the fact that I met someone new and amazing so quickly and found myself steamrolling towards another relationship. For the months after LA, all I wanted to do was eat a takeaway with Emily, go out for nice dinners with Emily, lie in bed all day with Emily, and partake in other endless activities that revolved around sex or food. Once again, it was almost as if I had taken what I needed from gay bars and then abandoned them in their time of need.

Thankfully, for others the closures were a call to action, and the closure of The Joiners in particular sparked an impressive response. When news spread in 2014 that it was shutting down, a disparate but diehard group of about fifty customers came together to form the Friends of The Joiners Arms. They would meet in the pub itself at first, then in living rooms and local community centres. They were trying to save the pub, of course, but they also wanted to prove a wider point: that queer people were tired of losing out to the forces of capitalist greed and homogenization. They loved the bar for the ways it stood in opposition to these things. 'We wanted to show developers that we won't take things lying down, that we can play them at their own game using legal mechanisms to resist them,' Kate, a Friend of The Joiners, told me. 'We basically wanted to say, "fuck you".'

Early on in their campaign, the Friends got The Joiners listed as an asset of community value (ACV), which is when a property is deemed by the council to be of special importance to a community group, affording it extra protection against redevelopment.

Now, at the Save The Joiners meeting three years later, I learned that after much back and forth with the local council, the developers had been told they could not take away a building with ACV status. For the first time in British history, the sexuality of the people using a space was to be included in a condition for planning approval. The developers were forced to agree to draw up plans for a new gay bar and to offer first right of refusal to LGBTQ+ owners, along with free rent for one whole year. The new bar would be on the same site and slightly bigger than the old Joiners, but it wouldn't have a late licence (the old Joiners stayed open until 4 a.m.) because of potential noise complaints from residents of the flats being built on site. It also wouldn't have a smoking area, and it would be offered up as an empty shell, without toilets or a bar or storage, throwing into question whether a community-led LGBTQ+ group would be able to afford to set it up.

'It's ridiculous,' said one ex-punter, as we went round the group discussing the proposal. 'The space they're offering is completely unviable. They want it to close at midnight. The old Joiners didn't even get going until then.'

'One year rent free doesn't mean much if the rent after that becomes prohibitively expensive,' said another.

The feeling was unanimous: the offer laid out by the developer wasn't going to come close to creating an iconic gay bar like The Joiners. It was a 'Trojan Horse draped in a rainbow flag', concluded Amy, who'd been leading the meeting. The mood was solemn; no one said it out loud, but we all knew that cooperating with a luxury property developer to create a watered-down version of the old bar seemed like a distinctly un-queer prospect. Then again, how long could the group keep saying no for?

After the meeting, I talked to Amy, a lesbian who'd moved to London from the Valleys in South Wales. I asked her why she had taken on the role as one of the campaign's leaders. 'What was it about The Joiners?' I asked.

'It's hard to put into words what it was about the place, isn't it? It had a very queer feel. It wasn't clinical in any way, and you didn't know what you were going to get when you walked in,' she told me. Hearing her say this put a lump in my throat; it brought back the feelings of anticipation I used to get before I went to the bar. Amy described the strange paradox of The Joiners better than I could: as a place that was thrilling and exciting, but also a second home. 'You'd talk to different people in the smoking area – it was friendly,' she remembered, of the poky outdoors space which was literally about three by two metres. 'And I always felt comfortable as a woman there, when sometimes in gay male spaces you don't.'

Then she told me that, if trying to save the pub had started out from a love of the place, it had evolved into loving the group itself – a bit like those recovering addicts who become addicted to going to addiction meetings instead of whatever drug they were on before.

'This group's like my therapy,' she said jokingly. 'I suppose it gives me the same sense of community that The Joiners did.'

In my limited experience writing about grassroots activism, people often drifted in and out. At the Joiners meetings, many people had dedicated three years of their life to saving a bar – a bar that they simply loved going to. Some might say: 'We all know the feeling of going on a night out, taking too many drugs and not wanting to go home, but aren't these people taking it a bit far?' Not me – despite my own inaction, I did understand why the Friends of The Joiners cared so much. Bars like this were part of the reason why, at eighteen, I decided to leave the quiet suburban Home Counties where I'd grown up, and return to the city where I'd been born. Like thousands before me all over the world, it was my personal great gay migration from the rural to the metropolis. Many people I met shared my experience: arriving in a Mecca of pubs and clubs that were full of flamboyant people, usually from regional towns that had one gay bar and an uninviting, un-diverse scene. After growing up as a teenager in a place where I didn't know anyone else who was openly gay at all, these bars were a place where I could fall into the crowd, no longer so different; they were playgrounds for exploring your type, expanding your mind and discovering the many different kinds of people who exist in the world.

As these bars closed, we lost with them places where we could be who we wanted to be (in fact, I felt so safe from prying eyes in East Bloc that I had once mounted a podium and danced for four hours, wearing a gold bikini top). In these bars and clubs, I somehow felt simultaneously like someone else entirely and the truest version of myself. This was their power: they allowed people to comfortably wear things they wouldn't on the street, to behave in ways they couldn't otherwise; they enabled thousands of personalities to flourish. They were Petri dishes for subcultures, which were then released back into the world, making it a much more vibrant place. The idea that they could no longer be necessary was a strange one.

Jeffrey Hinton is a man who fills me with joy. He is an iconic figure on the London gay club scene. Not everyone knows his name but many know his face. He's in his fifties; his platinum-blond hair falls around his kind, round face in ringlet curls. He always wears slogan T-shirts that say things like 'Andy Warhol Is Bad' or just 'SEX'. An important chronicler of gay history, over five decades he's DJ'ed in gay bars, taken photos of the life unfolding inside them, and eventually moved on to filming in them – the medium he is best known for. He hoards all these films in his flat, occasionally loaning them out, somewhat reluctantly, at the request of massive institutions like the Victoria and Albert Museum or the Institute of Contemporary Arts, for exhibitions with names like 'Club to Catwalk', about how nightlife influences fashion. He is a brilliant DJ and often, in a London club full of raging homosexuals, he will be the one playing the music, making everybody sweat.

I couldn't imagine anyone better to talk to about gay bar closures than Jeffrey, because he had basically gone out gay clubbing when he was young and never gone home. I had witnessed the unprecedented rate of LGBTQ+ club closures during the period that I had come of age in them, but as someone who had seen so many come and go for so much longer, Jeffrey might be able to tell me why we needed gay bars, and whether we should be sad when they're gone

Fittingly, he asked me to meet him in a London gay bar I'd never actually been to: Central Station in King's Cross.

The area used to be a well-known gay neighbourhood, run down and full of notorious gay bars, but as in Earl's Court before and Soho after, these had shut one by one, and were replaced with office blocks or posh hotel chains. Central Station, however, had held its ground. A corner pub that had been there for decades, it was a London gay bar relic, fitted out almost exclusively in mahogany. About three minutes after we walked through the door, Jeffrey fell into conversation with the barmaid, Nicola. They'd never met before, but once they got talking Jeffrey explained that he used to DJ in the basement of Central Station in the 1980s, at a night called Marvellous, attended by the likes of Leigh Bowery and Sheila Tequila.

'I remember whenever I came to set up it smelled of piss,' said Jeffrey.

'Oh yeah, that would be the piss dungeon. That's still there,' said Nicola, as I glanced ominously at my pint. She said that the pub was a multi-purpose space: they had an adult baby night ('boring – all they talk about is their corporate jobs'), a mixer for cis men to meet trans women, and SOP, which stood for 'streams of pleasure', a water sports night. It being a Saturday at 3 p.m., we had walked in on something a bit more pedestrian, some sort of meet-up for board-game enthusiasts.

After five more minutes of chatting, Jeffrey and Nicola figured out that they had both worked at the famous central London nightclub Heaven around the same time – Jeffrey had DJ'ed there, and Nicola had worked the bar. As she slunk off to serve someone, he turned to me, his face suddenly animated as he started to describe Heaven. He gushed that at its heyday, right after it opened in 1979, it was the most amazing club he'd ever seen.

'It was underground, sexual, and had these lights, these huge halogen lights that were really, really hot, so everyone was sweating. They were all mobilized on hydraulics. Not like these flat LED lights you have now – they were oper-ated by people so they could be timed to the music.'

He told me that, in Heaven, when men used to hit on him, he'd be so preoccupied with the music that they'd usually get bored and sulk off to seduce someone else; 'I always wanted to stay to the end, dancing until the last record,' he said wistfully.

I had seen him in action; I believed him.

Growing up in Barons Court in West London, Jeffrey started going out with his brother when he was just twelve years old, mostly because he didn't want to be at home or at school. His mum was thrown out of the house when he was eight, and no one really talked about it again. His main carer, his grandma, was a strict Victorian-style matriarch, and there was a pervasive 'what would the neighbours think?' atmosphere in the house, a strange and unspoken pressure to conform that didn't sit well with him as a young, closeted gay boy. At school, conforming was off the cards because Jeffrey was racked with nerves, had a stammer and breathing problems, was dyslexic, and everyone assumed he was gay.

'How did they know you were gay?' I asked.

'Cause I looked like a girl!' he replied in his almost-Cockney accent. 'Plus my brother had gone to the same school and he wore make-up and Gay Liberation badges. They called me "queer", "poof", any name under the sun. I never actively denied it or anything. In my personal experience I was instinctively of the notion I'm a minority of one, my sexuality is a minority of one, my opinions are a minority of one, and I'm the only one going through it. It was hard for me to sense anyone else was feeling the same, but I had my brother.'

The first distinctly gay place Jeffrey remembered his brother taking him was a cafe on Whitehall, just along from Trafalgar Square, that was open 24/7 – 'Barkley

Brothers, run by Maureen it was' – where 'rent boys and
cross-dressers used to hang out, take all the blues and stay
up all night. I thought they were all amazing, because they
had none of the hypocrisy, and they were so visually being
honest about who they were. I always felt protective of
them. I mean, they were always fighting with each other
of course, but for me they were really nice cause I was a
kid. People around me would use words like "degenerate",
"queer" or "freak", and they were talking about these
people I knew who I found really fascinating, so they've
always been a term of endearment to me, those words.
I've always been attracted to people like that.'

The first actual gay club Jeffrey went to was called
Sombrero. It was on Kensington High Street, owned by
'two Spanish queens'. He described it as his first great love.
He met his first boyfriend there. Back then you had to be
twenty-one to have sex with men so Jeffrey was under age.
Not that that mattered much to him. 'I would sit at a table
and get drinks bought for me cause I was sixteen, cute and
I looked like a girl. But I never let anyone take advantage
of me and I've never been a real prolific sexual predator,
I'm way more interested in the situation, the music, the
lighting, the ambience.'

'What was the ambience at Sombrero like?'

'To me, Sombrero was an oasis, full of Italian waiters.
There were tables and chairs so it was very social, a round
light-up dance floor with alcoves around it . . .'

'So Seventies,' I said, as if I had been there.

'So Seventies . . . the DJ played disco – the best disco! –
and Italo music, all that stuff. It was a really great time for

music. I just danced my head off like crazy. It was downstairs, too. I love when clubs are downstairs; I like the separation between the street and the club, like we've entered into another world. I don't smoke myself but that's why banning smoking in clubs was bad. People go in and out, in and out now, engaging, disengaging. You don't lose yourself. What I love is that anticipation and fear about going to a club, you feel anxious and that feeds into this euphoria. When you go into a space that's sexualized, people look at you in a different sort of way.'

Most gay bars were members' clubs back then, he said, meaning you had to know someone and there was a 'whole paraphernalia' to get into places. 'In Sombrero you had to have food to go along with a drink because they didn't have a licence, so you had to have a spam salad, you were given it. No one ate it, mind, so the place was full of spam salads. Except me. I used to eat it because I didn't have much money, and I used to go to the kitchen cause this really sexy Italian guy used to be in there and we'd snog over the spam salads.'

'Well, that really throws out the door my cardinal rule to never eat anything you find in a gay bar,' I said.

'The thing about that time was that they say they legalized homosexuality in 1967, but really it was just a containment law,' said Jeffrey. 'You had to be over twenty-one and in a locked room to have sex. So there was still a mentality that you had to be hidden. People were still in their denial state of mind. Gay clubs were still underground.'

The same went for New York, he explained, where he

travelled on a one-way ticket in 1978. At first, when he arrived, he only knew two people, whom he'd met in Sombrero, but luckily after the invitation to sleep on their floor expired he met a boyfriend with an apartment. For a while, he even stayed with William Burroughs in his famous Bunker ('I knew who he was cause of my brother's books') and hung out with Allen Ginsberg ('a bit lechy'), as well as other members of the group (whom Jeffrey describes as 'that poetry lot'). To meet people, he would go to gay bars, like Hellfire, 'a tiny bar, and by the toilets there was a door that you opened and the back room was like a whole block of people having sex'.

The similarity between London and New York in the seventies, said Jeffrey, was that they were both bankrupt cities. 'London had the three-day week, all that kind of bullshit, and in New York people were burning out their houses to make insurance claims. What's really good about a financial crash in any city is there's less police because the city can't afford so many, there's less rules about who can do what, and the opportunity to occupy spaces rockets sky high. People come from around the world with creative ideas, and when everyone's got no money they're on an equal playing field, meaning the creativity goes through the roof.'

The only problem was, Jeffrey was one of these people, and therefore utterly penniless. 'People would say, "How did you get here?" and I said I walked from there and they said, "WHAT?" It was really dangerous to walk around the streets then. I looked like a crazy person with a little jam jar of vodka, long black coat, curly hair. I was a child. I lived off going to private views, eating all the food, drinking all the drink, getting on the phone they had in the back rooms of the galleries and calling people up to find out where the parties were.'

Around that time he met all the 'Parsons School fashion lot' and they started going to other gay bars. 'The Ramrod in the Meatpacking District was – what's his name . . . Robert Mapplethorpe's favourite place. Then there was Ninth Circle, quite young crowd, indie boys. The Anvil I loved, it had a cabaret bit and the first time I was there a drag queen did "I Will Survive", the Gloria Gaynor song. When it next came on the radio I said, "That queen's got a record out!" because she had sung it so perfectly. GG Barnum's had a Latin mix about it, and in one room there was a dance floor with a trapeze going on above you. The other room was Puerto Rican trans women singing with their lovers on stage. That was always very beautiful to watch, this celebrated love between these men and these women.'

At this point, Jeffrey's own eyes filled with love. Clearly gay bars had provided not only a place of refuge from childhood to adulthood, but also a place to be with other people who were made to feel like outsiders, a place to be sexual, social, a place to actually *do* gay rather than simply be gay. For him they were spaces where the culture came alive, an alchemic blend of secrecy, hedonism, the unexpected.

'Has there ever been a period when you didn't go out?' it suddenly occurred to me to ask.

'No,' he said, taking a sip of his pint.

★

As Nicola brought us another drink and I sceptically surveyed the food menu, Jeffrey tried to pinpoint the moment when he, like me, first started noticing gay bars closing, or at least going in a different direction. It happened around the time he left New York, he said. 'Studio 54 was great. I wouldn't say it was the best club in the world but it was good,' he said, noting that the thing that was different about it was how gay and straight people came together on the dance floor. Back in London, where Heaven had just opened, the crowd was similarly mixed, the last days of disco were unfolding and the London nightlife scene was gradually turning to punk. Sombrero had started to attract people like David Bowie, the gay managers of various bands, while Adam Ant filmed a video down there for his song 'Antmusic'. Eloise's, a lesbian bar, was filled with punks, and the famous Vortex club turned queer. 'Punk was gay to me, it wasn't anything else. It was people dressing up and having a laugh, being challenging to the world around them.' But the punk club Blitz, which had formerly been a cabaret restaurant, summed up the shift that was taking place; according to Jeffrey, it was 'gay, queer, whatever'.

To Jeffrey, the seventies and eighties were the golden era of clubbing, before the nineties brought with them the commercialization of venues, before gay bars were bought by big brewery chains, and before banking made property so expensive that small independent venues could no longer survive. 'It can honestly make a huge difference, capitalist greed. In the age of the pink pound, and as gay people got a bit more accepted, people started marketing to gays as a disposable-income group, and then you get these homogenized gay bars like the G-A-Y franchise growing, making money. That's not a liberated format, it's just another construct. You can't manufacture a good club. For me, it's about the quirks. They're why venues with certain feelings are my favourite clubs. Sombrero was one of those moments. It was a place where people came together; the soundtrack was beautiful, the dancing, losing myself in the life and energy, in my minority of one. That's what I was searching for. That's the journey.'

I suddenly pictured Jeffrey in a slogan T-shirt that said 'Minority of One' and smiled to myself. 'All of the places you really loved, they must all be gone now?' I asked him, knowing that, other than Heaven, most of the iconic venues he'd mentioned weren't around any more. 'Doesn't that make you sad?'

'I'm used to things coming and going,' he shrugged. 'Sombrero lasted a long time, but now that's gone. Heaven's still there but it's morphed, it's a shell of what it was. Now we don't even have Soho but Soho has moved into other areas. Nothing does last forever. And even if you keep the outside of a building, the energy of a space is changed.'

'Where does that put the Save The Joiners Campaign then?'

'I don't know what will happen if The Joiners reopens. I agree that if you love somewhere, you should try and support it or protect it somehow. If they've been inhabited by outcast people or political groups, there is a point to keeping some of these places. But it won't be The Joiners any more, it'll be a civic centre gay bar that has to meet a lot of council regulations. The only reason it was what it was is because it was this illegal drug den, invisible to most people around it, but that all these fashion and art people came and adopted. The Joiners went through a whole arc of reinvention, the mix became really eclectic and, you know, it just fit that moment in the night. But right now I'm way more interested in finding new places to inhabit and I think frustration is a really powerful tool for invention. I was brought up on squats and situational parties and that was exciting. It's only recently, after the closures, that we've had this move back to more illegal things, which I'm very encouraging of. The only way to be underground is illegal.'

He swigged his pint again.

'There is no nirvana, so you can get over that idea. It's the act of making something that's most relevant.'

A few weeks after my meeting with Jeffrey, one of the people from The Joiners campaign got in touch. They had spent the month and a half since our meeting going back and forth between the council planners and the property developer until a decision was finally reached: the developer agreed to grant a twenty-five-year lease to an LGBTQ+ landlord, £130,000 to fit out the venue, and the same closing hours as The Joiners had before it shut down in 2015: 4 a.m. weekends, 3 a.m. Thursday and Sunday, and 2 a.m. Monday to Wednesday.

The Friends of The Joiners Arms had successfully done what they set out to do: saved the pub (or, at least, a version of it) and sent a strong message to developers that community organizing can speak louder than cash.

I phoned Amy. She was elated. 'I hope it's going to have long-lasting effects, in that developers will be aware that if they try to bulldoze a space used by a minority group they might have a PR disaster on their hands, or it's going to cost them a lot more time and money to get things approved.'

Towards the end of our call I asked her if she was worried about whether, if they won the new space, people would actually come to it. This seemed like a question she'd already considered. 'I think people will come, both old and new. A lot of people say that since The Joiners closed they don't go out that much – but maybe that's because it wasn't there.'

Still, she said, the plan for the new Joiners was to re-imagine it as even more inclusive than it was before, more accessible, run by different parts of the community, and serving that community around the clock – a kind of pastoral centre in the day, and a club at night. But all of this could only become a reality if the Friends of The Joiners first managed to raise the money to secure the venue.

One sunny Wednesday morning soon after, I loitered in the bookshop at the London School of Economics, waiting for a man who'd dedicated many years to trying to explain shifts in the way LGBTQ+ people take up space. His name was Amin Ghaziani, a sociologist at the University of Columbia, who had pored over archives of newspaper clippings and interviewed hundreds of people in an attempt to understand something he called 'the gaybourhood', an urban area populated mostly by LGBTQ+ people, full of gay bars, usually a few other gay businesses, and lots of visible rainbow flags around the place. In his book, *There Goes the Gayborhood?*, which compiles the research, Amin argued that it wasn't just the gay bar under threat from gentrification and assimilation, but the gaybourhood more broadly. If anyone could shed some light on why gay bars were closing, it was surely him.

He arrived, a man of lithe build, wearing a grey suit, and led me upstairs to one of the university's offices. I pulled up a chair and explained my interest in gay spaces, what they had given me. Then I asked him where his interest came from. He told me that it was personal too; in his late twenties and early thirties, when he was a doctoral student at Northwestern University, he lived in Chicago's Boystown district, the historically LGBTQ+ area of the city. In the nine years it took to complete his degree, he said, he watched the neighbourhood change, noticing more straight couples pushing prams, and that among the straight men in particular there were gazes of discomfort when they watched same-sex couples holding hands. It became a topic of frustration for him and his friends, almost an obsession, and so he told himself that after he finished his dissertation he would write a book about these areas. It would be a form of therapy and catharsis, but it also seemed like an interesting intellectual proposition.

'And what were the main findings of your research?' I asked him now.

'I found that gentrification, rising real-estate prices and rising rents, these factors are hugely important in explaining why gaybourhoods like Soho in London, the Castro in San

Francisco or Boystown in Chicago are changing,' Amin explained, quoting me a statistic that illustrated how neighbourhoods in America with a higher gay and lesbian population tend to experience higher increases in house prices, illustrating a pattern of LGBTQ+ people moving into poor neighbourhoods only to get priced out further down the line.

'But economics are only part of the story,' he continued. 'You could say some people are being priced out and others are *evolving* out. It's that latter group that we talk about less.'

'OK . . .' I said, readying my pen.

'To understand specifically what happens when gay bars disappear,' he said matter-of-factly, 'there are other factors to keep in mind. One, technology: the increasing popularity of geocoded mobile apps like SCRUFF and Grindr makes it easier to either meet someone for a night or a lifetime without having to go to a gay bar, a gay neighbourhood or even an LGBT community centre. Of course, not every-body who goes to a gay bar goes to hook up, so it is reductive to say that they'd disappear simply because of apps – it's an overstatement. However, apps like Grindr are extracting a segment of gay bar patrons.'

Kate from The Joiners meetings had said something similar: 'Even if we meet online, we still need somewhere to go on a date, and the fact is, gay bars are safer than straight bars.' I agreed, but from talking to friends this seemed truer for gay women, who tended to use apps to connect but still met in public places; except for my friend Lea, who lived in France, and who inexplicably always seemed to be going straight round to strange lesbians' houses before the first date. Even many of my gay male friends tended to prefer to meet in a gay bar first.

'Next: culture,' Amin continued. 'The reduction of stigma against homosexuality, the advent of what some people called "post-gay", a moment we're living in that is charac- terized by unprecedented levels of acceptance towards homosexuality. Surveys show that both gay and straight people these days are less likely to say anything about sexual orientation than they did in the past; we see much more homogeneity in the composition of networks, so straight and gay people mixing more, and earlier average ages of coming out. Also, if you look at the language LGBTQ+ organizations use, it's less of "lesbian", "gay" and "queer", and more shifting towards rhetorical expressions like "pride" or "allies". Sometimes "LGBTQA" means the "A" includes allies, whereby you're not demarcating any real slice of life because that could be almost anybody.'

Amin was describing a time after gay men had officially become marketable best friends that you could bring both shopping and to brunch . . . as per *Sex and the City*, *Will & Grace* and *Queer Eye for the Straight Guy* (all my favourite shows as a teenager, and still my favourite shows today, if we're being honest). It was the time when I'd come of age, a time when the term 'post-gay' was bandied about by academics as a way to describe the idea that being gay no longer had to define you. A time when 'gay ghettos' like gay bars and gaybourhoods might suddenly no longer be necessary. Amin's book is full of examples of this cultural shift. He quotes an article in *Newsweek* from 1998 in which

James Collard, then editor of *Out* – a magazine aimed at metropolitan American gay men – declared the death of the gaybourhood: 'First for protection and later with understandable pride, gay men have come to colonize whole neighbourhoods, like West Hollywood in LA and Chelsea in New York City. It seems to me that the new Jerusalem gay people have been striving for all these years won't be found in a gay-only ghetto, but in a world where we are free, equal, and safe to live our lives.' Another example Amin gives is a quote from the American statistician Nate Silver. When *Out* named Silver as Person of the Year in 2012, he told the magazine he defined himself as 'sexually gay but ethnically straight'. I quoted this last example back to Amin, like a suck-up.

'Right,' he said, nodding. 'And if societal change reduces the stigma, straight people start socializing at gay bars that they used to avoid because gaybourhoods had been where outcasts, perverts, criminals were hanging out and living. Now, you lift the veil of stigma and you see more straight people coming in. A lot of talk about how gay bars are changing looks at the influx of straight women to gay bars, like bachelorette parties . . .'

'Who in turn can sometimes put gay people off actually going to the gay bars.'

'Exactly,' he said. 'But also if there are LGBT people who are no longer likely to cite their sexual orientation as the most important aspect of themselves, then one of the differences in their behaviour may be their patronage of gay bars; they may not feel the need to go to them. And if these gay people no longer feel like the only place they can socialize is in a gay bar, well then you're distributing the economic base, meaning the net revenue of gay bars is decreasing.'

It made total sense but it didn't address the issue of safety; I thought of all my friends who had been attacked in straight spaces for looking gender non-conforming, or for exhibiting same-sex displays of affection, like the lesbian couple I know who had recently kissed in a South London pub and had a pint poured over their heads by some wanker. I put this to Amin: what about these people?

'Oh, I think physical expressions of gay sexuality are not entirely safe in straight bars, no,' he agreed. 'Anybody who says we can go to any bar we want and do the things we used to do in gay bars is overstating the nature of acceptance. In some surveys that show up, some people are comfortable supporting gay rights in theory – formal rights, hospital visitation, inheritance rights – but they remain uncomfortable supporting informal rights such as the freedom to express affection in public places by sharing a kiss or holding hands. I call this "performative progressiveness" . . . performing a liberal sensibility without the backing of action.'

Amin's words reminded me of a stat I'd seen recently, that said more than half of British LGBTQ+ people didn't feel comfortable holding one another's hands in public, despite the fact that we were living in an age when we could legally get married. This seemed to be what Amin was talking about: the idea that you could have legal equality, but still not be safe or feel safe. Performative progressiveness seemed to indicate that *being* gay was OK, while *doing* gay wasn't – and the latter was what we needed gay bars for.

That wasn't all, though. There was another reason we still needed gay bars, Amin interjected, unexpectedly handing me a book by a man named Howard S. Becker. He said it was about marijuana users. I must have looked confused because he began to explain: 'In there, he says that even these experiences that we think are purely pharmacological actually have a very social element. The experience of being high is not something you just have on a blank slate or something that is caused by chemicals, but that your interactions with other people teach you what it means to be high.'

Where are you going with this? I thought, saying something to the same effect.

'Well, to take that analogy and import it, even the notion of gay pride, for instance, was not something that just existed. For me to understand what that meant I had to learn it, through interactions with other gay people.'

He told me about the first time he had gone to a gay bar: when he was eighteen, in Ann Arbor, a few weeks after he started at the University of Michigan. He recounted the nerves, how he walked past the bar again and again, too scared to go in. Eventually, when he did go inside, he met someone he would see again, and later form a relationship with. As the relationship unfolded, he would write in his diary that he was going to hell, and then, terrified that the words existed in print, he would tear the pages out of the diary and burn them. But over time, the person he met in the bar that night helped to erode his fear. Older and already out, the person gently pushed and nurtured him into coming to terms with his own sexuality, to forget what he'd been taught growing up in a Muslim household: that being gay was shameful or sinful.

'There were many conversations in that relationship that would begin with a request like: "I would like to hold your hand down Main Street,"' Amin said. 'I was uncomfortable about being seen, clearly visibly marked as gay. But his response to my resistance was almost always reframing the situation, that it is a beautiful thing, an expression of intimacy, affection, potentially love. And over time, I relented.'

'So going to a gay bar allowed you to meet someone who could teach you how to be gay?' I said.

'Yes,' he replied. 'Being in London now, I go to Soho and see that, even if bars are closing or it's gentrifying, the ones I go to are heaving with people and they're very gay people. OK, so there's a generational difference, it's older gay men, and this is just anecdotal, but clearly there will always be some who feel a deeper connection with people in person rather than virtually. This is a fact of human life. Sociologists call it "homophily", the fact that it's a basic principle of our social life that like attracts like and that any amount of technological cultural or generational change will not undo the power of that.'

'Homophily,' I said, writing it down.

'The colloquial phrase we use is "birds of a feather flock together",' Amin added helpfully.

'Birds of a feather flock together,' I repeated back to him, as if to speak it into existence.

I left Amin and walked home, thinking about my own

use of gay bars: I had, at some point, stopped going to them so much because I no longer needed them, especially not as a white cisgender lesbian – cisgender meaning that my experience of my gender matches the gender I was assigned at birth. But just because I didn't need them, it didn't mean I couldn't want them. And I wanted them because they gave me a sense of belonging that I now had a word for: homophily. The time I had been spun around the room by my friend to 'Total Eclipse of the Heart' in The Joiners, the time I had failed to seduce the only girl not wearing a fedora in Candy Bar, the time I had danced on a podium in a bikini top at East Bloc because there were no straight men around . . . all of this time I had been learning to be gay. In some twisted way, then, the fact that being LGBTQ+ had retained some of its shamefulness forced us together, encouraged us to find places and people who would help dissipate the shame, and kept gay bars like Central Station in business. I wondered: without them, where else would we learn to be proud?

chapter four

WHAT HAVE WE GOT TO BE PROUD OF?

In the summer of 1970, the first gay pride parades began to spring up across America. First in New York City and Los Angeles, then Boston, these events weren't called 'Pride' just yet, but had names like Christopher Street Liberation Day or Gay Freedom Day. They were mostly organized to mark the first anniversary of the 1969 Stonewall riots, though a lot of what had happened in the interim year spurred them into motion too. LGBTQ+ activist groups like the Gay Liberation Front, Radicalesbians and the Street Transvestite Action Revolutionaries had formed in New York, with the goals of achieving freedom and visibility, and they wanted to go public with an event. One of the marchers at New York's first ever Pride, activist and organizer Fred Sargeant, described it to the *Village Voice* newspaper years later: 'There were no floats, no music, no boys in briefs. The cops turned their backs on us to convey their disdain, but the masses of people kept carrying signs and banners, chanting and waving to surprised onlookers.'

This early prototype of Pride was a protest, not a party, although in the archive photos from the Prides that took place that summer, the events look like both. A sense of joyful defiance is palpable; lesbians carrying signs saying 'Hi Mom', men holding hands on Hollywood Boulevard, and the crowds of people, mixed in terms of gender, race and age, embracing lovingly.

It wasn't until 1972 that the first Pride happened in Britain. It was called the 'UK Gay Pride Rally' and it was held in London, on 1 July, because that was the nearest Saturday to the anniversary of Stonewall. If not a direct tribute to the trans women who led the riot, the UK Gay Pride Rally was at least intended to echo their sentiments: that the LGBTQ+ community would not stand to be oppressed. There were only around 700 attendees, but by making visible and externalizing that which was only found in gay bars at the time, it offered a political statement to the world that proud gay people existed and would not be kept underground.

Five decades later, Pride in London is in some ways the same: a day when LGBTQ+ people, not just from across the capital but from the whole of the UK, will wake up and feel as though – maybe just for that day – London's streets belong to them. Many trans people will hopefully feel just a bit safer than normal in a country that still denies them basic rights, and drag queens will get the chance to flaunt a look that's usually reserved for the cover of darkness. Pride in London is undoubtedly the UK's biggest show of rainbow solidarity – silly and vital in equal measure – and every time I've gone, I have felt this energy. And yet, a kind of indifference to Pride has always persisted. I like doing poppers in the street as much as the next person, but the annoyance of being in a large crowd has, on a few occasions, outweighed my enjoyment of the spectacle. When I went in 2016, it poured with rain as onlookers shouted homophobic abuse at my friend; I got day-drunk and drowsy – it felt like any other miserable British day out.

There were other reasons I felt ambivalent about Pride in London, and like a lot of people in Britain's LGBTQ+ community, I believe that the event could probably do us more justice. Over the years, the ethos of Pride has become diluted by a number of factors. With gains in equality has come the growing appeal of Pride to hen parties and other tourists, the corporatization of Pride by big business, and its co-option by insincere political groups looking to pink-wash their image. In 2014, Barclays Bank became a major sponsor; in 2015, Pride was criticized for inviting UKIP – a historically homophobic political party – to have an official presence in the parade; and in 2016, it invited the Red Arrows of the RAF to fly above the event, as well as allowing BAE Systems, one of the UK's largest arms manufacturers, to march, angering pacifistic and anti-military LGBTQ+ activists. Brighton Pride, a regional UK Pride event, has even been sponsored by British Airways, an airline who offer up their planes to deport LGBTQ+ asylum seekers from the UK, while Pride in London's own marketing has come under fire, too: 2016 saw a trashy '#nofilter' ad campaign, and 2017 was worse – Pride was met with a brand-new level of criticism for its official advertising posters, emblazoned with slogans like 'Gay man, straight man, we're all human' and 'My sister is gay. I'm straight. Together we're graight'. The queer community immediately hit back at the campaign with the question: Why are posters for Pride putting straight people at their centre?

All of this crap advertising reminded me of the 2014 advert for Burger King's 'Proud Whopper' burger, which was released for San Francisco's Pride and came packaged in a rainbow-coloured wrapper. The advert showed customers unwrapping the burger expectantly, biting into it and trying to figure out what was so different, only to realize . . . the Proud Whopper was just the same as the regular Whopper! Enough to put you off your food, and a prime example of the hammy corporatization that shrouds Pride festivals today.

Of course, Pride is important: the pan-European LGBTQ+ rights organization ILGA-Europe explains that 'Pride is the strongest, most visible symbol of the LGBTI movement – it's a litmus test of how well democracies are functioning. Prides can be an indication of how well governments protect and promote human rights.' I had no doubt that this was true, that it was a moment and a means to hold countries to account for the way they treat their LGBTQ+ population. But it seemed that Pride had morphed into something different from what it once was; as I had sensed that day in the rain at Pride in London, the event had somewhat lost its potency. Perhaps this was why several alternative events in London had sprung up: UK Black Pride, Peckham Pride, Queer Picnic. Britain wasn't the only place where this was happening, however, and so, that July, I decided to go to the city where I had heard that tensions were running highest.

★

I wouldn't say I *forced* Amrou to come with me to Berlin Pride, but I was persuasive. I promised them a Pride that made London's look like a family picnic, a utopian city where all the best clubs are queer clubs and straight people queue for literally hours just to get into them. I also knew that Amrou hadn't been on holiday for four years. Truthfully, I had no idea what to expect; the only time I'd been to Berlin I had been mercilessly rejected from Berghain, its most notoriously difficult club to get into, and all I really knew about Pride in Berlin was that there were so many different versions of it that it was difficult to make out what each of them stood for.

Christopher Street Day was the big main event that took place in the centre of the city. Then there was the alternative Kreuzberg Pride, focused more towards the trans community. And then there was Dyke March, a lesbian-orientated option. They all happened, I read, over one weekend, and I didn't know how we could possibly attend all three. What I did know was that Berlin is the home of alternative culture, with a thriving BDSM community, a staunchly political gay scene and the most terrifying lesbians in the entire world. Wherever we ended up, that had to make for an interesting time.

I arrived in Berlin on Friday afternoon; Amrou had a drag event that night so they wouldn't arrive until tomorrow. To save money, I had booked a hostel in entirely the wrong part of town, so once I was out, there was no popping home. My plans to meet German friends fell through three times, and I began to experience the acute loneliness of being a tenuous friend to people in a strange city. I walked around and eventually settled at an Italian restaurant in the tourist centre. For some reason I couldn't stop thinking about Salka. It had been months since we broke up, but when you react to a break-up by pinballing around people and cities and jobs, the rare moments you find alone with nothing much to do become difficult. Frustrated, I gave up and walked the hour back to the West, where I was staying. Just as I got there a friend messaged me: 'Where were you tonight at Dyke March!' Drunk, lonely and emotional, I started to cry. My phone rang. It was Emily.

'What's wrong?' she said softly, ever patient.

'I've missed Dyke March.' I wept like a baby. 'I've spent all my money flying to Berlin to report on Pride and now I've missed Dyke March. I'm officially bad at my job.' My guilt about work was now exacerbated by my guilt at thinking about Salka.

'I'm sure all the dykes haven't gone home,' she said, taking my trivial problem quite seriously. 'Why don't you try and find them now?'

The unofficial Berlin Dyke March after party was at a bar called Südblock, in the precise direction I had just walked away from. The party was in full swing when I got there. I could see lesbians dancing under rainbow disco lights inside the building, which seemed barely reachable, given that hundreds of dykes were sitting on the floor outside, drinking beer out of cans. The floor was strewn with banners reading brilliantly confrontational statements like: 'You think I'm straight BUT I'M NOT'. It seemed like the natural conclusion of Dyke March. I searched for my friend – a self-described leather daddy dyke who was equal parts clever and condescending. 'You need to be going round here and interviewing these women about what you missed,' they pointed out when I found them.

'Yes, thank you, I am going to do that,' I said through clenched teeth.

Interviewing these women was not easy. Every time I walked up to a couple of dykes, they would kiss and I would have to back away slowly or pretend to be searching for a friend. The ones I did speak to all told me that they'd been coming to the event for several years, and that every year, they came to Südblock afterwards. 'Pride is very male-dominated and also very consumerist,' Julie, a thirty-one-year-old queer Berliner, told me. 'I think Dyke March has more of a tradition of showing female and queer struggles. I think it's more political and I feel more comfortable here – it's not so much about the gay cis male, but people as femmes, fags, females, transgender feminine people.'

Another person I spoke to, Kristen – who identified as 'lesbian dyke whatever' – told me: 'If you go to the main CSD Pride parade tomorrow and you saw Dyke March today you would know the difference, it's simple: one is a march, one is a parade.' For Kristen, who was Canadian, Pride had lost its way with police presence and sponsors: 'I don't think of Pride and think of being proud,' she said. 'I think we should have a shame march. Because when you see Pride sponsored by whatever corporation, it's nothing to be proud of. We have a power to disrupt shit and to present a different way of living in this shitty fucking world, and all of a sudden that suddenly gets absorbed. It's like we're made to think we belong, until something happens to remind us that we don't.'

Kristen told me about Pride in her hometown, Toronto, to illustrate this. They have a huge, all-encompassing event that's a testament to Canada's inclusivity, she said, but it's still not good enough. In 2016, Black Lives Matter protesters created a blockade to demonstrate against the police presence. Queer people of colour who suffer police brutality should not have to celebrate Pride under the watchful eye of their oppressors, they argued. 'I thought, this is intersectionality, this is people coming together,' remembered Kristen. 'Black Lives Matter did the most important political thing, shutting down this corporate police march.'

For Kristen, this sort of thing justified why, sometimes, one Pride simply doesn't fit all, and explained why Berlin has so many. She told me that Kreuzberg Pride was cancelled that year due to infighting – the radical queers behind it just couldn't seem to agree on what it should look like. 'That's a shame,' I said, having planned to go to it, and feeling slightly nervous that I would now be missing that as well as Dyke March.

'There's a queer picnic set to take place at the same time as the big commercial CSD parade was planned, at Hasenheide Park. You could go to that,' she offered.

Dyke March Berlin didn't spring up in opposition to Pride, but as an alternative. Its organizer Manuela Kay set it up in 2013 in the image of other Dyke Marches that had taken place in major cities like Washington DC (the original, dating back to 1993), San Francisco and Chicago. Manuela was the publisher and editor-in-chief of *L-MAG*, Germany's biggest lesbian magazine, and the company wanted to do something to mark its tenth anniversary but also to serve the community. 'Berlin didn't have one and we thought about how, at the time, lesbian invisibility is increasing,' she explained. 'Everyone at the magazine had been to Dyke Marches over the world at some point, so we took that idea of reclaiming the streets, and created something suitable for Berlin. A protest not with a distinct political message or a new model every year or any concrete demands, but a general message of visibility.'

Each year, Dyke March takes a different route to Südblock, and according to Manuela, the crowd has grown every year, from 1,500 in the beginning to 4,000 today. They keep *L-MAG* branding minimal, despite the fact that the magazine's staff pretty much organize the march on their lunch breaks. It has inspired four other Dyke Marches around Germany: in Cologne, Hamburg, Heidelberg and Oldenburg. Everyone is welcome, as long as they are respectful.

When Manuela and I spoke over the phone after Dyke March, I quickly learned that she was an out and proud lesbian raised in Kreuzberg, in the former West Berlin, and, at fifty-one years old, had been going to Prides every year since 1992. She knew about all the fighting over what Berlin's Pride should look like because she'd witnessed it from the wings. When I asked why there was so much conflict, she laughed at me.

'I'm afraid that's unexplainable to foreigners,' she said.

'The way the political discussion here is going is beyond belief. The more left they are the more they fight each other, so there were years when we had three different Prides happening at the same time. The people organizing it think of course it's a political statement which one you go to, but the people who are going to these events are totally overwhelmed with the decision. A lot of people I know would like to go to all three of them – they like the radical messages as well as the big commercial Gay Pride.'

'So you can't say the political people go to one and the apolitical people go to the other one?'

'It's not as simple as that. It's a challenge for the LGBT community to have all these Prides, but that's what Berlin is – a melting pot. It almost seems like people come here to fight over these issues. Sometimes I wonder why we don't have twenty Prides in Berlin.'

The fighting started right after the fall of the Berlin Wall in 1989, explained Manuela. Some people thought they should start in the former East; others thought the event needed to stick to the Ku'damm, one of the busiest and most famous streets in Berlin. The fights were over which location would get the best visibility; some wanted the walk to be where more tourists would see it and others said the walk needed to be where actual Berliners were living. As the CSD Pride grew in size over the years, people argued over that, too; something that also bothered Manuela:

'I don't think it's necessary to have it as big as it is. I think it should just end with a party but not a huge stage. All these drinks stalls and food, it's like a carnival. Most

LGBTQ+ people I know just go home after the parade, and the after party is for tourists and people who don't even know where they are. Over the last fifteen years, they forced it to be bigger and bigger without a clear vision of what they wanted it to be. Of course we can't turn back time to when CSD had five thousand people and everyone knew each other and it was like a class reunion. We fought for it to be big so we can't complain. But people at Dyke March tell me they miss that family feeling, and that's why they come to Dyke March. The more intimate an event is, the more you feel like a family.'

Kreuzberg Pride was tiny, according to Manuela. With its 'Queer Liberation March' it was the small, intimate affair that CSD wasn't, where friends could meet and soak up an atmosphere devoid of big trucks and company names. She wasn't sure why it was cancelled, precisely, but pointed out that CSD had taken note of Kreuzberg Pride's more political messaging: 'There was a break a few years ago where the old people stepped back from CSD and new people came, trying to re-politicize it – but it's not as easy as they thought.' She thought they needed to get rid of brand sponsorships from big banks and car companies and insurance brokers. 'Of course these businesses have more money to present themselves at Gay Pride than your local gay cafe or lesbian self-help group, but there's a big imbalance in that. It's a problem for all the big Prides all over the world.'

Towards the end of my night at Südblock, I met two gay guys called Joseph and Nick, PhD students from the USA living in Berlin. I asked them what they were doing at Dyke March. 'A friend of mine was marching and I wanted to express support and solidarity,' said Joseph. 'Attending an event that focuses on non-cis, white male people feels like a prerogative during a Pride weekend which puts those types of men above all else. And I say that speaking as one.' Joseph was indeed a skinny, white cis male.

'Are you going to Pride tomorrow?' I asked him.

'I'm not going to main Pride – it valorizes a body culture of very muscular white hyper-masculinized men that I don't feel that I belong to or want to be a part of,' he said.

I looked at Nick, a tall, handsome and built gay man in a snapback cap and vest. 'What about you?' I said.

'I think the body culture is totally fucked up; we end up subscribing to it,' he said, obviously noting his own complicity. 'As Joseph said, it's important not to valorize these body types or normative genders that are so hegemonic, but really centre the experience of the most marginalized queer people.'

I agreed. And we all hit the dance floor.

The next day, I woke up, got dressed and walked to the Berlin Victory Column, a huge, gold-topped monument on a roundabout in the Tiergarten, the city's biggest park. I knew the tail end of the CSD Pride parade was going to pass through here and felt that it was a good spot to inter-cept it. The people I met waiting didn't seem to fit the concerns Joseph and Nick had voiced the night before. There was Marianne, for example, an attractive blonde woman in her forties who was wearing a leather dress, sipping a Caipirinha at a cocktail stand that had evidently been erected in the name of the parade, just as cigarette vendors and people selling rainbow flags were targeting the slowly building crowd. Marianne was with her husband and a gay friend. She told me she was also writing a book – about the adventures she had with her slaves. A bisexual dominatrix, she felt that Berlin CSD represented the BDSM community well, and also pointed out that she might feel more reticent about wearing her fetish gear in the middle of the day in Miami, where she was from, compared to Berlin.

Günter, a gay man in his late fifties, told me that he was there to take up space, and believed that all lesbians and gays and trans people had a duty to go out and show themselves, to say 'this is who we are'. Just as Manuela had suggested, Günter was the type of gay who liked CSD and Kreuzberg Pride, and had been to both. But he was convinced that there should be one Pride to cater to everyone; 'Why should we be separate? We're the same people. Every person is an individual but we are all a community,' he told me in broken English, sounding forlorn.

'Do you think it could ever happen?' I asked.

'I have no hope that it will,' he responded.

When the parade itself approached the monument, I could hear it before I could see it. Gay Europop anthems and Katy Perry hits carried on the wind. I waited and soon discovered that a bus led the procession, blasting the music, with feathered drag queens dancing lazily on top of it while the audience cheered from the sides of the road. I immediately noticed that the parade wasn't shut off from the crowd with cordons or tape, but anyone was welcome to join. Taking advantage of this, I circled behind the bus and merged into the procession alongside a group of pups – men wearing leather dog-style masks for the purpose of puppy-play fetish. I overheard British accents coming from two of the masked boys closest to me who, other than their studded dog masks, were just wearing nondescript jeans and T-shirts. They were called Chris and James, and were also from London.

'What's the biggest difference you've noticed between this Pride and Pride in London?' I asked them, curious.

'Everyone seems much more relaxed about fetish and it's more in the open, whereas in London it tends to happen behind closed doors,' said James.

'It's a bit quieter than London – the crowd seems more chilled. In London everyone's screaming and dancing,' said Chris.

'I like the fact anyone can join in though,' said James. 'It's an open invitation to the march – you have to get a wristband in London, and if you haven't got one you're not marching with your friends. It seems much more democratic here.'

Another bus passed, emblazoned with a big banner that said: 'Skittles, taste the rainbow'. I cringed at how well the sponsor's tagline fitted in with the cause. Then my phone rang; finally, Amrou had made it to the parade. But just as I started looking for them, it began to rain – a terrible, biblical rain that felt as if it had been sent to drown us all for our buggery. I momentarily wondered what that meant for the queer picnic I'd planned to go to in Hasenheide, and then found myself preoccupied with trying to locate some shelter. Amrou was nowhere to be seen, and I spent forty-five minutes in an underpass with hundreds of other soaked, grumpy Pride-goers. People were smoking and drinking in the tunnels, drag queens with make-up running.

Eventually a dripping-wet Amrou appeared. 'God, this is miserable,' they said, cowering and shivering in the tunnel with me. We resolved to make a dash for it, and walked through the rain and the sad sight that was the outdoor Pride after party – a series of stages blasting music, and stalls selling overpriced cocktails. Marianne had warned me that her stand was the cheapest.

There were a few hardcore party animals dancing in anoraks, and Amrou and I joined them for a bit, or long enough to get drunk, before retreating to a nearby shopping centre to buy shoes that weren't saturated. Then we decided to do what felt like the only option left to us: go to Berghain, the club I had traumatically been ejected from six years before and which judges whether people are worthy of entry on the basis of how cool they look. 'This is the least queer thing we could be doing on Pride,' Amrou pointed out while we waited in line.

'I agree. It's so gross that a club that claims to be queer will reject people based on their appearance,' I said, internally praying that we would get in. After an hour in the queue, we still had a way to go, but the sunk-cost fallacy of the time we'd already invested made it too hard to give up. When we got to the front, we were, miraculously, admitted. The rest is forgotten, but what I do know is that

Berghain – with its attractive crowd, expensive cover charge and elevated sense of importance – reflected all of the criticisms people had made about CSD, and none of them, at least in my opinion, had applied to CSD at all. What I had discovered in Berlin was that the confusion around what Pride should look like had led to nothing but infighting. It was kind of a mess.

Amsterdam's Pride happens on the first weekend of August, two weeks after Berlin's. It's different from other Prides because it's structured around a boat parade along the city's canals, with people riding vessels packed far beyond what health and safety regulations ought to allow. I decided to visit it because it's supposed to be Europe's biggest and best, the website claiming it has over half a million spectators.

All of this makes sense when you consider how progressive Holland is; although buying weed and buying sex are not entirely decriminalized, they are legal under regulation, and the Netherlands was the first country in the world to legalize same-sex marriage, back in 2001. But as the head of the COC, the Netherlands' foremost LGBTQ+ organization, would tell me when I met him at a Pride event, the country had lost its footing in global polls on LGBTQ+ equality in recent years precisely because it was so far ahead of the curve in the past; it recognized gay equality in the law so early on that there was a feeling that equality had been achieved. The government had become complacent.

Still, I was impressed at just how forthcoming the Dutch

were when I reached out to speak to people. The organizers of Pride immediately introduced me to Hans Verhoeven, who I was told had been organizing Prides for over twenty years. Hans explained that I would need a bike – naturally – and that I could follow him for a day as he went about his various duties. As an ambassador for Pride, and one of the five people on the organizing committee, he needed to go between events to say hello, express his appreciation for the various societies and groups that held events under the overall Pride banner, and check that things were running smoothly.

Amsterdam Pride lasted a week, with the main events taking place on the weekends and a load of smaller events in between. Hans organized Pride Walk, which kicked things off on the first Saturday. It was an event designed to keep the protest in the proceedings, since it was ostensibly a march, followed by a bunch of political speeches. Then, once Pride Walk was over, Hans was free to breathe and focus on helping everyone else out with their events in the lead-up to the second weekend, which featured the big canal parade. I'd not heard about any splinter Pride or alternative Pride events in Amsterdam and I was beginning to see why: the main event was extremely comprehensive.

This was confirmed when Hans sent me the schedule. I was to meet him at a networking event for autistic LGBTQ+ people, before we moved on to an old people's home, and then the Mayor of Amsterdam's house for a drinks reception. The first was held in the leafy brick court-yard of the Amsterdam Museum, which was where I found Hans in a tight pink T-shirt with a leather body harness over the top, and butt-tight green jeans with army-surplus boots. He had a military-style short-back-and-sides haircut and was obviously a gym-goer. He sat me down, lit a Marlboro Red, and explained the basics.

'This is the way we've set up our programme over the last years: the week is activities with the beefy content, activities that have subject or meaning. And the last weekend: all about the party. But even when we have partying to do, we remind people that Pride has not always been a party but it started as a riot, and there's still lots of countries where Pride is not existing and where being homosexual is not fun at all, and we do that through power speeches.'

I would come to learn that moderating the party with the protest was Hans's entire MO. 'What's a power speech?' I asked.

'Every stage gets an ambassador to give a speech at the main stages of the party. We ask for attention, remind people where we came from, that there's a lot to do in the world, and we wish them fun in the meantime. I started it two years ago as a test: I took what I expected to be the most difficult of the stages, Amstelveld, where there's most heterosexual people. I thought, "If it works there it'll work on other stages as well." People had drunk a couple of beers and this guy came on stage and cut the music, and I gave the speech. Responses were good; people listened. So the year after we decided to do it on all stages. This year we're doing twenty-two speeches.'

'Who else gives the speeches?'

'Since 2013, Pride Amsterdam asks a new group of ambassadors who are community representatives each

year. I was amongst the first group in 2013, and the year
you're appointed is the year you're the face of Pride –
you're used in the media, you give speeches. We have
trans ambassadors, two people from the senior community, a drag queen . . .'

'So it's not a democratic process?'

'You see in Berlin where alternative Pride gets cancelled
from infighting; it doesn't work making this a democratic
process. There's a lot of money involved: €1.2 million.
When you're running a project like this, it's all about big
decisions. So we have five people on the board, an office
staff of four, and then we have coordinators . . . I coordin-
ate Pride Walk. The coordinators are very much on their
own: you're given a project, they say good luck. You find
a group of volunteers you work with, and you go for it.'

As Hans stubbed out his cigarette and went to say goodbye
to the organizers of the autism networking event, I considered just how obsessed with Pride he was. He had told me
before we'd met that, in 1991, the year I was born, he'd
launched something called the European Pride Organization.
The Berlin Wall had just fallen, and he and some friends
were discussing how they could support LGBTQ+ people
in developing Eastern European countries to hold their own
Prides. 'We thought, we'll make an event called EuroPride
which we'll award to different cities in Europe: the first one
was in '92 in London, '93 Berlin, '94 Amsterdam. We used
the first ones to set up the systems, to get things organized,
and then we exported them to countries that needed them
more than others,' he explained.

I knew that the previous year, EuroPride had come back

to Amsterdam, for the first time in twenty years. I asked Hans how it was.

'It was extremely emotional,' he said, 'after all those years . . .' He trailed off. 'Come on, I want to show you something.' He led me inside the foyer of the museum, where a fifteen-foot mannequin stood wearing a dress made up of national flags. They represented all the countries in which homosexuality was still criminalized within the law, said Hans. The dress had been made for the previous year's Pride, and was worn by a model in the parade. Then it had seventy-six flags on it, but three had since been swapped out for a rainbow flag. That was Belize, Nauru and the Seychelles, Hans told me proudly; they had all decriminalized homosexuality in 2016.

We stared at the dress for a moment. 'OK, let's go,' said Hans.

Cycling through the city behind Hans was a shaky business. He was a native Amsterdammer, weaving through traffic seamlessly, one-handed, smoking a cigarette with the other. Meanwhile, I was clutching my handlebars, constantly poised to brake and lightly sweating from the stress of being a non-cyclist in a foreign city attempting to keep up with the Dutch gay Action Man. My feet couldn't really touch the ground on my rented bike, so I panicked at every stop sign. But it was the best way to see the city: the dark, narrow stone houses along the canals, the boutiques and coffee shops.

Nestled among all of this vibrancy was the drab old people's home that Hans and I were due to visit. When we walked in, we were met with a room full of seniors, maybe a hundred people, mostly in wheelchairs pulled up to tables, angled towards a piano. At the piano a man was tapping out a jolly, old-fashioned Dutch song, while, circling him, singing to the crowd, was a slender drag queen in a dress emblazoned with ladybirds. The audience was hardly rapt: about ten people sang along as the rest stared blankly.

'Are they all gay here?' I hissed into Hans's ear over the music.

'About 85 per cent. The city has a programme for LGBTQI-friendly activities in elderly homes; it happens all through the year. We have eight elderly homes that work with Pride and we have more joining . . .'

After a few numbers, Dolly Bellefleur, the performer, moved on to conducting a raffle, and Hans and I ducked out, finding some plastic chairs to sit on in the beige linoleum-floored entrance hall. I asked him how Pride Walk had been. Apparently seven thousand people had shown up at the weekend, despite the rain. The focus was on the seventy-three countries where homosexuality was still illegal – just like the flag dress – and that year, they'd added an 'individuals at risk' programme, whereby attendees carried fifty signs to represent fifty LGBTQ+ individuals from around the world who had either been murdered or jailed for their activities. One such person was the long-blond-haired Iraqi actor Karar Nushi, who was murdered in Baghdad in July 2017 after rumours of his homosexuality circulated. Telling me about Karar, Hans began to sob. I was slightly taken aback that this six-foot, middle-aged man was crying in the entrance of an old people's home.

'What makes me very angry is people so easily forget about how lucky we are,' Hans started, wiping his tears. He looked at me. 'You know, we've been under attack the last couple of weeks; this discussion happens every year about how commercial Pride is . . . people say these companies who sponsor us have no interest and that is not true at all.'

I wasn't sure what this had to do with Karar's murder, but I sensed Hans was getting to it. He explained that, of the €1.2 million Amsterdam Pride costs to run each year, a small subsidy of €200,000 is from the city – 'that's the same cost we make for security and stages' – and the rest is paid by sponsors, usually a couple of big corporations. As in Berlin, people took huge issue with these brands' involvement. Time and time again, Hans said, he had received criticism for working with them – something he saw as irrelevant when so many people around the world don't get a Pride at all. He reeled off a number of things their sponsors were doing for the community:

'Yesterday I spoke to a general manager at IBM. He has three colleagues whose entire job is involved with our community worldwide, to see how we can work together, and also how to make an open, inclusive workplace for LGBT people. No one knows that's happening, so how can it be for the money? Three years ago, Vodafone changed the coffee cups in their shops across the world to have rainbow flags. Now, this won't change countries' laws, but in Bangladesh that one guy who is in the closet might pull out the cup and see the Pride flag, and that might be the closest recognition he gets from his employer there. This is more valuable than any money they can give us. And a few years ago, our other sponsor, KPN, put a 360-degree camera on their boat at Amsterdam Pride, so that you could log in and sail with the boat in countries where you cannot have Pride. They made it so people were safe to log in to the website, and we had thousands of people watching, from Iraq to India, people looking to have a little bit of the fun.'

According to Hans, it was 'very easy to sit in your comfortable chair in Amsterdam and not appreciate these things', but I also sensed that he felt personally affronted by the criticism of Pride as a commercial enterprise. Mostly because he'd brought it up before I'd even asked. For him, working with brands was a simple transaction: brands got to sail with the other boats, have their logo on the poster, and Pride got a handful of cash that they were free to spend as they wanted. 'Sponsors have no involvement in how we do things,' he assured me. 'If anything, it's more the other way around – we demand from our sponsors that they have an inclusive and diverse policy for their workers and staff, that they have the basic needs of LGBTQ+ people taken care of within their company. If they don't, then we don't want them as a sponsor.'

Complaining about Pride sponsors was clearly a first-world problem when compared to issues such as the criminalization of homosexuality or the murder of LGBTQ+ people, but the subtler point was that people who were sceptical of the corporatization of Pride, like me, might not be considering the fact that, although sponsors can change Pride for the worse, Pride might be changing its sponsors for the better.

Over lunch, Hans told me why he cared about Pride so much. He was fifty-three. His older sister, who had passed away two years before, had been gay as well. He was lucky in the sense that, growing up, she did most of the 'awareness creating' with their parents, the process of attrition that is coming out first. It wasn't hard for him at all, he said, never a struggle or a fight. At seventeen, his first boyfriend, a blond veterinary student called Eric, came over for dinner. After he left, Hans and his father were washing up, and his father told him to give in to his love for Eric if that was what he wanted. Hans almost dropped the dishes in shock.

He became an activist because his father worked for a company that moved them around often, to a lot of developing countries where Hans saw inequality first-hand. As he grew older, LGBTQ+ rights became his main interest, because it was the social issue closest to home. Especially given that, as understanding and kind as his parents were in regard to his homosexuality, they didn't have much information to impart to him; he had to hunt out his own history. Many second-generation children born to ethnic minorities were instilled with some background on their race, religion or culture, said Hans, but LGBTQ+ kids didn't necessarily have LGBTQ+ parents. He wanted to create a Pride that showed people the community they came from and where it might be going, something he had craved when he was growing up.

After lunch, we cycled to the gay fetish shop Hans owned. He needed to give his cat some antibiotics (they lived together above the shop), so I browsed while I waited. The room upstairs sold less kinky stuff and more tourist fare: soft porn, rainbow flag memorabilia, gay and lesbian DVDs, gay greeting cards, that sort of thing. I was more interested in the downstairs, a fetish store selling all kinds of specialist items. I browsed the rows of anal dildos, harnesses like the one Hans was wearing and full leather body caskets, which, once bound up, seemed like they might simulate the experience of death. I hadn't heard of it before, but I had no doubt it was a thing.

'Do people ever comment on the fact you sell butt plugs and are a cat-loving human rights activist?' I asked Hans when he re-emerged.

'They never mentioned it to me,' he smiled. 'I don't think it's too strange. The fetish scene is about acceptance and accepting yourself and your feelings in society. I call myself a social liberal entrepreneur: I do a lot of activism in my shop.'

Then he told me he'd tried all the toys on sale himself, for quality-control purposes.

As we got to our last stop, the Mayor's drinks reception, I told Hans that in Iceland there'd been a huge scandal after the country's BDSM community had been rejected by the main LGBTQ+ association and banned from walking in the Pride parade. In 2014, the head of Pride had refused to allow the fetish-lovers to take part, deeming it too offensive or risqué. And so in 2015 they didn't even bother applying, instead deciding to boycott the walk.

'Prejudice is not exclusive to the straight vanilla world,' Magnús Hákonarson, chairman of BDSM Iceland, had pointed out. The mainstream LGBTQ+ rights movement in Iceland had been so successful in integrating gay people into society, winning equality by law and marketing Pride as a family day out, they didn't want to run the risk of tainting their image with a load of mask-wearing, whip-toting fetish enthusiasts. Although in 2016, when I went to Reykjavik Pride, they were present in the parade, so the scandal couldn't have ended too acrimoniously.

Hans said that everyone was welcome at Amsterdam Pride – explaining why an alternative Pride hadn't sprung up yet. Pride Amsterdam was just a platform, and via its website anyone could apply to organize an event that would form part of the programme. That was why there were so many. In the canal parade there were more than eighty boats; an HIV testing centre had one, a BDSM group, there was one for the military, one for firemen, one for over-fifties. The sex worker community would even have a boat in the canal parade for the first time that year. The only way in which it wasn't inclusive was the access to the boats themselves, said Hans. It was incredibly difficult to get on one, he told me. 'You couldn't join in unless you jumped in the water and swam behind them,' he said, in a way that made it impossible to tell if he was joking. This was one of the reasons they'd started Pride Walk, he added: so Pride would be more accessible, like in Berlin.

After I left Hans to go to drag queen bingo (him, not me – I was too exhausted from all the cycling), I kept thinking about that sex worker boat. It didn't seem particularly inclusive to me that Pride would only have a sex worker boat for the first time that year, in a city so famous for its sex industry, and when sex workers and queer people have so much in common; both groups are destabilizing to mainstream ideas of sexuality and patriarchy, and as such, we've historically been both criminalized and ostracized (sometimes quite literally into the same areas, such as gaybourhoods like Soho).

Luckily, I knew some Dutch sex workers, having done a story on sex workers' rights in Amsterdam the year before. Two of the women in the article identified as queer, so I asked whether they could help me get onto the boat. 'You need speak to Lyle,' Hella, one of the sex workers, told me. She would be on the boat, she said, but Lyle was one of the organizers and he had 'a lot of opinions' about the inclusion of sex workers in mainstream LGBTQ+ rights.

I called Lyle. Lyle explained that the boat was going to be a big political opportunity because it was a great way to show 500,000 spectators all at once that Dutch sex workers weren't all cisgender women, that many were LGBTQ+, and that they came in all shapes and sizes. Sure, Amsterdam had its red light district, but this was about taking people out of that and making them visible. 'Pride is one of the biggest public events in the Netherlands so being there as a sex worker, out and proud, without any masks, I think that's a very important statement.'

I agreed, but Lyle still took a lot of persuading that I wasn't going to ruin the vibe of the boat by being bigoted, pushing someone in the canal, or asking sex workers stupid questions like how much they got paid. I even had to quickly pen a letter to everyone on the boat, to convince them in turn that I would protect their names and personal details if they wanted me to. Once that got the all-clear he told me to be at a ferry point about a mile from Centraal Station for 9 a.m. I asked him what to wear and bring and he told me, 'Whatever you want,' which I thought was nice and inclusive, but also incredibly unhelpful.

At nine the next morning, no one was at the spot Lyle had sent me to. It was just me, cycling around a closed and empty dockyard, bewildered. Thankfully, I had decided to wear my regular clothes, so wasn't dressed in anything too ostentatious, which might have made the feeling of being stood up more embarrassing. I had decided to pack two bottles of white wine to help ingratiate myself with everyone on the boat and overcome my nerves about being stared at by 500,000 people – which had nothing to do with being on the sex worker boat and everything to do with being the type of person who desperately craves attention until they actually get it.

After leaving Lyle a few missed calls, I was about to give up when I located the people I was looking for. One of them was Martin – who ran P&G292, the catchily titled government think tank that had coughed up the cash for the sex worker canal boat – and the other was Sharon, our choreographer for the day.

Sharon was dressed in a black T-shirt that said 'VOGUE' – in the same font as the magazine, but in reference to the dance style. My stomach lurched as she explained that we would be doing a dance routine to 'Lady Marmalade' to entertain the crowds along the canals, and everyone – *everyone* – on the boat, including me, had to learn it.

Martin was handsome, in his thirties and blond. He was wearing an ever so slightly shiny suit, which I guessed might have been the glitziest thing in his wardrobe: why else would you wear a full suit on a searing hot day in August? Martin explained that the idea for the boat had come up in a focus group P&G ran with male sex workers about three years earlier, but it had taken a long time to come to fruition, mostly because of funding. The boat had cost €6,000 to hire for the day, not including the sound system, decorations, food and drink. Lyle later told me that funding P&G was a way for the local government to reconnect with sex workers after a restrictive policy had closed down a large percentage of Amsterdam's windows, creating a lot of hostility in the community. This wasn't a bad thing, he added, because without the P&G groups the idea for the boat might not have come up.

By 11 a.m., about a dozen more people had arrived, a few blaming a hangover or work the night before for their lateness. There were a couple of middle-aged Hispanic women, a couple of gay boys in tight hot pants. My friend Hella arrived, wearing a baseball cap and dark glasses – because she wasn't quite out as a sex worker to everyone she knew yet. Lyle arrived, and given his authority on the phone I was surprised at how young he was – twenty-three, he told me, but he looked even younger. He was short and confident, speaking to the Hispanic sex workers in fluent Spanish, before switching to English and then Dutch.

I chatted to a beautiful man called Ricardo, who told

me he was from Bonaire, a Dutch colony in the Caribbean, but had moved to the Netherlands to study tourism. I also got acquainted with Foxy, a pink-haired porn star from Utrecht, and as Sharon started coordinating us into formation, we decided to crack open the white wine I'd brought.

Foxy told me that she mostly did gang bang or shame porn, as well as BDSM work, which I could have guessed from the 'joy' and 'pain' tattoos on her knuckles.

'Don't you think "Lady Marmalade" is a little trite?' I asked her, as everyone started rehearsing in the car park. Foxy agreed, but Sharon was beckoning us over. She was very strict in enforcing her routine, explaining that we would have to restart the song and launch into it anew every time we emerged from one of the bridges along the canal over the four-hour period we'd be sailing.

'How many bridges are there?' I whispered to Lyle.

'About fifty, I think,' he replied.

I looked over to Foxy, who was also trying to copy Sharon, and wondered how this level of humiliation compared to shame porn.

More people were assembling in the dockyard now, canal boats sailing across the water to pick up the various Pride parties. One was made up of drag queens dressed in pink. Another had people all wearing white polo shirts and looked very wholesome, perhaps linked to a brand. I felt we were especially malcoordinated as a group; a motley crew of about twenty people, nobody seemed to be able to memorize the dance routine and everyone was dressed very differently – some in leather, some in sequins, some in jeans and a T-shirt. We also seemed to have fewer people than the other boats, maybe because not everyone wanted to make their debut as a sex worker on Dutch national television. In that moment I felt a pang of respect for the sex workers who had turned up; as many of them reminded me throughout the day, they knew well the stigma that came with choosing to do sex work, particularly as an LGBTQ+ person. Lyle had given me examples of this before we'd met: LGBTQ+ sex workers might be less likely to come out as such to people they knew. Trans women who were sex workers were often prone to violence from men struggling with their own sexuality. And then there were migrant sex workers who had come from homophobic countries and were doing sex work to survive. Being an LGBTQ+ sex worker didn't necessarily grant you respect from other LGBTQ+ people either. Lyle said he often encountered discomfort in what he called 'normalized or integrated parts of LGBT culture': people who didn't want to associate themselves with what they saw as promiscuity. In that sense, it was a bit like the BDSM organization that was rejected from Pride in Iceland. I could see why that made being in the canal parade so important: by outing themselves as queer sex workers, the people around me were doing what little they could to erode all of these stigmas, not just for themselves but for other sex workers too.

Lyle told me afterwards that he hadn't just dealt with the stigma of coming out as gay and a sex worker, but coming out as HIV positive as well, something he'd decided to do recently in a YouTube video. He had got into sex work when he was still at school and working in a supermarket for €3.50

an hour. At the same time, he was discovering the excitement of travelling on his own, as well as his sexuality – rites of passage for any teenager. 'I was earning less money and spending more,' he recalled, 'and I remembered this one time that I'd been in a chatbox online when I was younger and guys were offering me money for sex. I would say no because I was afraid of STDs, or afraid that they would kidnap me or something, but now I was older, eighteen, I thought I should give it a try, and when I did, I really liked it. I expected that I had to take my clothes off, have sex, get my money and then leave, but my first time couldn't have been more different. My client was even more nervous than I was. He shared his life story. How he had been struggling with his homosexuality in rural Belgium for decades and how this was one of the few ways for him to be able to experience intimacy.'

The decision to become an activist came more easily than the decision to be a sex worker for Lyle. Despite being born in the Netherlands, Lyle moved with his parents to Belgium for ten years, where he joined the Belgian Green Party when he was just fifteen. He later got involved with high school politics, eventually chairing the student union at eighteen. 'While I had that position I started doing sex work, and I was enjoying what I was doing, giving nice moments to my clients,' he remembered, 'but I couldn't speak honestly about it. I had to cover it up, and I found that uncomfortable.' Around this time, Lyle's parents had begun to figure out what he was doing. 'My mum, she is a sensitive woman. I was working late hours and had weird excuses for how I earned the money I all of a sudden had.

She put it all together and it hurt her initially, but she always told me she loved me and never made me try to change my mind or stop.' Lyle said his mum's open attitude helped him to make a decision: in the summer holidays, after a year of being president of his student union, he wrote a blog post in which he came out as a gay sex worker. He said the news became a big story in Belgium, and particularly in Bilzen, the sleepy town he was living in. 'I was seen as this good student with good grades and involved in politics, and then this person turned out to be a sex worker,' Lyle explained.

He eventually decided to relocate to Amsterdam because he'd visited it with his mum and seen all of the cultures, the freedom, the LGBTQ+ people. 'It was so different from where I came from – I came from a small countryside city where diversity was not the norm. In Amsterdam I fitted in right away.' Continuing his sex work, Lyle quickly became involved with launching PROUD Netherlands, a union for sex workers, and even acted as their spokesperson for a while. The PROUD office, which sat beneath the stunning eight-hundred-year-old church Oude Kerk, was where I'd interviewed Hella and her friend the previous year, and now, as we boarded our Pride P&G292 sex worker boat, we were handed red umbrellas with the word PROUD printed onto them. The red umbrella was the union's logo – a symbol of shelter, but also inclusion – and the idea was that we'd open the umbrellas and spin them around at some point during 'Lady Marmalade', to do a bit of PR for the PROUD brand, which supported its members through crises like extortion from brothel owners, police harassment and having next to no workers' rights, as I had found out on my last trip.

The boat set off at around midday, and the moment it started moving I became extremely conscious of the fact that I wouldn't be able to get off for four hours. As we entered a kind of queue where the boats were lining up to start the actual parade, we practised the dance routine one last time without Sharon, who had left for another appointment. We poured glasses of box wine and filled our stomachs with catered sandwiches. I didn't ask anybody what kind of sex work they did, but no one minded telling me as I chatted to them. Some of the guys worked in boys' clubs – closed establishments where punters could come in, have a drink and take a guy upstairs, they explained – others were window prostitutes. There was a girl who did webcam sex, a straight porn actor, and Lyle was an escort who went to his clients directly. He later told me he'd seldom been in a space full of sex workers in such diverse areas; often they were segregated along class lines. The boat itself was decorated like a window brothel, or at least that was the idea – along each side there were windows which were, inconveniently, too tall to pass under the canal bridges, meaning we had to collapse them every time we went through one or else the boat would be destroyed. As we approached the first bridge, the crowds along the water were beginning to thicken: families waving rainbow flags, drinking from plastic cups. Some onlookers stared, others didn't, and I couldn't decide which I found more offensive.

We assumed our positions.

'Where's all my soul sistas? / Lemme hear ya'll flow, sistas.'

We glided through the waterways seamlessly, but the routine was a mess. No one could remember what Sharon had taught us, and the more we drank the more disbanded we became. The sun was glaring down on the entire event, and as we sweated through the nineteenth chorus the crowds seemed to be giving us an A for effort. People were cheering, throwing flowers, raising their glasses to us. And if they weren't, we didn't care because we were too drunk on warm box wine and adrenaline and pride. I wasn't a sex worker but I still felt emancipated as a queer person, openly dancing in front of all those people, and my face hurt from laughing as Foxy and Hella rubbed their fingers together and pretended to solicit from the boat, poking fun at the ridiculousness of the song playing.

By the time we had heard Lil' Kim's voice for what must have been the fortieth time, the boat had descended into a sort of Bacchanalian orgy – most of the boys had taken their shirts off and were kissing. I too had taken my shirt off to reveal my bra, and didn't really think about it until later when my Dutch aunt sent me a clip from the TV coverage with a message saying: 'Is this you?'

The boat was strewn with empty cups and fag butts and clothing. Everybody was embracing. Ricardo and I swapped numbers so that we could stay in touch. It felt as if something magical had happened, but we'd probably need a few days to process just what that was.

I called Lyle later in the week to ask him how he thought it had gone. He said he was happy with the amount the

Pride organization mentioned our boat in the media, something he took to be a sign of their support for the project.
Having gauged the crowds' reactions after the fact, he felt
that we'd surprised a few people by being there, another
good thing 'because that's when change happens, when
the people with the least familiarity of sex work see you'.
And most importantly, being there with his community,
being open, had changed something for him on a personal
level.

'You saw it yourself – everyone was cheering and happy
and there wasn't that much difference between our boat
and all the other boats on show to the world. We're part
of that LGBT community just as anyone else, doing a job
just as anyone else,' he said excitedly, explaining how the
day proved that, even in Amsterdam, for all its progressiveness, Pride was vitally necessary for certain groups of
people, and how even for him, the most out and proud
sex worker there was, it gave him an unprecedented feeling
of self-worth.

'The canal parade is a moment of Pride and to have
sex work there, portrayed like that, as something that is
joyous?' he concluded. 'That's just something you never
see.'

I travelled to Belgrade with Emily in mid-September.
In England, summer was bowing out. Belgrade, like
Amsterdam, promised thirty-degree heat, a much more
appealing prospect than a Berlin-style washout. Less promising was the idea of having hundreds of protesters shout
'death to homosexuals' at us, as had happened at Serbian

Pride in 2010, part of the reason Belgrade Pride is still cordoned off from the rest of the city by armed police. I looked at Emily sleeping angelically next to me on the plane and worried about her safety. I thought about how she wasn't out to her parents, meaning that if anything did happen to her, I would have to explain somehow why she was: 1) in Belgrade, 2) in Belgrade with me, and 3) at Belgrade Pride. My neuroticism could only mean one thing: that I was completely falling in love with her.

In 2017, a study revealed that 59 per cent of people in Serbia think that homosexuality is a disease, so it was easy to understand why Pride hadn't been as big there as it had been in Berlin and Amsterdam. LGBTQ+ activists thought that after the fall of the war criminal President Slobodan Milošević's regime in 2000, things in the country might become more liberal and Pride more accepted. But the 2001 event, the country's first Pride, was attacked by various right-wing groups.

According to Goran Miletić, probably the most well-known voice in Belgrade on LGBTQ+ rights, a gay Serbian activist and Director for Europe at the Swedish not-for-profit organization Civil Rights Defenders (who now co-fund Belgrade Pride), there was just no desire to have a Pride in 2002 after the 2001 attack, and the Serbian government banned the event anyway. Though activists thought about organizing another Pride in 2003, they were deterred by the shooting of Prime Minister Zoran Đinđić by a member of the Serbian mafia. As Goran put it: 'If you see there is a force that can kill the prime minister, what can you as gay or lesbian expect?'

2003 to 2009 became a period of fighting for legal wins, as far as the LGBTQ+ community in Serbia were concerned. In 2005, they didn't get a Pride, but they did get a law banning discrimination based on sexual orientation in employment, and another in higher education (although this law has never actually successfully been used in court). In 2009, there was what Goran described as a 'huge scandal' when an umbrella anti-discrimination law was withdrawn by the government just hours before its adoption, at the behest of some Serbian Orthodox priests. 'The Church is that powerful, and the only reason for the withdrawal of law is sexual orientation,' Goran explained. 'But for the first time, we got some kind of sympathy from the public about it, and some media were on our side. For twenty-five days, there was a huge campaign, and eventually parliament adopted the law. We thought, "Aha! We have some sympathy, this is the time to try Pride again."' Once again, however, the government banned Pride (by changing the location to an area that would have been unsafe, according to activists). A small number of Serbs held their own Prides in the spirit of funerals, laying down flowers in political protest, as you would if someone had died, as if mourning the broken promise of democracy.

When Pride did eventually happen, in 2010, the security level was understandably high. Thousands of police were deployed to protect the parade-goers. 'Hooligans', as they say in Belgrade, moved to the police front lines and threw petrol bombs, rocks and bottles – mostly at police, as they couldn't get near the parade. Frustrated by this, the mob then proceeded to vandalize the city in a statement to the authorities that Pride should not be permitted. They torched cars and trashed government buildings. The government tried to pass this off as general hooliganism, with the Mayor of Belgrade, Dragan Đilas, telling the press at the time: 'What's going on now has nothing to do with the Pride parade. Unfortunately there are always people who will use every opportunity to destroy their own city. Fortunately no lives were lost – this is the most important thing.' Around forty police were injured and sixty people arrested.

'I was in the media team, monitoring fascist forums and websites, where people were brainstorming how they wanted to attack the Pride,' Aleksandar, one of the volunteers in 2010, told me. 'They were planning what kind of weapons to use, where they wanted to store rocks to slingshot. At the Pride we were so disconnected from what was happening, we didn't know anything, but the city was burning. The police interrupted the party before it even started, saying they have to evacuate us.'

All Pride events were cancelled by the government in 2011 and 2012, until 2013, when a guerrilla Pride was planned. Organizer Adam Puskar explained that, after the official ban when the prime minister made the statement on prime time news that he would not stand for Pride, a group of LGBTQ+ people and their friends went to the main office building of the government, inviting left-wing media to report. 'In that moment a police cordon surrounded us, so anyone who wants to join the celebration, they cannot come. Police say they will arrest all of us 'cause we are doing something against the law.

'We tell them we are not marching on the day of the ban, as the official ban was for tomorrow, so we use a hole in the law and march,' Adam told me over Skype, before I arrived in Serbia. 'A lot of the media called this Stonewall for Eastern Europe, because we don't want to be funny, smiling people on the streets; we want to send a political message that we exist, that we won't have pressure on us any more.'

By 2014, under Prime Minister Aleksandar Vučić – a former nationalist who had pivoted to become the main champion for Serbia's bid to join the EU – Pride was finally permitted. The night before, protesters gathered in Belgrade's main square, demanding the protection of family values and the banning of Pride. In a VICE Serbia video, they can be seen sharing sentiments like, 'Pride is a stab in the heart with the Serbian flag.' But Pride went ahead, though Vučić himself was conspicuously absent, despite endorsing the event. About 1,000 people showed up to join the parade, among 7,000 armed police, according to Goran. Despite a few anti-gay protesters, there were no incidents. It was the same for the 2015 and 2016 parades, which Goran claimed had 6,300 and then 4,500 police in attendance. The Pride we were attending was set to have the lowest police turnout ever – with 2,000 officers. I wasn't sure if that made us, the people going to Pride, more or less safe.

As the plane touched down in Belgrade, I kissed Emily to wake her up. 'You can't do that here,' she said, opening her eyes. I was confused for a second and then remembered where I was.

'Legislation and the things you have on paper in Serbia might seem wonderful and amazing but the reality is totally different,' Adam had warned me, although I didn't think it did look that amazing. 'There is no implementation of all those things. There is one picture in the media and another in real life. You will see.'

Belgrade is a delightful city. It has the relaxed atmosphere of European cafe culture with none of the pomp of Paris or Rome or Berlin. It's slightly dilapidated – some of the buildings are still bombed out from the Yugoslav Wars of the nineties – and you can smoke in restaurants, which is so popular that the no-smoking areas often have the only empty tables, where no one is eating. There are few tourists and people are incredibly friendly, like our Airbnb host who greeted us with Turkish coffee and illustrated an old map of the city with sights we might be interested in. We pretended the reason for the trip was just a cultural visit. Two gal pals on a city break.

The Pride Belgrade calendar had a few events listed for each day of the week-long festivities: panel discussions on living with HIV, film screenings of camp classics like *Priscilla, Queen of the Desert*. After putting our stuff down, we decided to check them out, and headed to a venue called KC Grad, a bar down by the Sava river that held monthly *RuPaul's Drag Race* screenings (yes, even in Serbia) and other queer cultural events that might not find a home elsewhere in the city. I was supposed to be doing a talk for VICE Serbia on gender neutrality (a concept one Serb described as 'first-world problems' in the ensuing Q&A)

but my main reason for being there was to catch Ines, a trans rights activist who I hoped could tell me about life for LGBTQ+ people in Serbia.

In person, Ines was formidable. She was dressed in long, black lace Gothic clothing, with a dramatic side fringe. She was with her boyfriend, a big masc Swedish man whom she jokingly described as 'her bodyguard'. As we sat down to talk she brushed aside my precursory line of questioning – 'So are you from Belgrade originally?' – with, 'First, let's talk about intersectionality.'

The idea of the meeting was for Ines to give me some background on the state of affairs for trans people in the country, but I would learn hers was a very unique experience. Ines was from the southern part of Serbia, a city called Novi Pazar, which was the only Muslim-majority town in the country, in the region of Sandžak: 'That means I have a specific religious and ethnic background – my parents are belonging to an ethnic minority in Serbia called Bosniaks, which are a Muslim ethnic group on the territory of Balkan countries,' she explained. This brought specific dynamics when it came to being trans, she said. Her local community, when she was growing up, was highly conservative with a lot of religious fundamentalist groups. 'If you google my hometown you will see the political rhetoric of independence, because they do not want to be a part of an orthodox country.'

According to Ines, her childhood was 'just terrible', as was probably to be expected. 'I have always known that I am a trans woman, although in childhood you do not have that identity category of "I am trans",' she began. 'I just knew that I am a girl. I liked everything that a little girl is supposed to like. It can be influenced by the media or whatever – what is femininity and what is not is a different conversation – but in elementary school it was difficult to express myself. When I was in first grade I would always take a towel to school and put it on my head and pretend that is my hair! The other pupils would tease me and my parents were really angry, like, "If you take that fucking towel once again!" But I was only being myself.'

Ines began her activism when she was just fifteen, getting involved with a human rights organization in her home city – the *only* human rights organization in her home city, and one that had never touched on LGBTQ+ issues. They agreed to let her start a series of workshops on LGBTQ+ rights.

'Did anyone go to your workshops in Novi Pazar?' I asked.

She lit a cigarette. 'Honey, it is 2017 and I am still the only public trans person from my hometown; it is 120,000 person big. But there is always a hipster community everywhere and they are willing to listen to everything related to LGBTQ+ rights, even if they're not LGBTQ+.'

Ines's main priority at this time was to get as far away from Novi Pazar as possible: 'My strategy for saving my own life was to study, to be a good student and get a foreign scholarship or internship.' Ines left Serbia for the first time when she was eighteen after getting a scholarship for undergraduate studies in sociology at the American University in Istanbul, a city where she said virtually everyone assumed trans people were sex workers, and she would be offered money for sex on the bus to classes, 'even when I was wearing bad clothes like a sweatshirt'. She did her exchange studies in London, and after university landed a paid internship in Stockholm, followed by a master's in Lund, Sweden, where she was living when I met her, researching the forced sterilization of trans people, and where she said she felt safe. It was also where she met 'the bodyguard'. She planned to stay there for the immediate future, to do a PhD and to conduct her gender confirmation surgery, although she told me there was a long waiting list. In Sweden, gender confirmation surgery was free (hence the long wait), whereas in Serbia, only 65 per cent was paid for by the state.

The reason Ines left her hometown, and part of the reason she wouldn't go back, was that she had become a figure of hate in local newspapers. The discrimination she faced as a teenager had led to days of crying in her bedroom, until the only thing she felt she could do was the opposite of hiding away. On one transgender awareness day, she walked down the street alone with a blue, pink and white trans Pride flag. People didn't really know what it was, but her presence alone garnered the wrong kind of press.

'The title of the first page of newspapers was "First Tranny Muslim in Serbia" – people react to that. I received death threats.' It wasn't usually out-and-out violence she suffered, though, she said: 'It was more like middle-aged women spitting on me in the street and shouting, "You're a disgrace to your family, how can you do that, walking in those clothes?" – those types of things.'

'What do your parents think?' I asked, Ines's openness making me feel entirely at ease with her.

'My parents were not OK from the very beginning, but

now I have contact with both of them. My father came to
Sweden three months ago and he bought me a dress. He
thinks I dress like a slut so he wanted me to wear something a bit more decent. He said, "OK, you can be trans
but at least be a lady."'

As we laughed, I got the sense that Ines's humour was
probably her best weapon. She must have sensed I was
thinking this because she stopped laughing and admitted
that she had found the incident tough. 'I'm generally
speaking about things in a happy manner because I'm that
kind of person, but all of these things are emotional.' Then
she straightened up. 'Regarding my mother, we just talk
via the phone because it's not safe for me to go to my
hometown now. I haven't been back for two years.'

'What about Belgrade? Do you feel safe here?'

'Not really, but I don't seem to have a problem on the
street this time. Maybe because of the boyfriend and the
fact he looks like a lumberjack. Communicating with
people in the pharmacy or the store, I'm still always so
concerned: how should I stand that they do not notice me,
what should I do with my voice, those kinds of things. I
was in Belgrade a few years ago, when I had come from
Turkey. I got off the plane and I was in the airport waiting
for my friend. I saw her and I waved and called, "Oh my
God! Hi!" and a guy walked straight up to me and punched
me in the face. I was bleeding on the floor.'

'Jesus,' I said. We were all silent for a moment, to
acknowledge how horrific this was.

'How long have you been with the bodyguard?' I asked,
getting the feeling Ines would prefer a change of topic.

Ines leaned in. 'Not much. Like three months.' She grinned: 'But it is INTENSE.'

That night, after dinner, with Emily passed out from tiredness and me wide awake, I decided to go to a drag show that had been organized as part of Pride. When I arrived at the building there were about fifteen police outside – my first taste of the police presence at Pride. I met my friend Masa, who worked at VICE Serbia and had organized my talk. Masa gave a whole new meaning to the term 'straight ally', as did her on-off boyfriend. He had once been beaten on the street in Belgrade for sticking up for a friend who was gay. Masa went to Pride every year and was one of the people who laid down flowers in 2009, giving her name to the papers and speaking out on gay rights, despite the attached risks. Now she was helping me by introducing me to LGBTQ+ people and translating for me.

The drag party was like a school disco, with groups of friends awkwardly milling around a big dark empty room waiting for some action. There were people of all ages and gender expressions there – well over a hundred – which gave me a restored faith in the freedom of the Belgrade queer nightlife scene after seeing the police outside. I bumped into Ines and the bodyguard, and we grabbed a drink and stood together. Four drag queens performed in rotation, doing about five or six numbers each. That impressed me; most drag I'd seen in the UK or at DragCon only required one performance per queen. You really had to sing for your supper in Serbia. Ines was there, shaking her head and critiquing some of the performances next to me. 'Lazy,' she quipped

at one queen. Another did a four-song medley of Lana Del
Rey and Lady Gaga, fake-hanging herself on stage at the
climax of 'Marry the Night', which sobered the crowd a little.
A lot of the other performances, Ines informed me, were
impersonations of famous old Croatian pop stars; a lot of
the jokes were also in Serbian, flying way over my head.

'She just said an old Croatian saying – something like,
"You can take a girl from the village but you can't take the
village from the girl,"' Ines explained over the music.

'Ah, we have that one too,' I shouted back.

By the time a queen in leopard print was miming jacking
off to Elvis Presley's 'Always on My Mind', the bodyguard
was protesting that he and Ines should leave. He complained
that it was his favourite song and that the performer was
'butchering it'.

With Ines having headed out and Masa flirting with her
sort-of boyfriend, I chatted to a young queer called Nicolas
and he agreed to show me Grindr on his phone. 'Look, 90
per cent of guys do not have a picture of their face,' he
pointed out.

'Why not, is it dangerous?' I asked, thinking of how
male dating apps had been used to entrap young gay men
in countries like Russia and Nigeria.

'It's not dangerous, it's just the quality is not great, the
emotional quality. Everybody is looking for sex and they
are discreet. I don't like people that are in the closet –
because if I'm not in the closet why should you be? I want
to meet people who are out so I could try to lead a normal
relationship, not be with some guy who wouldn't associate
with me.'

'Where do you meet people then?'

'Through friends. Or at gay bars maybe.'

I had been told that there were just four places in the city that held gay parties. The venue we were in for the drag night was one of them, Masa explained, and it also held 'rainbow parties', big queer discos where young people, straight or gay, would all be making out with each other. Then there was a club called Pleasure, well known for gay nights, although it wasn't officially a gay bar.

The next day, I tried to drag Emily to a 'Gay Balkan EDM' night at Pleasure, because it sounded so fantastically niche. But we got into two consecutive taxis that refused to take us to the venue, telling us to get out and walk. The third driver – to whom I gave a vague address, not the club name – drove us around the city in a circle three times before suggesting I pay more than I've ever paid for a trip in a black cab in London. After a screaming fight – me in English, he in Serbian – Emily paid him off with a quarter of the sum he'd asked for, and we slammed the doors and solemnly walked home. When I told my new Serbian friends how much he'd tried to charge over the next few days, they exploded with laughter. My experience with gay clubbing in Serbia was extremely short-lived. But apparently so were a lot of people's; Masa told me that more than half of her LGBTQ+ friends had left Serbia for warmer political climates: London, Paris, Chicago.

However, the reason for leaving was not always homophobia alone, it was homophobia combined with economics. Adam had told me that he and his boyfriend Boban struggled to find jobs anywhere in Belgrade as out homosexuals. In a country with a youth unemployment rate of 30 per cent, things were tough for all young people, but throw being LGBTQ+ into the mix, alongside no implemented anti-discrimination laws for the workplace, and the decision to emigrate seemed like a no-brainer. For many, staying put was the bigger challenge.

On Sunday morning, I walked across the city early to get to the Pride location. As riot police milled around in groups on street corners, I felt distinctly nervous and, for one of the only times in my life, self-conscious about my sexuality. The closer I got to Pride, the more aware I became that passers-by on the street were staring at me walking intently towards the event. After moving through police barricades (I wasn't sure of the criteria that allowed me to pass) and undergoing a bag check, I picked up a press pass. Other Pride-goers were wearing pink entry wristbands that they'd applied for ahead of time, although I was confused when they told me that anyone could apply for a wristband. Was it just the fact that they were neon pink that was meant to deter homophobes?

The part of the city we were now in, although central, felt quiet and barren, as if it had been evacuated – at least until I turned a corner and saw the small but growing crowd of people carrying rainbow flags expectantly. It was 11 a.m. and there were about a hundred and fifty people present. A drag queen I recognized from Friday night was dancing to Katy Perry as thirty riot police stood silently in a long, formidable row ten yards away, watching over her.

As the crowd slowly thickened, I stood on some steps

and watched Goran buzzing around greeting people. I asked two young women next to me what they were doing there. Malina, a lawyer, said she was there because she wanted a Serbia with better human rights; the other, Zorana, was there to support Malina. They were a couple, both twenty-five, and had been together for two years. They lived together, pretending to the world and to their families that they were just flatmates. Zorana said she hadn't wanted to come to Pride because she didn't want someone seeing her on TV. They said this was common, avoiding the cameras. I told them I had felt nervous walking towards where we were and they looked at me sceptically. I assumed they were thinking, 'Try feeling like that all the time,' but then Zorana said, 'Why? You don't *look* gay.'

My phone rang and my own girlfriend and lawyer informed me she was at one of the gates. The night before, she'd told me that she'd never been to a Pride parade before. Now, as she joined me on the steps, I pointed out the minor similarities and differences between Belgrade Pride and every other Pride I'd been to. Rainbow flags, shit Katy Perry songs and the cameras were normal. The number of police, the lack of children, the relatively small size of the crowd (now about five hundred people), the fact that no one was drinking, and the absence of any fetish communities were the immediate differences. There were, we were told, a lot of straight people in attendance, as well as many foreign diplomats and activists. I even bumped into Hans from Amsterdam Pride, which made me smile. It was hard to miss him as he was carrying a ten-foot rainbow flag, for which I accused him of dick-swinging.

He told us he was there to help educate Serbian organizers on how to try and gain sponsorship.

'I've learned through the years sometimes people need an excuse – not for themselves but for others – so what we're offering these people from Belgrade companies is they can say to their secretary or colleague or wife, "I was invited by my colleagues from the Netherlands, that's why I'm thinking of funding Pride," and they might get away with it.' It was smart, and had Hans written all over it. Through his eyes, sponsorship would help to scale Belgrade Pride. They currently had a budget of just €50,000, which came from Goran's organization, the Civil Rights Defenders, the Dutch Embassy and the German Embassy, with no money from the government. 'The police are obliged by law to be here,' said Goran, 'but we are paying security ourselves, which is very expensive.'

Despite the city and state's lack of contribution, the country's first ever lesbian prime minister, Ana Brnabić, turned up at the parade to give a speech. She was elected in June 2017 amidst continuing attempts for Serbia to join the EU, and as such seemed to divide opinion among LGBTQ+ people I talked to in Serbia; some said her appointment was a pink-washing, essentially a diversity hire with no real outcome for the community (accusations that Brnabić had publicly called 'nonsense'), others thought it was a step in the right direction for representation. Either way, here she was, giving a speech on bettering LGBTQ+ inclusion just one year after the EU stated that Serbia had a long way to go in terms of inclusion, not just for LGBTQ+ people but also for Roma citizens and people with disabilities.

'The government is here for all citizens and will secure the respect of rights for all citizens,' Brnabić announced to the crowd. 'We want to send a signal that diversity makes our society stronger, that together we can do more.'

A week before, Brnabić had also appeared at a Pride conference on hate speech, and expanded on her reasons for attending the parade: 'As a citizen, I want to live in a society where the Pride parade is news only at the level of information related to the closure of streets for traffic. Where that event is significant to those who are organizing it, along with citizens who want to participate in it. Without tensions several months before and after. As prime minister, I have the obligation and duty to say that this state and its institutions decisively stand beside their citizens, equally protecting their rights – regardless of whether they belong to the majority or are members of minority groups by birth, orientation or personal decision.'

Her choice of the terms 'obligation and duty' seemed telling, almost as if there was a disconnect between the state-sponsored equality that she was asked to talk about and the kind of equality she actually wanted. The Mayor of Belgrade between 2008 and 2013, Dragan Đilas, once told the city that homosexuality was best left in private, and 'should be kept behind four walls'. And there was more. Interestingly, almost every single LGBTQ+ person I talked to in Serbia about the government endorsing Pride had the same thing to say on the topic, a conspiracy theory of sorts: they believed that the government puppeteered the very people who attacked Pride.

'There was seven thousand hooligans in 2010: football

hooligans, extremists, Neo-Nazis,' Goran told me. 'Seven thousand,' he repeated. 'Then, in 2014, zero. Those hooligans still live somewhere here, they haven't left . . . how do you explain that we have not even a stone [thrown] on Pride? They are still around us, but someone tells them to stay at home now. Who? I don't know,' he concluded with a sarcastic shrug.

We started to march. Some of the thousand-strong crowd of people held banners emblazoned with the official Pride slogan *Za Promenu*, meaning 'For Change', and danced to the music blaring out of the sole truck. At one point confetti was blasted onto us from a high window somewhere. It felt celebratory, bar the fact that no one was watching except for maybe three elderly women who had failed to be evacuated from the area, and who stood on their doorsteps, faces gnarled into frowns while they shook their heads disapprovingly. At one point, a counter-protester appeared, shouting things at us, but he was promptly swept up and away by the riot police like a leaf in a gust of wind.

After half an hour's marching, we congregated at the end point of Pride, Belgrade's Republic Square. At least 60 per cent of the crowd chose to go home at this point, stuffing rainbow flags into bags and removing Pride badges as they dispersed. Hans came onto the small stage and gave a speech, pointing out how rare it was for a country's prime minister to attend Pride, before asking everyone to hold hands with a stranger in solidarity. After about another half hour of celebrations, which involved more speeches and more drag, it started to drizzle. I watched from a cafe in the square as the last stragglers – including Masa – danced in the rain before moving off too.

It was at this point that other strange groups started to appear. There was a religious group, who held photos of Russian Orthodox emperors and cast holy water onto the ground to cleanse the streets after Pride. Then came a 'pro-family group' of about twenty people with banners reading 'Serbian Home Never Sodom' and 'Stop Faggotization'. From their meagre numbers, these groups seemed to be in a minority. The police couldn't do anything about a bit of non-violent, indirect hate speech, said Goran, as there was freedom of assembly in the square. But a week before Pride, the head of the Serbian Orthodox Church had compared homosexuality to incest. Clearly there was a divide between the state, endorsing Pride publicly by permitting Brnabić to attend, and the Church, who vehemently opposed Pride. Then there were just the regular Serbian citizens who wished Pride would go away, to make life easier for everyone.

On the doorstep of our Airbnb, dampened from the rain, we ran into one of these people, our host.

'How was your day?' he asked.

'Nice thanks, just had a walk around the city,' I responded.

'We saw some police . . . was something going on today?' Emily interjected, as I shot her a worried look.

He started shaking his head and tutting, like the old ladies along the streets where Pride had been. 'It is the Pride,' he said. We feigned surprise while he searched for something more to say. 'I don't have anything against it,' he assured us. 'It's just . . . monk should not come out of monastery, and these people should not be on streets.'

'Ah, I see,' Emily responded. 'You think they should stay behind four walls?'

He nodded, avoiding our eyes. We immediately went and had sex in his guesthouse as revenge.

During my last days in Belgrade, I decided to learn more about an aspect of Belgrade Pride that had surprised me. During my trip, someone I met had explained that there was not just one Pride in Belgrade, but two. As in Berlin, Pride had divided people here.

In 2015, an alternative Belgrade Pride had materialized, more radical, and, they would argue, more community-minded. It started as a trans gathering at the main event, which many had felt was not very trans inclusive (punters at Pride the day before had told me the event was very cis-male heavy just three years ago). By the next year, this splinter Pride saw around two hundred people gather in front of the National Assembly and march to Republic Square. Adam had warned me about the event over Skype. He told me a group of 'so-called activists' organized a gathering in the city centre and named themselves Belgrade Pride.

Emily and I met Andela, one of the organizers of this Pride, the day after the official Pride, at a bar in one of Belgrade's trendier tree-lined streets. She was a stocky, straighttalking lesbian, who had a compelling way of explaining things from her own perspective, though I didn't necessarily agree with everything she said. She used to work for the government, she said, but was now full time with an LGBTQ+ rights organization called Egal.

'We mostly do field work, direct contact with community members, on violence and discrimination, harsh situations. We address all human rights violations against LGBT people,' she explained. 'And we're about to be the first organization to get institutional support from the state to start a drop-in centre at a permanent location. It will provide aid and support for the LGBTI community. Our work is very focused on trans community members, so there will be services for persons who have undergone gender confirmation surgery. We also do advocacy, lobbying, legal work.'

'What are some legal cases you've worked on?' asked Emily.

'In May there were three major attacks on trans persons in one month. One was attempted murder: a trans girl went out of a club at 4 a.m. – and Belgrade, by the way, is usually a safe place to go around when you're alone, especially at weekends because everyone is on the street, but if you're any kind of different, not passing . . . there were five young boys and they started calling her names and then one of them pulled a knife while they were beating her. There were concrete blocks from a construction site nearby and they started throwing the concrete blocks on her and they demolished a car with them nearby. Right after the attack, she had a broken arm and wounds on her head, but a taxi driver didn't want to take her because he said he's not going to give a lift to a faggot, a hooker or a person who is bleeding. And then, when she got to a police station, the policemen didn't believe her. Then they said: "Why do you have to dress like that? You were asking for trouble." When she asked, "What are you going to do now?" they said: "Kennedy was killed and we don't know who killed him."'

'Have there been any charges?'

Andela explained that they hoped this case would be the first time the country's anti-hate-crime law could be used to prosecute someone. It had existed since 2012, but as of yet, nothing.

Still, it was this kind of groundwork that put Egal in the position of understanding the community's needs, said Andela, which was also how their Pride event came about. She told me it looked just like the main Pride, only smaller. There was music, rainbow flags, posters, but it wasn't closed off from the city, traffic wasn't stopped, there were few public figures, no private security and scarcely any police in attendance. The only threatening thing that happened was a taxi driver giving the crowd the finger.

'We've had two June Prides so far and nothing happened on either one of them,' she said matter-of-factly. 'We had no fences. The city was open, it was a beautiful Sunday morning and I walked to the place. There were tourist buses, just an ordinary day, and people started coming and they were very like, "Where's all the police? Are we OK?" And we were like, "Yeah, you're safe."'

I understood the wider argument against the militarization of Pride, but I couldn't quite reconcile what Andela was saying with the violent hate crimes that she had just described.

When I put this to her, she brought up the four walls idea: 'Yesterday they had four entrances to the Pride . . .

they could have put three, or five, but no, they had four.'
She almost laughed, but not quite. Her point was that
closing Pride off to the city was just reinforcing the idea
that LGBTQ+ people should be hidden away, the antithesis
of the message that used to be at the heart of Pride. 'Maybe
ten years ago there was a need for all this, but look at our
lives – we live openly 24/7. Having to pass corridors of
police cordons is kind of an insult for somebody who lives
as LGBT, and adds more pressure for anyone who would
like to attend but is scared. You don't see armed police in
the street on an ordinary day.'

'But 2010 was so violent,' I appealed.

She explained that one of the reasons they held their
event in June was because schools were off for the summer,
making it harder for young 'hooligans' to mobilize. Then
she told me the other reason: that it was closer to the
anniversary of Stonewall. 'When you advocate the idea in
public, it's much easier to explain to people in Serbia, who
really don't know anything about LGBT issues or history,
that we do this in June because this thing happened years
ago, the first time the community rioted against the repres-
sion from the police – that's why all over the world we
march in June.'

'But so many Prides across Europe happen later in the
summer,' I replied.

'Yes, and there are two types of Pride marches now: the
celebration of achievements and everything that's been
done, like Berlin, for example. And then you have other
Prides – as it should be in Serbia – where it's a protest; it's
a moment when you say, "We suffer violence, we need

changes of legislation, because we're citizens of this country," and you ask your state to recognize your rights. This year for September, you have the press clippings all about who came, who wore what, but you cannot hear demands and that's wrong on so many levels. Pride is important but it's not just about that one day or one month of campaigning – it's like, what do you do the rest of the year?'

Her point made sense, I thought, but in her voice there was some real animosity.

'Did you go yesterday?' I asked.

'Yes. I felt awful yesterday but of course I went. We support the idea of public assembly of the LGBTI community so we attend all events, whether we agree or disagree with the politics. But something felt deeply wrong . . . the weird-looking guys in black with glasses, a security company that get paid to be there.' She was referring to the security details, the men (badly) undercover in dark glasses and black clothes. 'It didn't feel right. I can't even explain it rationally. I'm not saying violence isn't an issue – of course it is, it's a huge issue – but it is possible to be visible, to be exposed, and it's an offence for every one of us exposed in that kind of way to go on this protest where we were all gathered and surrounded by so many police enforcement, blocked off from the rest of the city. Do I need that every day? Do I need to live in a different place? Should I go outside of Serbia?'

Andela's answer was poignant, but it made me sad in more ways than one. Because when I talked to Goran in the Civil Rights Defenders office, he explained that despite all the 'juicy arguments' that had happened between the

teams behind Andela's Pride and his Pride – of which there
were a lot, from 'you stole our name' to 'you're funded
by suspicious foreign investors' to 'you're in cahoots with
bent politicians' – at the end of the day, it kind of felt as
if both sides wanted the same thing: a Pride that was
political and demanding, a Pride that was safe for the people
who attended it, and a Pride that was visible to those who
feared it.

'You think we have any influence on the number of
policemen? You think I can say I want more or less please?'
Goran had exclaimed when I asked him about their presence. 'The event they have in June is not announced much
in advance. They announced it ten days before, it's summer
and no one is in Belgrade. We have a press conference here
and we'll announce Pride in 2018 to be 16 September, one
year in advance, it's very public. The police assess the
amount of officers needed. We say we want less police,
they say, "If you want less we can ban Pride." Every year
they exaggerate the assessment and then they realize and
next year they decrease it. This year there were two thousand police.'

Goran continued with implied reluctance: 'You can
accept these things,' he said, 'but you cannot accept that
nobody can observe Pride. We have some people watching
here or there, but we don't have people that will watch
Pride as observers, and that's a big, big problem.'

On the plane home, Emily and I discussed Andela and
Goran's feud. 'I'm sorry to sound like Miss World, but I
wish they could just get along,' I said.

'Maybe their disagreement isn't such a bad thing,' she

said. 'It's more queer in a way, isn't it? Having multiple Prides?'

'I guess you're right,' I said. But Goran had left us with a more empirical question: What is the point of a Pride parade if no one can see it?

chapter five

NOW YOU SEE ME

I was discovering 'coming out videos' late in life, or at least, later than everyone else, but after my summer of Prides, I fell down the rabbit hole. They'd been there for a decade, these YouTube clips of LGBTQ+ vloggers opening up about their sexuality online. I'd dismissed them as irrelevant to me: too saccharine, too earnest. I had gone through the process of coming out and 'coming to terms'; why would I want to watch other people do so?

Now I was eating my words.

I got started with Rose and Rosie, two attractive British vloggers who were married, lived in Hertfordshire, and made videos where they bickered, teased one another, phoned up their exes and sometimes made out on camera for their fans. This formula had – perhaps unsurprisingly given the girl-on-girl content – helped them to accumulate 145 million views on Rose's YouTube channel and about 30 million on Rosie's.

I told Emily about them with the excitement of someone who had discovered some new, untrodden pocket of the Internet. She was shocked that I hadn't heard of them before.

'Yes, Rose and Rosie. Emily and Amelia . . . we could have made a fortune by now,' she said, as though I had deprived her of the right to become a YouTube sensation.

There was a time when I would have responded to that comment with, 'No one is interested in the boring ins and outs of our prematurely middle-aged lesbian life,' but having scrolled through the comments under Rose and Rosie's videos, I could see that people clearly were.

'These TWO FUCkerS are The REAson I REIlizaD I WAS gaY AND afTER WATCHING THIS I REMEBER WHY,' wrote one fan, under a compilation video of Rose and Rosie that was created by yet another fan.

Rose Ellen Dix and Roseanne Elizabeth Spaughton had come out on camera separately, the first as a lesbian and the other as bisexual. They met through a mutual friend, and then started vlogging as a couple. They had announced their engagement on YouTube, posted footage of their wedding on YouTube and, more recently, begun sharing the details of their attempts to have a baby. If I had presumed this type of YouTube content was aimed exclusively at a teenage audience, they soon proved me wrong: one episode detailed their search for a sperm donor, another discussed IVF. Watching these, I was actually learning something, and kind of enraptured by seeing into another lesbian couple's domestic set-up. It was like what I had experienced when I went to visit Patty, only broadcast direct to my home: a glimpse into the future that was cheerier than those I'd grown up watching in lesbian films, where someone usually died at the end.

Rose and Rosie's coming out videos led me to others: I discovered the American twin models, the 'Rhodes Bros', two twinkie angels whose video showing them come out to their dad down the phone put a lump in my throat. It had 24 million views and counting. I saw the coming out video made by Ingrid Nilsen, a young female vlogger who explained how supportive her ex-boyfriend was about the process. That video had 17 million views, more than the video in which she interviewed President Obama. In lesbian couple Bria and Chrissy's '10 Worst Ways To Come Out' video, they jumped out of actual closets in the most laboured visual metaphor I'd ever seen: also around 17 million views. I watched the videos of celebrity YouTube star Gigi Gorgeous, who after coming out as a gay man came out as a trans woman, and later a lesbian, all over a period of several years. And finally, I watched Emma Ellingsen, a Norwegian blogger who was just fifteen years old, tell 3 million viewers that she was transgender. Each vlogger had a strong look, a logo, an HTML identity. Most seemed to take themselves quite seriously, and were comfortable with crying to camera.

Until now, the only similar videos I'd seen were my Belgian sex worker friend Lyle's – the beautiful and genuine video in which he came out as HIV positive – and before that, the British Olympic diver Tom Daley, who had made one in 2013 and posted it online via his own YouTube channel, getting 4.5 million hits in the first day. 'I was thinking I could do a newspaper interview, but you wouldn't want somebody to twist your words,' Daley later told Simon Hattenstone at the *Guardian*. 'You could do a TV interview, but you don't want to be asked questions you don't want to answer. So I just said exactly what I was comfortable with saying at the time. And nothing could be twisted.' For Daley, already famous, making a video himself was about control, about ownership. While this seemed true for some of the vloggers I had come across, others gave me the feeling that if they weren't vlogging about being gay or bi or trans they'd just be vlogging about something else – maybe free holidays or make-up (actually, some were already doing that too) – but it felt significant that they had chosen their gender or sexuality as noteworthy content, and that we, in our anonymous millions, had chosen to watch it.

I contacted Rose and Rosie for an interview but failed to get a response. Then, after emailing again, nothing. I got mildly irritated. I even tried going through a friend who knew them, but to no avail. I was beginning to realize what I had been too out of touch with youth culture to realize before: that YouTubers are more famous than God. At one point, I got a tweet back from Rosie about the interview, further fuelling my obsession, but then they went quiet again. For a while, it was sort of like when you fancy someone and they ignore your texts: them stone-walling me only made me more pathetic and eager. I began to bring them up in conversation, and even planned to go to a pre-teen vlogging conference they would be at, which was ordinarily my notion of hell. When I told Emily about this, she looked concerned, so I decided to drop the Rose and Rosie idea altogether, and instead asked myself why I had watched an accumulative ten hours of vlogging content over the last three weeks to begin with.

On some level, the sense of spectacle in these videos made me uncomfortable, especially the fanfare made of coming out. But on another level, I found the vloggers compelling; for most of my queer friends, humour and privacy were the two most vital tools for existing in the world, but these people were poker-faced, invested in themselves, happy to share their 'journeys' with the world. The thought of coming out in front of so many people would have been a waking nightmare to me at fifteen or seventeen, but maybe that's because this type of content didn't exist yet. I'd come of age in a time before same-sex marriage and before YouTube and social media, when dial-up Internet and MSN messenger were the height of technology. From my Nokia phone, I had no access to the Instagram accounts I follow now, the ones that post pictures of campy LGBTQ+ icons and chronicle LGBTQ+ history. In fact, in hindsight, I can see that my teenage years were a barren wasteland of LGBTQ+ people. We had our suspicions about certain pop stars but they were in the closet; UK TV had several gay men presenting chat shows on prime time but far fewer gay women. There were peripheral gay storylines in sitcoms, but no main characters who lived fully formed gay lives.

The only gay woman I knew while growing up was my school hockey teacher, and from the age of eleven to thirteen, my classmates and I would screech, run and hide whenever she came into the changing rooms. We used 'lesbian' as a term to insult one another. At fifteen, when news leaked that two girls in the year above had made out at a party – not for the entertainment of boys (I went to an all-girls Catholic convent school; we really didn't know many boys) – we were scandalized; being bisexual automatically meant you were a lesbian, and being a lesbian automatically meant that you were a predator. When a friend came out to me as bisexual at sixteen, I didn't know what to say, so I said nothing at all.

At seventeen, I too realized I had feelings for a girl. From the minute I saw her, I knew. I didn't tell anyone; as far as I can remember, no one in our college of two thousand students was out. If we became friends, maybe it would go away, I thought. So, like a double agent, I gained her trust. Every day, we would hang out; every night, I would look at her Facebook photos. I never did anything about my attraction. I just waited to get over it, but when I realized that wasn't happening quickly enough, I did the most homoerotic thing I could do given the context: I slept with the guy she was sleeping with.

Years later, when I was twenty and out (she'd forgiven me long ago about the boy), she came to visit me in London. I took her on a night out – to The Joiners – where we hung out with my friends, danced, and I kissed someone else.

'Why did we become friends in college?' she asked, over a drink back at my house.

'I think I might have had a crush on you,' I admitted.

She didn't flinch. Or run out of the room, or do any of the things I'd imagined she'd do if I ever told her years before.

'Do you still have a crush on me?' she asked, avoiding my eyes. Then we had sex, and although I can't remember it now I do remember what it felt like – it was as if all my gay teenage self-hate dissolved away in one perfect evening. Until the next day, when she told me she was straight and made me promise not to tell anyone. I felt seventeen again, and as though I should be locked up.

This would happen repeatedly to varying degrees for the next three years: different girls but the same story. I learned that shame is contagious; just when you think you've rid yourself of it, someone passes it back to you. In the pub with my friends, I would joke that it was a compliment that girls like this were 'only gay for me', but in private, I would wonder why, if they had feelings for me, it would be such an awful thing to be with me. The hours spent crying behind closed doors were not glam or cinematic like the final credits of *Call Me by Your Name*, or as tragic as the sparse queer films I'd seen growing up, like *Boys Don't Cry* or *Milk*. They were tinged with the feeling of self-indulgence mixed with self-hatred, and the thought that, if I could get turned on by sex with men, why could I never develop feelings for them? Why did it always have to be girls? And, for a long time, girls who made me feel guilty about it?

I never mentioned this to anyone because it was an intense privilege that these were my only encounters with gay shame. I was lucky to have moved through life without my parents burning all my gender-non-conforming clothes as Amrou's did (although I'm sure if Amrou saw some of the ill-fitting dungarees I wore, they would agree that they should have been destroyed), and with no one pouring a pint over my head in a pub. It felt as if a bit of internalized homophobia was the best possible outcome you could hope for as a gay person. And as I got older, and met more LGBTQ+ people from different walks of life, I realized I was right: I really had had it much better than everyone else. As these people, many of whom had had more shame and stigma to overcome, taught me to love myself the way they had managed to love themselves, I started to love people who would love me back. Or people like Salka, who didn't love me just because they didn't love me, rather than because of my gender.

When I looked back and asked myself whether anything could have made a difference, the YouTube videos seemed like the obvious answer. Watching them, amazed at the confidence with which young people publicly talked about their sexuality, only reinforced how much I had needed something like this when I was younger. If I'd known anyone gay who I could relate to, if I'd seen anyone that might look like the future version of me in the media, if I'd been able to access something as basic as Rose and Rosie's videos, secretly, from my bedroom, would I have come out earlier, felt less shame, spent less of my early twenties sobbing over 'straight girls'?

There was no way to know. But what I could be sure of, mostly from the viewing figures, was that these videos were now one of the places where young people were going to learn to be gay, either before they could go to gay bars, or because there were fewer gay bars for them to go to, or because they lived in a place where they had no possibility to explore what their gender or sexuality might be, out in the open.

The videos made me think about visibility – both a cause and an effect of how things had improved for LGBTQ+ people since I was a kid. There weren't just these YouTubers now, but also pictures of gay people getting married in the press, *Drag Race* on television, and countless out celebrities, including many women, from Kristen Stewart to Cara Delevingne to Ellen Page. There was so much that hadn't been around ten years ago. But what difference did it actually make that people who were once marginalized by the media were now visible? Did this mean anything for the lives of regular LGBTQ+ people? And was the world actually as progressive as the media would have us believe?

The only thing more annoying than going all the way to Berlin, missing Dyke March, Pride being rained off, and then blacking out for most of the eight hours you're in Berghain (I would have explained what happened if I knew), is flying to New York to meet trans models, suddenly getting ignored by all of them, and then realizing that you have accidentally booked the trip over Thanksgiving, when most people are off work or out of the city.

'It'll be fine,' said my friend Helene.

Ironically, Helene herself was a model, just not a trans model. She was in New York to meet American casting agents, and I was staying with her. We had booked a room on Airbnb in Bushwick, Brooklyn. When we arrived, it turned out the flat was occupied by four lesbians. Helene, not a lesbian, was confused by some of their living arrangements, like why they only had soya milk and why there were so many cats everywhere.

'If I help you understand lesbians will you help me find trans models?' I said.

'Go on Insta,' she replied dismissively, eating some room-temperature sushi. Helene always seemed to be eating something she had pulled out of her pocket from earlier. Once, most horrifyingly, some old pork that was wrapped in foil. When I saw it, I vaguely remembered it from a meal a few days before.

She was probably right: I should go on Insta, for Insta was the home of all models, and there were a few trans models that I followed. One of these was Teddy Quinlivan, a beautiful redhead who had come out as trans in the media recently and whom I also had a huge crush on.

'Always trying to interview people you fancy,' tutted Helene, as I emailed Teddy's agent.

The fashion world embracing trans models wasn't a new phenomenon. In fact, I remember seeing a trans model on TV for the first time back in 2008, when Isis King became a contestant on *America's Next Top Model*. King had been asked if she would apply during a photo shoot in an earlier season where the show's model contestants dressed up as homeless people. King, living in a homeless shelter at the time, was asked to be a backing model (in an interview later, I asked her if she thought this might be a problematic shoot concept and she told me that she was not offended, just grateful for the opportunity). King was 'outed' on TV, with the other girls asking her questions about her genitals, making her feel 'like a caged animal' (her words, when we spoke). For a lot of people, King's appearance provided the first notion that a trans person could be a model, and by the time she returned to the show in 2011, trans models were featuring in magazines more regularly. Most famously, Lea T posed naked on the cover of *Love* magazine kissing Kate Moss. The same year, Andreja Pejić, a Bosnian-born model from Australia, who had been spotted at the age of seventeen when she was working in a McDonald's, starred in a campaign for Marc Jacobs and walked for Jean-Paul Gaultier. Two years later, she came out as trans, becoming the most famous trans model in the world.

If this felt like a landmark moment for trans visibility, the truth was that trans models had actually been around much, much longer. One of the first British people to undergo gender confirmation surgery, April Ashley, modelled for *Vogue* in the 1960s, until a friend 'outed' her as trans to the press for a fee of £5. African American trans woman Tracy 'Africa' Norman appeared in *Italian Vogue* and as the face of Clairol hair dye in the 1970s, until she was 'outed' on a shoot for *Essence* magazine. And Bond girl Caroline 'Tula' Cossey was shot for *Playboy* in 1981, until she was 'outed' by the tabloids.

The explosion of openly trans models in the fashion industry in the 2010s came at – or heralded – a wider moment of visibility for trans people. My friend Paris Lees, the one who reminds me of Samantha Jones, grew up trans in a small town in the north of England and recently summed it up well: 'When I was growing up you rarely saw trans people in the media and only then as objects of pity, ridicule or disgust,' she told me. 'I'm not sure I could even begin to explain what effect this had on me and the way that I saw myself. Early on in my transition, when I didn't blend in as well as a girl, people would often shout abuse at me in the street. For about a year or so I thought that was OK, because what did I expect? After all, I was a "boy dressing up as a girl", and I deserved it, right?' Paris said that every time she'd seen someone like her in public life they were being humiliated, so she naturally believed that she deserved to be humiliated, that she was, in her words, perverse, fake, ridiculous. 'I remember walking home with my best friend Steffi, who was also trans, and talking about how we'd like to make things different one day. I must have been sixteen or seventeen back then. Trans people didn't appear on news shows to give their opinions on important issues, they didn't win awards or appear on the cover of magazines, and they certainly weren't celebrated as feminists or indeed anything, really. We were literally just a joke. But I felt it was possible. That gay people had been on that journey. That people of colour had been on that journey. Why couldn't we try and take part in society – in life – as equal members too? Then Nadia Almada won *Big Brother* and everything changed in my mind. I'd never seen anyone transgender celebrated in public before.'

Some time after Nadia won *Big Brother* in the UK in 2004, the broader climate started to change slightly. Paris became a prominent spokesperson, presented on Channel 4 and Radio 1, and became the first trans person to appear on *Question Time*, our biggest political debating show. Something similar started to happen in America: in 2014, *Orange is the New Black* star and trans activist Laverne Cox graced the cover of *Time* magazine. A year later, Caitlyn Jenner was shot by Annie Leibovitz for the cover of *Vanity Fair* and debuted her inane TV show *I Am Cait*, a spin-off from *Keeping Up with the Kardashians*. Around the same time, trans TV presenter and *Allure* beauty columnist Janet Mock published two iconic autobiographies. One of my favourite artists, Anohni, formerly of Antony and the Johnsons, became the first trans woman nominated for a Brit Award (and the second for an Oscar, but she boycotted the ceremony). And the TV drama *Transparent* attempted a nuanced portrayal of a father from a Jewish family in LA transitioning to become a woman (before the lead actor, Jeffrey Tambor, was released from the show following sexual harassment claims).

In March 2017, French *Vogue* ran its first ever issue with a trans cover star: then twenty-year-old Brazilian-born model Valentina Sampaio. It wasn't just the first edition of *Vogue* to put a trans person on its cover, but also the first magazine in French history to do so. What stood out to me, though, was the headline, which read: 'Transgender Beauty, How They're Shaking Up the World'. I decided to write an article about it, and spoke to Shon Faye, a brilliant British journalist and commentator on trans issues who objected to the headline quite strongly.

'Most trans people are not trying to "shake up the world",' Shon said, pointing out that, although kinder than the coverage of recent years, it was still a 'sensational representation' of trans people. 'Being trans is not a political statement designed to make everyone rethink gender,' she explained, with her usual acerbic eloquence. 'It may have that effect sometimes, which is good, but we are not a style aesthetic. "Shaking up the world" is not always positive for trans people. Shaking people up often means they won't give you a job, or that they throw you out on the street, or that they rape you.'

I agreed with Shon that the headline was offensive, that 'they' seemed to denote trans women as other. For me, it summed up everything about the strange moment we were living in for LGBTQ+ representation more broadly. There was a thin line between visibility and spectacle. There was the question of how sincere a gesture it was to put a trans model on the cover of your magazine or in your latest campaign at a time when it seemed to be a sure-fire way to garner publicity. And then there was the blatant fact that this assertion had come too late: if trans people were shaking up the world, they'd been doing it for a while.

A couple of days after we got to New York, I received a helpful email. Not from Teddy's agent, who had fobbed me off – 'YouTubers and trans models, more famous than God,' I noted – but from a woman called Cindi Creager. Cindi's company, CreagerCole Communications, taught LGBTQ+ celebs how to handle vicious right-wing media and tense television interviews. 'Before the premiere of my VH1 reality show, *TRANSform Me*, Cindi Creager prepared me for a myriad of press interviews about the program,' wrote Laverne Cox in a testimonial on the website. 'I employ the spokesperson techniques Cindi taught me to this day and I highly recommend her services.'

When I learned that Cindi had coached Teddy to announce that she was trans at the start of 2017, I suddenly wanted to interview Cindi more than Teddy. I emailed asking if I could meet with her and I quickly got a message back: she told me that she was too busy to meet me face to face while I was in New York, which seemed like exactly what I would say if I were a New York PR guru trying to manage my own public image. Instead, she generously offered to let me call her for a chat. I had come all the way to New York to phone someone in New York. Still, if this woman coached gay and trans people in coming out, she would be the perfect person to talk to about what positive LGBTQ+ representation ought to look like: she was one of the people who shaped it.

Cindi had set up CreagerCole with her spouse Rainie Cole in 2012, she explained over the phone.

'We founded CreagerCole as a boutique public relations firm with expertise in LGBTQI issues and we offer media training and message development,' she told me.

'What does that mean?' I asked.

'Really that means we get great press for LGBTQI organizations, individuals and causes. We help clients deliver clear, compelling and concise messages when speaking to the media. The care and sensitivity we bring to the issue, that's our value proposition.'

Cindi was an advert for her own business: very clear, compelling and concise. She explained to me that after working as a TV anchor in Alaska, she went to Columbia University's graduate journalism school in the late nineties, then landed a job producing documentaries for ABC News, which was when she started to identify that she might be a lesbian. It was 2005 when she scored the job as Director of National News at GLAAD (the Gay and Lesbian Alliance Against Defamation), where she worked with Laverne Cox,

she said. There, she ran campaigns that held the media
accountable for homophobic, transphobic and defamatory
journalism, campaigned for the Associated Press to change
their style guide to be more inclusive and modern (switching
'transsexual' to 'transgender', for example, or using 'gay'
and 'lesbian' instead of 'homosexual'), and advised celebrities
and activists on representing the community appropriately
in the media.

Another part of Cindi's job back then was to work with
everyday people who wanted to get a story in the news,
in order to raise awareness about the difficulties LGBTQ+
people and their families experienced. She had worked
with Elke Kennedy, whose son Sean W. Kennedy was
punched in the face by a man called Stephen Moller in a
homophobic attack that took place in South Carolina in
2007. Sean fell to the pavement, hitting his head so hard
that he died. Elke, with the help of Cindi and GLAAD,
ran a media campaign that highlighted South Carolina's
lack of hate-crime law at the time (Moller ended up serving
less than two years for involuntary manslaughter), and
Cindi believed the work they did contributed to the Hate
Crimes Prevention Act of 2009. She also worked with Janice
Langbehn, who in 2007 was about to leave on a cruise from
Miami with her wife Lisa Marie Pond and three of their
four children when Pond collapsed and was rushed to a
local hospital. Langbehn and the kids were barred from
seeing Pond, a decision justified by a member of staff who
told her that Florida was an 'anti-gay city and state'. Pond
died of a brain aneurysm without her wife and children
by her side.

'These were serious stories, but stories that helped persuade politicians,' said Cindi. 'The woman turned away at the hospital helped persuade President Obama to say hospitals need to provide visitation for same-sex couples; the law was changed.' Cindi's experience at GLAAD taught her the power of the media to shape not just representation but legislation too. A lesson, I would learn, that she carried over to her next endeavour, at CreagerCole.

Cindi described the PR firm's work with models as 'proactive work: you know you're going to be making an announcement and you plan for it', as opposed to 'crisis PR: when someone outs you or you find yourself having an unexpected media moment and you need to respond to it'.

'Say I was a model,' I started, 'which I am about two feet and one face graft away from ever becoming. Say I was a model and I was famous and I wanted to come out as a lesbian . . . how would you help me?'

'Well, we can't all be models!' Cindi laughed cheerily. 'So we'd start by asking you questions in a safe space: Why are you coming out? What is your reasoning? Do you want to speak out for lesbian rights? Once we get those messages down we'd start to write a press release, shape that with you. Does this seem accurate to you? Possibly you want to get into your childhood: What was it like being gay growing up? We'd sit in a room and practise talking across the table, then we'd get a camera out and start to put you on camera, longer interviews with someone who has more time . . . or pretend you were on CNN for three minutes. We'd make sure you're ready for any curveball questions as well. Who do you vote for? What do you think of Trump? I would caution the client to keep the interview on the topic at hand. We'd teach you how to speak to things on your terms. Then we'd plan and strategize media outlets that would handle your story properly. We'd bring you options, and then when the time is right, a few months in advance, we'd plant the seeds . . . and when you're ready, and you feel comfortable, the interview takes place. We field and vet the requests that come in the door.'

For the first time, I was grateful not to be a supermodel; the whole process sounded gruelling. But to come out as bisexual or a lesbian – when there were a number of women like Cara Delevingne, Heather Kemesky and Freja Beha Erichsen already out, as such – or as trans, when models like Andreja Pejić, Hari Nef and Lea T had done so, was one thing; Cindi told me she had also helped Hanne Gaby Odiele come out as intersex, a first in the world of high-profile models.

Hanne Gaby has been on the cover of *Vogue* and has modelled in campaigns for Balenciaga, Mulberry and DKNY Jeans. She's from Belgium originally, and is instantly recognizable to anyone who's ever opened a fashion magazine: platinum blonde; a naturally stern brow; a pretty, petite, bird-like face. Although there are many ways to be intersex, it basically means that you're born with variations on what people think of as male or female physical characteristics, so variations in your genitals, chromosomes or internal organs. Hanne was born intersex due to a condition called androgen insensitivity syndrome, which, simply put (and it's not very simple, medically), means that you have the genetic make-up of a male but are resistant to male hormones, so you have some or all of the physical traits that are considered typically female. The condition can also affect the genitals, so those born with it are often given involuntary 'corrective' surgeries as children that can be psychologically harmful. This was what had happened to Hanne. She also had to endure the stigma that comes with being born intersex, which still exists despite the fact that approximately 1.5 per cent of the global population are intersex. That's roughly the same percentage as people who have ginger hair.

Hanne's modelling agency, Women Management, approached CreagerCole in June 2016. Her agent had already spoken to several publicists and he wasn't getting a good feeling about how they would handle Hanne's story, Cindi explained to me. Then someone at the group InterACT, which advocates for intersex youth, suggested Cindi, so they set up a meeting. 'He didn't even tell us her name at first, they just came to our office and we had a very informal meeting. Hanne said she felt instantly comfortable with us and that was it: once they felt comfortable and wanted to hire us, we'd soon guide her to becoming the most high-profile intersex person in the world.'

'What did you do first?' I asked.

'We said: let's break down what your story is. It's one thing to be a model but to be able to talk about your own personal story, to talk about intersex issues in a way that you can be that advocate . . . We really started working very, very intensely at the end of October 2016, through November, December. Certainly what Hanne went through as a child was very traumatic, so we needed to work hard to make her feel strong to talk about these things, and unapologetic about being intersex. You're taught to live in shame all these years and all of a sudden you're talking about it and it takes time to practise it, to be able to mitigate emotional triggers that come up for you.'

CreagerCole broke Hanne's story on *USA Today*. It went out, purposefully, at the start of New York fashion week, three days after Trump was sworn in. 'There was all this Trump news that morning,' remembered Cindi, 'and then all of a sudden this gleaming light of Hanne in all the top news stories. After it broke it was like wildfire – we were inundated with media requests, to speak on panels, to do press, to talk about the issue. We had many, many lists of journalists wanting to interview Hanne. She could pick and choose; book deals, documentary deals, offers to maybe be in movies.'

The coming out process was similar for Teddy, who had the same media training and made her announcement around New York fashion week in the autumn. After hours and hours of practising her story in CreagerCole's meeting room, she was ready. CNN Style broke the story, but Teddy also posted a series of videos to her Instagram about the decision. Like Tom Daley, she wanted to take control of her own narrative. 'I remember living my whole life as male, but feeling like I was playing a part. I always knew I was female, just in my soul, in my heart, in my brain,' she told her fans in the video. 'I kind of knew I had to pretend to be male to appease everybody else. At one point I just stopped giving a fuck.' After Teddy came out, Marc

Jacobs and Andreja Pejić immediately and publicly expressed their support. She, too, was inundated with interview requests, said Cindi. From her Instagram account, it seemed so effortless, but now I knew how much work had gone into the decision and process of telling the world.

'Why do you think Teddy decided to come out?' I asked Cindi.

'She was living as cisgender, and tired of seeing so many things happening to trans people in the world: murders, attacks, and this administration's attacks on trans people through policy. Teddy said: "I really need to use my voice. I'm a successful model and I need people to know I'm a trans woman also. It's just one aspect of who I am but I wanna fight for what's right, stand out." Plus now she gets to go up the runways at Paris and Milan fashion weeks and know she's doing it as her authentic self.'

'What about Hanne?'

'Hanne was told when she was young by doctors: "You're the only one like this, don't tell anybody, don't talk about it." She wanted to represent the community positively, being new to speaking about it, and she wanted to shed light on the human rights abuses inflicted against intersex children, abuses that she herself experienced.'

'So they've basically done it for the greater good?'

'They're both changing the world just by being out and visible,' said Cindi. 'I know just from the messages of support that Hanne and Teddy have got on their Instagrams, people writing to them – families out there that thought they were alone, particularly on intersex issues, people who have said they don't feel that they're alone any more. I just know that it's given a lot of courage to families to share their voice.' I knew it was Cindi's job to say all of this, but I could also tell that she believed it and that she cared.

'I think they'll both help with policy changes too,' she added before we hung up the call. 'Hanne is sitting on a lot of panels: with InterACT, with people from the UN, working with Human Rights Watch occasionally.' She was out there, lobbying for policy change.

'So it really can make a difference?'

'In the end, you hope that leads to something.'

The lift floated up to the twenty-sixth floor of One World Trade Center. On the site of Ground Zero, this building was a kind of replacement for the twin towers that were destroyed on 9/11. In the late November sun its glass exterior reflected the cloudless blue sky. When I asked the doorman how high it was, he told me it was the tallest building in the Western hemisphere.

I reached the floor I was looking for, the *Vogue* floor, and was told the person I was after was elsewhere. I glimpsed the view across the office, filled with partition desks just like any other, and headed all the way back down.

I still hadn't found any trans models, but I did have a meeting with Meredith Talusan, the first transgender executive editor at Condé Nast. As well as being a trans woman of colour in a rare position of power at a huge media company, Meredith was in charge of the brand's latest digital title, the first to launch in a decade: *them.*, a website aimed at young LGBTQ+ and non-binary people, which used pretty much exclusively LGBTQ+ and non-binary models. With a sleek design and intersectional ethos, *them.* was like a newer, shinier and queerer version of *Teen Vogue*, not just for teens but for millennials too. Articles included: 'This Makeup Transformation Is WILD – But Don't You Dare Call It "Drag"', a diary of top surgery, a regular column 'about the people, places, and events that have shaped our queer lives' called 'them.story', and listicles like 'Trans Jokes by Trans People'. ('Q: How many trans people does it take to change a lightbulb? A: One to change it, literally everyone else to tell them to wait and slow down first.')

A few nights before my meeting with Meredith, Helene and I had been having dinner and talking about trans models.

'Did you see what Rihanna said?' she asked.

'No.' I never knew what Rihanna had been saying.

'Yeah, someone asked her why she didn't use a trans model in her Fenty campaign and she was like, "cause I don't wanna tokenize". You should google it.'

I googled it. At the dinner table. (We had been together for more than twenty-four hours and all common courtesy had gone out of the window.) A fan had indeed DM'ed Rihanna asking her why she had not used a trans model in the campaign for her make-up brand.

'I've had the pleasure of working with many gifted trans women throughout the years, but I don't go around doing trans castings!' Rihanna wrote in her response, which the fan later posted on Twitter. 'Just like I don't do straight non-trans women castings! I respect all women, and whether they're trans or not is none of my business! I don't think it's fair that a trans woman, or man, be used as a convenient marketing tool! Too often do I see companies doing this to trans and black women alike! There's always just that one spot in the campaign for the token "we look mad diverse" girl/guy! It's sad!'

Apparently the fan then apologized for any offence that might have been caused, to which Rihanna replied again: 'You absolutely didn't babe! Just didn't want you to think I intentionally leave anyone out!'

I agreed with what Rihanna was suggesting, in that sometimes inclusivity benefits the brand more than the model, but I also felt that making the most invisible people in society visible could only ever be a positive thing. And yet: *was* it anyone else's business who was and wasn't trans?

Her attitude to casting trans models was a lot like the rapper Angel Haze's reaction to me asking her about her pansexuality – that's attraction to people no matter their gender – in an interview: 'If we were in a sexual situation you would know exactly who I am sexually,' she told me over the phone in 2014 (quite flirtily, I liked to think). 'But if we're just having a conversation, you don't need to know what I do in private. Sexuality is not the most interesting detail about a person. It's like me saying my favourite colour is red all the time. After a while you'd kindly tell me to shut the fuck up about it.'

To her, being pansexual was a private matter, and to make a fuss out of it would be at best intrusive and at worst fetishistic. It was her business and her choice, sure, but if no one talked about their sexuality or gender identity in public then who would kids look up to? We'd be back at square one in terms of having no visible role models. I agreed that trans women should not be included in campaigns or videos only for the sake of their being trans. But equally, the result of Rihanna's approach was that zero trans women were included.

'Don't you think we just need to be deliberately inclusive until the world naturally gets a little more inclusive?' I said to Helene.

'Sometimes I get asked to do stuff just cause I'm mixed race,' she shrugged. 'In fashion, diversity basically just is tokenism.'

We were silent for a moment, mulling over her words. Then I broke the silence: 'Imagine if Rihanna DM'ed you,' I said.

'I know, mate. Twice.'

After my failed visit to the *Vogue* office, I found Meredith across town at The Wing, a bougie New York members' club for working women that was decorated like the inside of a bag of pick'n'mix, all pink and white stripes. I was half an hour late, thanks to my detour, and we headed straight up to The Wing's rooftop, with views of the Empire State Building, where the sun was setting. Meredith started telling me about herself, and when she said she was forty-two years old my jaw dropped because she didn't look a day over twenty-five.

'Have you seen the TV show *Younger*?' she laughed, when I expressed my surprise. 'It's about a forty-year-old woman who pretends to be in her mid-twenties to land a job at a millennial publishing firm. There are days when I feel like my life is that.'

Meredith was – in her own words – a queer, disabled, trans, albino first-generation immigrant and person of colour. I knew that, because of this, she would have been on the end of a few token gestures, but also, as an editor at a big media company, that she might be in a position to tokenize other people. When I put this to her, she immediately acknowledged it; 'Absolutely,' she said. 'I'm a product of early nineties elite college diversity initiatives, which weren't perfect, but if you were a poor immigrant kid and happened to be nerdy and do well in school, it meant it was possible for you to enter the halls of privilege.'

Meredith grew up in the Philippines until she was fifteen. Her parents were divorced when they emigrated to the States. Her mum moved to LA, her dad to New York. She lived with her mum until college, when she went to Harvard as an undergrad, at which point her base shifted to New York. She made her career as a journalist, writing breakout pieces for *The Nation* and *American Prospect*, calling bullshit on transphobia in LGBTQ+ movements or organizations that were failing to support the 'T'. But she wasn't interested in only writing for LGBTQ+ publications – because wouldn't that be preaching to the converted? – so she wrote for the broadest audience possible. This won her the attention of a lot of editors on Twitter, as well as a lot of anonymous Twitter trolls.

It was in 2015 that she got a staff job as a writer at BuzzFeed, where she says she was the only trans person

in editorial. This meant that, if anything remotely problematic was published about trans people, she would hear
about it, or even be held culpable. She was a token by
default. 'At a 4,000 to 4,500-person company that's difficult,'
she sighed. 'I felt pressure to get involved with anything
to do with trans culture.'

Teen Vogue wunderkind Phillip Picardi, the man behind
the idea for *them.*, called Meredith up to sound her out
about the job of senior editor in 2017. He knew her work
at BuzzFeed and her vocal Twitter presence. They also had
a mutual friend in Janet Mock. Meredith wasn't really interested in a full-time editorial position but, a few months
later, Phillip contacted her again to ask if she could suggest
someone for the role, preferably a trans woman of colour.
This was annoying, she said, because apart from Mock,
she couldn't think of anyone. How few trans editors there
were in East Coast America only highlighted further that
she ought to go up for the job. In fact, Meredith had just
written an article about how there needed to be more trans
voices in editorial positions, so it was time to put her money
where her mouth was.

'Did you have any reservations about taking it?' I asked
her. 'Were you worried about working on something queer
created by a big company? Were you sceptical about their
reasons for doing it?'

'Basically all of that, all of that,' she said, almost laughing. Meredith was very agreeable. She was also not a Condé
Nast PR mouthpiece.

'I think, for me, I'm deeply aware that we live in a late
capitalist society,' she continued calmly. 'If I was an

ideological purist I wouldn't be a journalist working in mainstream media; I would be living on a communist, separatist queer island. Like, if I'm going to play the game of being a journalist in this particular environment I'm going to have to make strategic decisions about how I'm going to negotiate it and how my politics play into that. Even if Condé Nast doesn't play into my own personal values, if I engage with my job with integrity and am constantly looking for ways for the result to be a net gain for marginalized queer people, well then I feel OK with that.'

I asked for an example and Meredith told me about a time when *them.* was casting for a video and one of the people they were thinking of casting had a disability. 'Someone else on staff said it would be inconvenient to cast this person in the video because they were disabled in a particular way. I said, "As a disabled person, I think we could see this as an opportunity to have the able-bodied people adjust for the disabled person, not the other way around."'

She then explained that this was one of both the positives and the negatives of what we might call tokenization: that once in a position of relative power, a marginalized person might be able to use their position to help others; that she could 'leverage' her privilege against her marginalized identity. But, she said, it was worth remembering that this wasn't always the case for trans people or people of colour.

'I think tokenism has a couple of different meanings,' she said, explaining that traditionally it used to be about 'a person only existing in the room in order to excuse the fact that the entire system is unjust', whereas more recently, she'd been thinking about a different, perhaps subtler kind of tokenism, whereby you were a minority hired on merit but you still had to be an exceptional outlier to even get in the door and once you were through it, you still had to fit the standards of the majority. Part of the reason she was able to have a job like hers was the amazing work done by people advocating to see more trans people repre- sented, but it was also because – and she was very aware of this, she said – she was a child prodigy who scored insanely well on standardized tests and went to Harvard. Her success didn't necessarily mean the system was skewed any better towards trans people; she wasn't the rule, but the exception. And until that changed, the system wasn't really improving. The same went for trans models and actors, too – most of the time, Meredith explained, they had to fit a mould of cis beauty to be successful. 'I'll see models who fit into particular tropes of femme, white, waif, female blondeness, who are using their modelling visibility to continue to advocate for social and political change, and that's been really important. But it's also a paradoxical position, simultaneously saying, "I'm here because of these outlying conditions that make me atypical as a trans person, but it's important for trans people who are not like me to also be in more privileged positions too."'

For Meredith, putting queer and trans people in positions where they have the agency to steer representation was a good thing, and an imperative for companies who wanted to do better. 'It's hard to objectify people who are like yourself. So as sensitive as one can be about these issues, having the people you want to represent on staff is the *only* genuine way to diversify,' she shrugged.

'Is that the start of what "real diversity" looks like?'

She thought for a second. 'I don't necessarily believe in the binary poles' – she said this in such a way as to imply sarcasm at her choice of term – 'of what we might call "tokenism" and "real diversity".' Not only because they were on a spectrum, but because whatever 'real diversity' was, it was difficult to achieve. 'The media doesn't just shape society, it reflects back the way society looks, and besides, you can never really represent *everyone. Them.* tries to counter the forces of tokenism in society – at the same time we're really aware that we exist within a market and there's never going to be any piece of representation that is going to be fully diverse.'

'The photo frame isn't big enough for a photo of literally everyone.'

'Right,' she said.

On that note, I asked her what she thought about Rihanna's quote.

'It's a tough quote because, on the one hand, I agree that the ideal situation is for trans people to be able to operate in the world in ways that are equal to cis people, but at the same time, that's not the world we live in. It's simultaneously good that trans people aren't being used as a pawn in some kind of diversity game; at the same time it's important to acknowledge that a trans person working with Rihanna would be a good thing. So I guess I'm at odds with that quote.'

'Yeah,' I sighed. 'Me too.'

After a few more stressful days in New York, one of the trans models I'd contacted finally got in touch with me. Her name was Peche Di, and she was the founder of Trans Models, an agency exclusively for trans and non-binary people. I asked Peche if I could come to the Trans Models office, and she told me that actually, she ran it from home, so the evening before Thanksgiving, I found myself walking to Peche's house. She lived in Greenpoint, one of Brooklyn's most gentrified neighbourhoods, its tree-lined streets peppered with vintage warehouses and boutique coffee shops. I walked there down Bedford Avenue, past the Apple store and busy bars, which I stared into from the freezing cold outside, like a jilted lover from a Richard Curtis film. I went into a chocolate shop, the only store that was open, and panic-bought Peche some macaroons. Then I walked across McCarren Park, which was floodlit and eerily empty.

When I found Peche's house, she let me in and I followed her upstairs. I noticed how bouncy she was, full of energy. Her home was a spacious one-bed apartment with a long corridor that stretched from the entrance hall through a kitchen, a living room and into a bedroom. Peche joked that it was perfect for practising her runway walk, and showed me just to demonstrate that this was possible. I followed suit, doing my best Linda Evangelista. We sat on her bed, which gave me the feeling of being a kid again, at a sleepover. It was also quite camp getting straight into bed with someone you'd never met before, like a Nineties breakfast TV show or *In Bed with Madonna*. This was not Peche's intention; she had recently moved in, and the other rooms were cluttered with boxes. She pointed to an Apple Mac on a desk in the corner of her bedroom. She told me this was where she ran Trans Models from.

I asked Peche where the idea for Trans Models originated and she told me that the story really started when she was eight or nine. This was when she first understood what it meant to be transgender, she said, because her mum showed her a picture of a cousin who had moved to Germany and transitioned. 'I never met her but I saw her photo and was like, "Wow, she used to be a man? She looks good!"' said Peche, laughing.

Back then, her dream wasn't to become a model, but to become a beauty queen; a dream that was thwarted by the other kids at school, who would kick her in the crotch, call her names like 'sissy' and tell her she'd never be a girl. Undeterred, Peche stuck to a strict beauty regimen. She would read about how to make her skin softer, make her own coffee scrubs for her face and put coconut oil in her hair. I made a note to ask her more about this later.

When Peche was a teenager, she met another role model, this time in the flesh. 'One day a girl who had graduated from my school and had transitioned came back to visit the teachers. She had long hair, a gorgeous face. I asked her how I start and she said, "Go to buy hormones right now." So that day, after I finished class, I went to the pharmacy to get hormones. I took three because I'm impatient, and then I vomited it all up. So then I was like, "OK, let's take one from now on," and I kept taking it every single day.'

'Did you tell your parents?' I asked.

At this Peche let out her infectious, high-pitched giggle again. 'No, but my mum caught me because I left the hormones in the pocket of my student jacket. She thought I had a girlfriend and it was for preventing pregnancy.'

'Wait, so it's the same hormones?' I said incredulously.

'Yes.' Peche seemed a bit impatient with me at this point, so I explained that I hadn't taken the contraceptive pill in eight years. This once again resulted in the 'What! You're gay?' conversation.

'Did you have anyone else to look up to, any trans celebrities?'

'Yeah, there was a trans celebrity. She used to be a trans model walking with big Thai fashion designers, and after she turned to be a commentator on television, on *Thailand's Got Talent*. Her name is Ornapa. She was very well respected, everybody knew her and people are accepting of her. She didn't really start out as a model – she was a make-up artist before and then one day a model got sick and the designer was like, "Can you wear my clothes and walk for us?"'

I gasped at how *Devil Wears Prada* the story was.

'Yes! And she slayed!' Peche exclaimed, nattering on. 'I read her book in Thai. I always carried it with me. That was the book that inspired me to be a model. But first, I had to join beauty pageants, and I was very shy because I'd been attacked at school and I never felt comfortable with my body or with my look, so learning how to dance, be on stage at beauty pageants for a few years, helped me be comfortable, to go from a very shy person to a more outgoing person.'

'Did you see the *Vogue* cover, with Valentina Sampaio?' I asked.

She told me she had, and that she had read *Vogue* religiously ever since she was a kid in Thailand. If she had seen a trans woman like Sampaio on the cover back then, she said, she could have shown it to her family, and they would have thought that being trans was acceptable, desirable even. Role models weren't just for us to see, they were for the people around us to see too.

'What do you think of the headline?' I asked.

'I think labelling is important for young people. When they have that term "trans" they know they have found their representation. Some people think we shouldn't label but if we don't, what about the younger generation who have no idea who is and isn't trans? It's important for young people to see the label.'

It was this belief that you had to see it to be it that carried Peche to America in 2010, when she was twenty, where she would try to become not just a model but a role model for others. By this time she was twenty she had transitioned and had been working as a model back home, including national campaigns and walking in shows during Bangkok fashion week. But she hadn't been able to find an agency that wanted to sign her. Transphobia was rife, she said, so some girls would use a fake ID to join the big

Asian agencies. 'In Thailand we don't have any law or regulation to change your gender marker,' Peche explained. One of her friends was even arrested for changing her documents illegally to model. America seemed a more promising landscape in which to pursue her dreams. She had seen that the models Isis King and Yasmine Petty were featured in different magazines and working with top people in New York, so she decided to follow suit, believing that America might also allow her to change her legal gender, that she might find a partner and build a life with someone. (Incidentally, two days before we met, Peche had just had her new passport come through, identifying her as legally female for the first time.)

Peche worked in a Thai restaurant for cash, took English lessons to improve her pronunciation, and pursued styling and modelling on the side. Around this time, she met a friend who became a mentor and would take her portfolio to different agencies, but she would hear nothing back. She felt she was being discriminated against, so she tried to hide that she was trans. She scored her first job, but then her campaign was dropped when she had to show her passport to be paid and the agent realized she was lying about the gender she was assigned at birth. Eventually, it seemed best to be transparent about being trans. The emergence of trans models like Lea T, who modelled for Givenchy, was a comfort.

'It was much better to be honest . . . I felt like I didn't have to lie to people.'

'So did you start getting jobs?' I asked.

'No!' That giggle again. 'People didn't want to take my photo because I'm trans. Except for a lingerie brand for trans women.'

In 2014, Peche landed her first big US campaign, for Barneys New York, called 'Brothers, Sisters, Sons & Daughters', in which they cast all trans models, seventeen in fact. It was shot by Bruce Weber. *Vanity Fair* described it as groundbreaking. But it didn't change much for Peche; she still couldn't get an agency. This was when she had the idea to start an agency for trans models herself, given that there seemed to be a market.

'I made a list of names. My friend said, "You shouldn't put 'trans', people are still negative towards that word. It's not a good idea to expose yourself." I said, "I know that there's negativity towards it, that's why I want to use the name." I wanted to purify the word, add positivity to it. When you google about trans on the Internet, porn shows up. I want to add something that's not just porn when I google the word "trans". When people say, "Don't use that word!" it makes me want to use it more.' And so, in March 2015, Trans Models was born.

Peche started casting models through friends of friends. Her roommate was also trans, so they called on people they knew. They aimed to include not just people who passed for cisgender but people who did not pass, or were androgynous, or who identified as non-binary. 'I wanted to represent the actual person . . . you don't need to pass. And I don't like the idea of passing and passable, it's like white privilege . . . passing is a privilege for a trans person. I didn't want to represent that as what's considered beautiful: that you have to pass. It's not fair.'

They set up their first photo shoot with nineteen models at a friend's loft, and Peche gave an interview published in *The Atlantic*. The story travelled fast and the first jobs started coming in: *i-D* magazine, *Time Out*, *Teen Vogue* – later some brand work with Puma, W Hotels, Kenneth Cole. Then a big job for *National Geographic*'s special 'Gender Revolution' issue, which featured several of Peche's models.

'Money-wise, it was not that great. I'm not good with numbers, I'm more a creative visual person, and some work with brands paid but only like once a month. We got a lot of exposure, but we were struggling.'

'What happened next then?'

'Nineteen models was a lot. I thought I needed a lot of models to make a lot of money but after I met with my friend – I represent her, Yasmine Petty; she's my role model and my mentor – I realized you don't need a lot of models to create a successful agency. I felt like I couldn't handle it, it was too stressful. She said, if you can represent just one person, like Laverne Cox, that's all you need. After she said that I decided to release everybody. Now we have four models.'

'Do you still represent yourself?'

'Yes!' Peche started giggling, the most she had giggled yet.

'What's so funny?' I asked.

'That I'm *still* looking for someone to represent me,' she laughed.

I wondered whether Peche wasn't having much luck

with getting signed or getting many gigs for the same reason a lot of talented drag queens weren't – because their industries were getting crowded, and there was only one proverbial golden ticket in a world increasingly rife with tokenism. Trans men, who had always been less visible than trans women, were even starting to become more visible in the world of modelling: Casil McArthur walked for Marc Jacobs at New York fashion week, and underwear model Laith Ashley, who'd been represented by Peche, had 200,000 Instagram followers and had been featured in *Vogue*. Trans Models wasn't the only trans model agency any more; the LA-based agency Slay Models had even been followed by a TV show.

When Peche and I talked about this, she told me she didn't see more trans models as a threat, but rather as a good thing – both for business and for politics. The problem was the type of model who would get exposure.

'For me personally, when trans people get to be on covers, it's still mostly Caucasian models who look cisgender. The beauty contracts trans people get signed to are all Caucasian trans women: Andreja Pejić, Caitlyn Jenner. I want to see the change include trans people of colour, and gender-non-conforming trans people.'

This applied to Teddy and Hanne, I supposed. Without diminishing their incredible activist work, they were shaking up the world in many of the right ways: they were thin. They were white. They passed. And they were already famous when they came out.

'Fashion is still lacking portrayal [of the] beauty of Asian trans women and African American trans women,' said

Peche, sitting up. 'I'm shocked when I hear brands call darker skin tones a minority, because Asian people are a majority of the population, and African people are a majority. I get frustrated and pissed by that term, "minority". I wish magazines would be more inclusive – we are women and women need to be represented in different shapes, sizes and forms. Isn't that better for the magazine in the long term?'

'So all these trans models . . . is it just a moment or is it actual progress?' I asked, processing what Peche had said about the tyranny of passing privilege and Eurocentric beauty standards – the supremacy of white, Western ideals that are upheld by magazines and the media. How there still seemed to be a particular 'type' of LGBTQ+ person we were happy to see in a magazine, or on TV.

'Thankfully progress is happening. I think it will happen more . . . I'm not saying this against the fashion industry – I'm in the fashion industry and I love this industry – I just want to work towards something that's more inclusive. It's trans women of colour that get attacked and killed,' said Peche, 'so I want to see the change include those people.'

chapter six

NOW YOU DON'T

At some point during my conversation with Meredith, I had 'circled back', as the Americans say, and asked her why *them.* needed to exist to begin with. I told her about my own experience, working for magazines like *VICE* and *i-D* and *Dazed* and *Refinery29*. They weren't LGBTQ+ titles, I said, but they widely covered LGBTQ+ issues as well as 'straight' issues, long before and after I was there encouraging them to do so. So why did Condé Nast need a separate LGBTQ+ publication?

She told me that she perceived culture to be changing; that, for people who were millennials or younger – younger than thirty-five, really – queer culture *was just culture*. 'Surveys show that Generation Z – after millennials – more than 50 per cent of them consider themselves not straight or cisgender.'

I didn't know, off the top of my head, whether these stats were correct. (When I looked them up later, they were backed by trend-forecasting agency J. Walter Thompson Innovation Group, which found that only 48 per cent of American Gen Zs identified as exclusively heterosexual in 2016.) However, I knew the stats in the UK said roughly the same thing: more people than ever before placed themselves somewhere on the scale that said they weren't entirely straight. A UK survey from 2016, for instance, found that half of young people in Britain aged eighteen to twenty-four identified as something other than heterosexual.

Meredith carried on: 'So, to me, *them.* feels like a queer publication in name, but I feel like as audiences get younger and younger, the idea that only a small percentage would be reading a publication like *them.* disintegrates.'

I wasn't sure I was following. Wasn't that the point I had made? If queer culture *was* culture, why would you need to distinguish it?

Meredith smiled. To her, being separate didn't mean being ghettoized, it meant creating a dedicated space where LGBTQ+ voices were the dominant voices; to her, *them.* being its own entity was just 'putting queer culture in its rightful place'. In a perfect world, she said, *them.* wouldn't cease to exist because LGBTQ+ people would find it unnecessary to read a separate LGBTQ+ magazine. It would be read by *everyone*, and be just as big as the *New Yorker*, or *Vanity Fair*. This, she said, was her goal.

'That's an interesting outlook,' I said, a little embarrassed that I hadn't seen things this way myself.

Then she said something that struck a chord with me, something I was still thinking about a week later, after Helene had left, as I was riding the subway to Queens to stay with my gay friend Patrick.

'People forget that before Madonna's "Vogue" there was an entire history of queer trans people of colour,' she said, 'or that, for every make-up look you have for a pretty cisgender model, it's extremely likely that a queer person was a part of creating that look. So many cultural products we perceive to be innovative or mainstream were created by queer and trans people.'

Keeping queer culture separate was a way of staking a claim to that, she concluded, rather than once again letting queer culture be subsumed by the mainstream.

If I had gone into my conversation with Meredith feeling dubious about Condé Nast's decision to market itself to an LGBTQ+ audience and sell ads off the back of it, Meredith's politics left me feeling optimistic. Condé Nast had put its money where its mouth was, by hiring a trans woman of colour in a position of power, and the result felt truly inclusive, unapologetic, beneficial to actual queer people.

But what Meredith had said about queer people having their culture co-opted stayed with me because it was still happening everywhere, all the time. While the media had diversified to include the representation of queer people in recent years, genuine or otherwise, so had brands, and as with some of those brands who sponsored Pride events, this often felt distinctly disingenuous. Every time I passed a billboard of two men kissing for an advert for a bank, I wondered how that bank supported its LGBTQ+ staff. Every time I saw an advert for a vodka brand featuring trans women or drag queens, I thought, *What does this have to do with marketing vodka to the masses?* And every time I saw a luxury fashion brand or a make-up brand adorning queer bodies of colour for an advert, I wondered, *Why didn't you do this before it was fashionable?*

It was just as Rihanna had warned us: brands wanted to score themselves points for being inclusive, without really improving inclusivity. Or worse, they tried to be inclusive, and got it wrong. While some brands like Burberry or Adidas created LGBTQ+-inspired clothing lines in order to give the money to LGBTQ+ charities, others did the same without giving back or standing by the values they were claiming to promote. L'Oréal asked the British activist and model Munroe Bergdorf to be the first ever trans woman in one of its major beauty campaigns, only to drop her when she posted comments on Facebook after the Charlottesville rally in August 2017 in which she explained that all white people are conditioned to be racist (she was talking about structural racism). L'Oréal wanted Munroe, but a palatable, censored version of her.

The token use of LGBTQ+ people in brand campaigns gave me the same feeling as seeing a Hollywood film about gay or trans lives starring straight or cisgender actors. I remember watching *Transamerica* with my mum when it came out in 2005, a film that cast a cis woman as a trans woman. Then there was *Dallas Buyers Club*, with Jared Leto playing a trans woman trying to get hold of AZT drugs to treat her HIV. And *The Danish Girl*, in which Eddie Redmayne played Lili Elbe, one of the first people to undergo gender confirmation surgery, sustaining complications that eventually killed her. The problem with these films is that there aren't enough gay or trans actors visible at the top of the media to begin with, so for roles about their lives to be taken by straight or cis actors seems to be unnecessarily perpetuating a disparity. There are a lot of

LGBTQ+ actors out there. Plus, you know, it's just annoying to see someone try on a marginal identity that they have no experience of for a role, and then later take it off and throw it away.

If all of this frustrated me, there were other people it frustrated more. As Meredith had said, in terms of cultural production, no group of people had contributed more to culture and had its efforts co-opted and pillaged more often than queer people of colour. If tokenism was using an individual to look inclusive, then appropriation was stealing the cultural signifiers of a community of people for profit, and giving absolutely nothing back. I thought of one of the people I'd had the most honest and insightful conversations about this with before, and remembered that she lived in New York.

I had been a fan of Kia LaBeija's art for a while. Kia's identity, like Meredith's, comprised a lot of marginalized intersections: she was queer, black, female and born HIV positive. She was a photographer, a dancer and an activist. I discovered her work online via Visual AIDS, an organization that archived art by people who lived with HIV or died from AIDS-related illness, and provided a platform for HIV positive artists to upload their own work, whatever the medium, and receive grants or become involved in art shows and panel discussions. In her early twenties, Kia uploaded a self-portrait, which was immediately selected for one of Visual AIDS's shows. It was called 'In My Room', an image of her sitting in her bedroom in red lingerie. In another image from the same series, she stretched her body out across a balcony above New York, in a beautiful red dress, channelling one of her first and only HIV positive role models, Rosario Dawson's character Mimi from the film *Rent*. Like all of her photos, they captured the various, intricate sides of her character, as well as the stories she had to tell, but they also highlighted how politicized her body was. In each shot, she reinvented herself with costume, lighting and poses, creating a catalogue of glamorous, cinematic images, where she sometimes appeared powerful, and other times vulnerable.

'For me, my work is about releasing trauma out of your body, through movement,' Kia said, when I interviewed her over Skype in 2016. 'I've endured a lot of physical and emotional pain that I've pushed down. I have all these experiences I've never dealt with and now they're manifesting in my photos.' As well as trauma, a lot of Kia's work focused on memory. One of her photos pictured her lying on the floor of her bedroom with an image of her mother in a frame. Another was titled 'Eleven', after the day it was taken: the eleventh anniversary of her mother's death. Looking like a film still, it was a photo of her wearing a red prom dress and holding a rose corsage in her doctor's office, the same doctor's office she'd been going to since she was four years old to get her meds.

'As a child born with HIV, I wasn't expected to make it as far as my high school prom,' she said. 'I was born in 1990, and medication that put you on a regimen that was expected to save your life didn't come around until like 1996, so people weren't sure babies with HIV of my age would survive.'

Kia described her mother, Kwan Bennett, as 'in the 1 per cent of people living with HIV, because she was a woman, heterosexual and Filipino Native American'. Bennett was an activist herself; 'She was a survivor of rape and incest when she was a child and HIV was one more thing added onto her plate of very traumatic things,' explained Kia. 'She wanted to cope with it so she got involved with different organizations, such as Apicha – an organization for Asian Pacific Islanders, particularly with HIV. She wanted to spread the message that Asian people can contract HIV too.' Bennett passed away in 2004 and Kia picked up where she left off. Tackling AIDS and representation through her art and her activism helped to assuage the feeling of loneliness her status gave her, especially given that her mother wasn't around and that she felt she couldn't tell anyone at school she was HIV positive, due to the stigma attached to the virus.

After growing up feeling like this, Kia found community when she started to vogue around nine years ago while training as a dancer. Later, when she was working at a big nightclub in New York City called Webster Hall, she met someone in a voguing group called The House of LaBeija, which she proudly took up as her last name. 'A house is a family and the family walks under a name that is chosen by the founder of the house,' she told me. 'A lot of houses are named after actual fashion houses like Dior or Chanel or Saint Laurent. These house families compete in balls – underground competitions where queer people enter into different categories: performance categories like "voguing", fashion categories like "best dressed", or "realness" categories like "butch realness" or "femme realness", where you have to try to pass as a heterosexual man or woman.' She would train with her house once a week and go to clubs and practise. 'That's how you learn – you learn all the elements and go out and make them your own when you compete.'

A lot of people date the emergence of ballroom culture back to *Paris Is Burning*, the 1990 Jennie Livingston documentary that captured the culture on film, but historians have found evidence of African American drag queens in Washington DC as far back as 1888, and The House of LaBeija is over forty years old. According to Kia, LaBeija was the first ever voguing 'house' and still one of the most famous in the world. It was founded by Crystal LaBeija, who appeared in the 1968 documentary *The Queen*. An African American drag queen, Crystal was competing in a pageant against white drag queens and felt it was because of the colour of her skin that she did not win. 'She made a fuss about it and someone close to her suggested she host her own function under the name of LaBeija,' said Kia. 'So she did. She was the first one to create the blueprint for ballroom culture, and slowly new performance categories have been added.'

After Crystal, someone called Pepper LaBeija became the mother of the house, but when Pepper died, the house became a little inactive because she was the leader; 'She was the star, the icon, the glue that held everything together,' said Kia, who was recently asked by the fathers of the house if she'd take on the role. She'd been winning lots of voguing competitions, being very vocal in terms of her activism, as well as very present within the community

– all criteria of a house mother. Practically speaking, being mother meant organizing balls and meet-ups, and being there for members of the house when they were in need. For Kia, taking a more active role in the house was more than just a job. 'When we get together it is beautiful, it's a political statement,' she said. 'There's so much love, so much art and so much acceptance.'

When Meredith mentioned Madonna's 'Vogue', she was talking about how Madonna had turned it into a worldwide phenomenon by writing the song and voguing her way through the video. As folklore had it, Madonna first saw voguing at the New York Love Ball, a fundraiser for AIDS. She asked Willi Ninja, a voguing expert, to teach her how to do it, and then put Jose and Luis from the House of Xtravaganza in her video. She had, in other words, taken something subcultural, repackaged it for the mainstream and profited from it. A similar argument was made against *Paris Is Burning*: Livingston, a white lesbian film-maker, was accused of profiteering off ballroom culture since she didn't pay the participants in the film. Others defended her, by suggesting her status as a genderqueer woman gave her a stake in queer communities more generally, that documentary film-makers don't usually pay their subjects, or by pointing out that she'd spent seven whole years working on the film, which didn't sound like someone trying to make a quick buck.

The point was, it wasn't only straight people who could appropriate. RuPaul had come under criticism for making money from a culture that he didn't have a whole lot to do with any more. Drag was heavily indebted to ballroom, and what we saw on *Drag Race* – particularly the runway section at the end of the show – was a lot like a glitzy televised version of what took place in Harlem ballrooms in the 1980s. This threw up a lot of difficult, perhaps unanswerable questions: Is there really a polarity between 'OK' and 'not OK' when it comes to appropriation, or are the lines more blurred? Can you call out the appropriation of ballroom or drag culture if you've never contributed to the production of it yourself?

For someone like Kia, the result of the historic interest in ball culture was complicated: the enduring popularity of voguing meant that not just artists or film-makers but brands too wanted a piece of it. There was an opportunity for her to make money, but at what cost? The same went for her art as an HIV positive, queer woman of colour. While showing work at the Whitney and the Studio Museum in Harlem was good for her career, the interviews she was asked to do sometimes felt bittersweet – her identity turned into hashtags for intersectional clickbait. 'Sometimes I think this association will follow me for the rest of my life,' she told me. 'Sometimes you wonder, "Would they be as interested in my work if I was not living with HIV?"'

In this sense, she embodied a lot of what Meredith was talking about: she was living at the site of conflict between inclusion and tokenism; she had experienced first-hand what it was like to have your culture appropriated; and she was exasperated by it, as I found out when I finally went to meet her at her apartment in Hell's Kitchen that week.

Over tea, Kia told me about the work she'd been doing

recently: namely, more work for brands, like a 'Voguing Tour of New York' for Airbnb. When this type of work came to her, she had to ask herself why she was being asked, and whether she was being reimbursed properly. 'People really try it,' she told me, visibly tired. 'They lowball you and assume you're not on top of your game, or make assumptions that because of who you are you might not understand how things work. For me, because I've been working so much lately, I'm like, "You're not gonna put nothing past me, I know what I'm worth!"'

Kia also thought a lot about the fact that every time she was asked to do a job, someone lower down the food chain didn't get paid; sometimes she even turned down work because of it. 'I have a particular story, experience, relationship with vogue culture, for example, but it's not the only one. Sometimes I'm asked to be part of things and I say, "I know you want to involve me but maybe you should involve someone else whose experience is a little bit closer to what you're looking for." At the end of the day, ballroom is majority male-driven and trans-driven.' She told me that, because she'd been doing this work, tokenism and cultural appropriation had been on her mind more than ever before, particularly the question of why black queer culture *was* so often appropriated and what that meant.

'It's hard, right? Cause diversity is so in right now,' she said, emphasizing the last part sardonically.

'It gets fucking annoying. You see something and you're like, OK, I see myself, but you'll be like, they're really trying it though, they're doing it because everyone is doing it. Being culturally diverse is in vogue, being black is in vogue.'

Literally. Weeks before we'd met, British *Vogue* had a much-needed overhaul, with white Editor-in-Chief Alexandra Shulman stepping down for Ghanaian-born Edward Enninful, who promised to drastically diversify the magazine. More generally, a seismic shift seemed to be happening, where those who were once treated as marginal were suddenly embraced as beautiful. Kia was talking, inadvertently, about all of it – the rise of trans models, the launch of *them.*, even DragCon. What I wanted to know was when she thought this movement became problematic. It took her about thirty seconds to think of some examples.

'When Pepsi did that Black Lives Matter commercial,' she said, referring to the trivializing advert where Kendall Jenner handed a Pepsi to a riot cop as an olive branch during what appears to be a civil rights protest, a nod to recent police clashes with Black Lives Matter protesters in America. 'It's like, are you doing that cause you really wanna include people,' continued Kia, 'or cause it's the hype right now, and you don't wanna get backlash for not doing that?'

She carried on: 'Oh, and I *hate* seeing the word "slay" everywhere! It drives me up the fucking wall. Oh God, stop with slay and werk. I see it everywhere! I was looking at something on Instagram today. Maybe Maybelline or CoverGirl – one of those brands – they had this Instagram ad. First of all the make-up looks terrible, it was like thin winged cat eyeliner, and then it comes in and you fill it in' – I started laughing at her scathing description – 'and then they're like, "catch the shade" or "get shady". I'm like, *Noooo, stop will you already!* Just stop.'

I thought about a pair of pants I had seen in H&M that said 'Slay' on the bum and shivered. I told Kia about them. 'I think some people are buying them with no irony, and I say that as a white person.'

The trouble with these words, I knew, was that they had somehow wound their way from African American communities through the LGBTQ+ culture of Harlem's ballrooms, via *Paris Is Burning*, the Internet, *RuPaul's Drag Race*, Beyoncé and *Broad City*, into the popular consciousness. The first use of 'yass' – the word everyone was shouting at the *RuPaul's Drag Race* viewing parties – had been traced back as far as 1893, but now Instagram had stickers you could add to your photos that said 'yass'. I had seen online that the frequent use of the word 'banjee' on *Drag Race* even had teenage girls using it (it's a street term from the eighties, used by queer black and Latino communities to describe masc gay boys who look tough, later evolving into a more general byword for 'ghetto'). Quite often, I'd hear a white gay man or a straight female friend of my own using words like 'werk' and 'fierce'. Had I misguidedly used them once or twice? Probably. I knew what these words meant because they were everywhere – you couldn't escape them – but I asked Kia to explain their meaning anyway.

'To "read" somebody is pretty much to tell somebody about themselves,' she said, not as impatiently as I had expected. 'When you're reading it's like you're giving somebody an inside look and you do it with "shade" – in a way that's not necessarily nice. And you can read and read and read and read as long as you want to, but sometimes it can be a back-and-forth situation. A read can also be playful.

It can be nasty and serious but it can also be funny. And "werk" is a praise,' she continued. 'When you see some-body doing something sick, you're like, "Werk – that shit is hot." Giving somebody props for something that they're doing. It's all about the way that you use the word as well: "Werk bitch, killed it, nailed it, you are excellent."' She said it with conviction, to show me how it was done. But by the time we came on to the word 'yass' – an affirmation, a version of 'yes', an encouragement – she gave up, letting out a sigh.

'The thing about these words is, they sound so crazy when you explain them, but queer people of colour created this vernacular because they've grown up around a mother, sister and aunts who have a certain vernacular. The inspir-ation comes from women of colour, specifically black women. Queer men of colour have recreated it in a way that's super playful and fits into their community, but they're words heard in the home growing up.'

'How does it make you feel when you hear other people using it?'

'The vernacular is used by white queer men in a way that to me feels offensive. Like now you're just mocking a black woman, not using it with black femme power the way that black queer men are using it,' Kia weighed in. 'White queer men using it feels offensive given the history of violence against black women. White queer men use it with a sense of entitlement. If I say, "Excuse me, you sound nuts, these words belong to my people and you can't just use them in a way that's nasty and offensive," they'd be like, "Oh, I can do whatever the fuck I want."'

'But it's not just white queer men. I feel like this language goes from black women to queer black men to white queer men to white teenage girls to everybody else,' I said.

Kia shook her head disbelievingly. 'Why would teenage white girls want to use this language?' she said, sounding genuinely confused. 'Black culture is appropriated by mass media so fast. I see this language all over the place, and the inflection and the way people say it sounds . . . ugh . . .' She trailed off and gathered her thoughts. 'When you're used to people speaking with this kind of language and you hear it you're like, oh' – she snapped her fingers – 'you feel it's true, you know? But then you hear it and you feel it's dishonest. People have the right intentions – "you slayed that" – but the way it's being said, it doesn't really come from you, it doesn't make sense in your vernacular.'

'What about you, when do you use it?'

'I use the vernacular but I don't overuse it. I use it in moments that I feel it. It's something I came into in my late teens. I grew with it, kind of, but it's bits and pieces here and there.'

'Why do you think ballroom culture is so borrowed from?' I asked, simultaneously understanding that this was a huge, complex question, and having no doubt Kia would give me an answer.

'It's been happening over time, you know? But so many people have romanticized what ballroom is based on what they've seen in *Paris Is Burning*. It looks very glamorous – it *is* quite glamorous in its own way. It's a lot about fantasy, about embodying who you feel you are, being able to express one piece of you for that night. Whether it's a runway diva or a grandiose performer or a fashionable person, it gives you a chance to play, in a world where it sometimes feels like everything can be so serious.'

I told her that a lot of my friends told me they experienced something similar when they did drag. It was easy to see the appeal.

'And why do you think the culture of queer people of colour in particular is so appealing?'

'I think it's because black American people have so often been left with nothing that they've had to be very creative. This creativity, this language, these attitudes, these stories we carry, they become interesting to people who are not of colour, or people who have privilege. And when you come from a marginalized group of people, or from spaces where you don't have as many opportunities, or situations where your economic background isn't as affluent as others, or where you're not accepted by your family, all these different things that queer people of colour have to go through, that's what creates the best art. People fall in love with any romanticized struggle, and queer people of colour have struggled because they're in two marginalized groups. I think people are attracted to that, the art that comes from the struggle.'

As we carried on talking, Kia explained to me that while Madonna didn't necessarily take credit for coming up with the concept of voguing, people still thought they were indebted to Madonna for it. 'Because it was on the body of a white woman with the platform to put it in a big place in media and in history, people think voguing comes from her,' said Kia. 'I'll say "vogue" and people will go "Madonna Madonna Madonna". They don't remember that Queen Latifah was one of the first people to put voguing in a video, or Jody Watley in "Still A Thrill". But these are African American women. It's about visibility – and who has the most of it.'

'Couldn't you say that, when it comes to language, or dance, it's all bastardized?' I asked, playing devil's advocate: voguing itself had evolved from the Old Way to the New Way; one language was usually derived from another.

'In this day and age you can't say anyone owns anything,' she conceded. 'Voguing comes from poses in *Vogue* magazine. LaBeija comes from "beautiful" in Spanish. Everything is a copy of a copy of a copy – a mirror image of something else. But there are so many influences in ballroom that ballroom has become its own thing. Borrowing will happen, it's just the way it goes – the problem is when people aren't getting credit where due.' She gave the example of when big companies or brands co-opt trends from marginalized groups and take the credit, or when something is taken from a community and popularized – be it a fashion trend, a dance style, or a word – and the origin is forgotten.

'At first braids, dreadlocks, hoop earrings, gold teeth and long nails are "ghetto",' Kia continued, understandably more pissed off now. 'But then it slowly gets picked up and one person influences one person and suddenly it belongs to them [white people]. Especially in America. Black art in general, not just queer art, started so many of the most appealing forms – jazz, hip hop, R&B, blues, all this kind of stuff – and it all comes from pain. Hip hop started out of the South Bronx when they were literally burning down buildings and kids had no place or nothing to do, and kids started gangs, started fighting each other and all the other bullshit, but the music came out of it. Fighting became about dance forms, breaking, MC'ing, DJ'ing. And now that doesn't really exist any more because it's a commodity.'

In other words, the sense of community or culture these things represent comes to be diluted. The appropriation or commodification ruins something pure – it's a kind of colonization. Kia linked this process back to the very beginning of American culture: 'It's one of the biggest problems with this country,' she sighed. 'Christopher Columbus came over here and said, "This is my land now," and that's how this country works – off taking, stealing and appropriating: that's our history. The entire foundation is based on taking what does not belong to you. Not only are things appropriated and stolen but we [people of colour] are written out of the history.'

'So what's the solution?' I asked.

In the age of social media, Kia pointed out, when anything pops up that feels exclusive or unrepresentative then, in her words, 'your shit's gonna be on blast'. Brands should be wary. But there was more that we could all do, she said: 'It's all about knowing your history and digging deeper.'

'I suppose if people dig they might be pleasantly surprised by what they find.'

'Exactly. Because the people that take and don't make

things their own might get the credit, but the people who don't will always be the creatives, the trailblazers, the true avant garde.'

I agreed. But the problem was, when it came to the people who pioneered ballroom, most of this true avant garde weren't around any more to claim credit where due. Many had succumbed to HIV, homelessness, or homophobic and transphobic violence. Pepper LaBeija died from complications related to diabetes in 2003. Willi Ninja died from AIDS-related heart failure in 2006. Meanwhile, *Paris Is Burning* lives on via Netflix and *RuPaul's Drag Race* appears to be immortal. The language of ballroom permeates memes across the Internet and circulates the globe. Some people see this as a beautiful thing, others as a travesty. But while we could never all agree, one thing was clear: that when it came to the mainstreaming of queer culture, certain people were forgotten.

Much of what had been sanitized and corporatized came from spaces of collective safety and support that arose out of desperate situations. When Kia described ballroom houses as 'self-sustaining, underground communities of queer black and brown folks', what she meant was that they provided safety to people who may not even be safe in their homes, or, for that matter, even have a home. Appropriating from ballroom meant cherry-picking the good parts of a culture and community of poor black and Latino queer people with none of the risk that came with those politicized identities. Madonna might have sung the words 'It makes no difference if you're black or white / If you're a boy or a girl' in the song 'Vogue', but whatever her intentions, the fact was, it did matter. Or, as Kia aptly put it, the reality for many of these people 'wasn't always that fabulous' – for every bit of visibility for queer people, there was and still is someone that is invisible; for every fabulous moment, one when your life could be thrown into danger.

With this in mind, on my last day in New York I decided to pay the NYC Anti-Violence Project a visit. The organization had a simple goal: creating a world where all lesbian, gay, bisexual, transgender, queer, HIV positive people and their allies are free from violence. Not so simple was trying to achieve it.

The AVP started up in 1980, in response to violent homophobic attacks on gay men in Chelsea (a predominantly gay neighbourhood in New York), but today they aimed to look after all sections of the community. From their base, a modest floor of office space on a small street a couple of blocks away from One World Trade Center, where Meredith worked, they offered a twenty-four-hour bilingual hotline, legal advice, counselling and support groups, and organized community outreach and educational programmes. They also produced reports on the state of violence towards LGBTQ+ people in America, which could be used to lobby local and national governments (theoretically, at least) to implement protections.

Before my meeting, I sat in a Starbucks around the corner and read some of their reports on my phone. One of the most recent was an emergency report, released in August 2017. NCAVP (a national coalition of around fifty

LGBTQ+ organizations coming together under the banner of AVP to share vital information) had found, despite being less than eight months into the year, the highest annual level of anti-LGBTQ+ homicides on record in their twenty-year history of tracking the information. After August, I read, the problem had continued to worsen, and we now know that in 2017, there were fifty-two hate murders of LGBTQ+ people in America. That's the equivalent of one a week. And those were just the ones that were registered; it is likely there were more. Of the 2017 deaths, 71 per cent were people of colour, 67 per cent were thirty-five years old and under, and 42 per cent were trans women and femmes of colour. It was no coincidence that these demographics largely described the people who had found refuge in the ballrooms that Kia and I had talked about.

I climbed the stairs and waited in reception for AVP staff member LaLa Zannell. When I had looked her up on Twitter I saw that her bio read: 'Goddess, Mother, Lead Organizer #LaLa4President' (the last part, after having met her, I would definitely get behind). She appeared, shook my hand, and led me to her office, explaining on the way that she was a community organizer, meaning she did activism work through AVP but also on her own, particularly working to empower and inspire trans people, as well as trying to create broader shifts in cultural consciousness.

'What kind of shifts?' I asked, as we sat down.

'Conversations with LGBT parents, conversations with black men about masculinity, or with men who consider themselves to be trans attracted, to create supportive spaces for them.' LaLa reeled off these points as if the work wasn't as important as it was, as if she was describing any old job – but I guessed that was because she'd seen it all.

'At AVP I do a lot of outreach, getting people to our services, to learn about our programming,' she continued. 'I have two community action groups here. One of them works on the trans economic empowerment campaign, so we had a survey to collect information on employment discrimination of TGNC [trans and gender non-conforming] New Yorkers to create analysis on why, particularly, trans women of colour can't seem to get employment here in New York City, why with all the policies we have here folks still aren't being able to access jobs. I'm about to finish up the TGNC leadership academy, where we taught a group of eight how to get involved in policy or get further education or internships. Paid internships,' she added proudly.

Over the next twenty minutes, LaLa told me what she could of her story. She was from Detroit, Michigan. She'd been working at AVP for five or six years. She moved to New York City from Atlanta, where she had been working in a Starbucks and experiencing a lot of discrimination around being trans. She wanted a fresh start; her income wasn't panning out the way it should and she didn't want to wind up homeless in Atlanta, where she knew they didn't have a shelter that would feel safe for her. A friend told her to come to NYC – they had insurance, different services for trans women, things were easier to navigate if you were in that in-between situation. But she wasn't ready to commit to a shelter, so when she arrived in the city, she ended up getting back with an ex-partner. The situation soon turned violent, and she wasn't sure how to get out of it, until a friend encouraged her to go to a centre called the Female Spectrum, run by a woman called Cristina Herrera from the Translatina Network.

Here LaLa was around trans people, but she still didn't fit in – they were older, had transitioned later in life. She had transitioned at fifteen. They were a little more privileged; they already had jobs, money, things she didn't have. But they did tell her about AVP, where she set up a meeting with a counsellor to talk about her predicament. That meeting would change everything for LaLa. It was the first time in a long time that someone seemed to actually care about her and be in a position to help. 'When you're a trans woman of colour, the chances of people really caring seem slim to none,' she said. But they were putting words to what was going on with her: the abusive relationship, the discrimination that had happened when she'd been in work, and most importantly, they told her that there were things she could do about it. Her first reaction, she said, was 'Wow'; she just wanted more trans people to know about AVP, and to have access. They helped her get into a safe shelter, and she ended up volunteering with the charity as a hotline counsellor, then joined as an intern, then got a job at the front desk. From there she moved up to Anti-Hate Violence Organizer, and then Community Organizer. She's also spoken at the White House – twice – and testified for Congress. 'I guess you could say there have been a lot of transitions along the way,' she joked. 'People reached out to me for help, so it just became my life.'

Like Kia, LaLa used to be involved with ballroom culture. She compared what AVP gave her to what that experience gave her: community. 'The best part of the job is coming to work with people who understand you and trying to create a world without violence. When you're able to help people – get them in a shelter, get them a protection order, get them a U visa [for victims of crimes who have suffered mental or physical abuse and are willing to assist in their investigation and prosecution] – that's the good part of the job.'

'What's the bad part?' I asked tentatively.

'The bad part is when I come to work and a trans woman has been killed. Nine times out of ten I know the person. I've lost lots of friends throughout my life but more so the last few years – or I find friends of mine calling me to get support because it was their friend they lost. When it's someone you personally know, it's harder, but then it's also the ones people don't know, that don't have the community or don't have the support to try to find some recourse to what has happened. The bad part is knowing that when I come to work I'm gonna hear about the pains, the violence, the inter-partner violence, the sexual violence, the police violence, the hate violence, and trying to balance when to feel and not to feel so you can continue to move in the work, to numb what's going on personally as a trans person or a black woman. The emotional labour is high in the workplace; you never get used to it.'

When I thought about the nature of the crimes LaLa was dealing with, I couldn't comprehend how she went to work every day. Especially as they weren't just violent assaults on a life but violent assaults on a certain kind of life – a trans life, her life. Not only that, but she'd experienced attacks herself. 'I'd been in fights and scuffles in my neighbourhood in Detroit, nothing to do with me being trans,' she told me. 'But blatantly being attacked for me being trans? I didn't experience that till I moved to New York City, and I was so shocked cause it was not like any other fight I'd had in my life. It wasn't even a fight like when I was fighting with my ex-partner. It was clearly a hatred of a life. I felt like they were trying to take me out – and I had to fight literally for my life. It felt different. I felt that hate first-hand.'

I had never experienced what LaLa was talking about, but I began to understand the severity of the hate when I waded through the gory details of the kinds of murders she was dealing with. The website for the Transgender Day of Remembrance attempts to keep a record of all trans people who are murdered. For the years 1970 to 2012, a Google Doc listed more than seven hundred murders globally. You could see the nature of the crime, the brutality of the killings: mutilations, beheadings, dismembering, faces disfigured, genitals removed and discarded in dumpsters. For 2017, around two hundred and fifty deaths were listed, most in Mexico or Brazil.

Scanning this website, or reading about murders of trans people in the news, it didn't take long to realize how frequent the killings were, the scale of the violence trans people faced. In the first week of 2017 alone, two trans women were killed in America: Jamie Lee Wounded Arrow, a two-spirit woman living in South Dakota, followed by Mesha Caldwell in Mississippi. In February 2017, two transgender women were killed in New Orleans within forty-eight hours: one shot, the other stabbed. Another trans woman was killed in Louisiana a week before, bringing the state total up to three people in one fortnight.

The perpetrators are mostly male. Some victims were killed by strangers, like gender-fluid teenager Kedarie Johnson, who sometimes went by Kandicee, murdered at the age of sixteen in Burlington, Iowa. Others were killed by lovers or friends, such as Ally Lee Steinfeld, a seventeen-year-old transgender woman who was found dead in a chicken coop in Missouri in September 2017. She'd had her remains set alight by a woman she had been dating, who had conspired with her roommates to murder her. Others were killed by cops, such as the twenty-one-year-old Georgia Tech student Scout Schultz, who identified as non-binary and was shot by police while experiencing a mental-health crisis, following two previous suicide attempts. Or Sean Hake, one of three trans men whose murders AVP logged in 2017, who was twenty-three when he was shot by police during a mental-health episode. When I combed the news stories of these particular killings, I noticed that all of the victims were younger than me.

What was tricky when it came to tracking all of these crimes with the AVP, said LaLa, was how often trans people were misgendered after their own murder, their name wrongly reported, or their lived gender dismissed in favour of their legal gender, which might not have been changed.

When LaLa lived in Detroit, she said, she saw girls go missing 'all the time', but if there was any discussion of it in the news, it often wasn't in a way that was respectful to that person's gender. Of the trans people killed in 2017, several were misgendered. This made things difficult for the AVP, who had to spot the relevant murders in the news in order to know about them, since there was no central database where law enforcement departments around America were required to report these crimes. While there were a handful of trans people visible on magazines, walking down catwalks and writing newspaper columns, these trans people's lives and deaths were not just largely invisible to society, but to the organizations actually looking for them.

I asked LaLa about a case that stuck out for her, and she didn't have to think before she told me about the murder of twenty-one-year-old fashion intern Islan Nettles, who was attacked in Harlem in August 2013. Her attacker was a twenty-five-year-old Brooklyn man called James Dixon who, as he later told police, had attacked her when he realized that she was transgender because his friends had started teasing him for trying to pick up a trans woman. He knocked her to the pavement with a punch, and then hit her again as she lay on the ground. She died in a coma five days after her attack. The police made a wrongful arrest at first, then Dixon handed himself in to the police. He was eventually sentenced to just twelve years – a bargain struck for pleading guilty. The murder sparked protests across New York City, including one in January 2014 outside the New York Police Department that was attended by around a hundred people, roughly half of whom were trans women of colour like Islan. LaLa told me this was the first case she'd been involved with all the way through, from the murder to the protests, the court hearing and the convictions.

The Nettles case was a prime example of one of the most common circumstances of these killings: a man who felt 'tricked'. But when I tried to grasp the 'reasons' for these murders more broadly – although really, there was no reasoning – all I could think of was that to be trans must really offend people's basic beliefs. A fixed and binary gender is the first thing that we experience or are given when we come into the world. It becomes something we think we know to be true. When those foundations are rocked, or when people go changing their gender, all structures start to give way and people can feel a deep-seated sense of discord and panic. It is incomprehensible to me, but this is how I tried to make sense of it.

LaLa told me she had the same kinds of questions when she asked herself how anyone could do this. 'Where did you learn that from, that you hate someone in that way, that you think it's OK to attack someone simply for who they are, in the United States? It shouldn't happen nowhere, but this is the United States, New York City, where the Stonewall riots happened,' she exclaimed, visibly furious, but also puzzled. 'I was attacked in the Village, where we had trans folks fighting the police in a riot that liberated the LGBT movement fifty years ago. For New York City to not have an analysis around these things, it's really shocking to me.'

'What part does Trump play?' I asked, thinking about how the 2017 spike in hate crime coincided with the first term of his presidency.

She tutted. 'People say Trump did this, Trump did that, blame Trump. These things have existed, he just opened up the door as permission to be more hateful. Because as the leader of this country you have made it a clear mission of yours to show that there's no room for LGBT folks.'

LaLa was talking about how, under the Trump administration, federal protections for trans students had been rescinded, there had been an attempt to ban transgender people from serving in the military, the Justice Department had decided to stop applying workplace discrimination protections to trans people. On top of that, since the Republican win, sixteen states considered employing bathroom bills in 2016, after President Obama outlawed them. Later, an anti-trans bill surfaced that sought to define gender as unchangeable and based on the sex assigned at birth. Mix this government-sanctioned transphobia with a climate of top-down misogyny and racism, and you had a truly deadly concoction, one that went some way to explaining the disproportionate deaths of trans women of colour. According to the *New York Times*, the National Center for Health Statistics found the annual murder rate in 2017 for Americans aged 15–34 to be about one in 12,000. Mic.com found the rate to be one in 2,600 for black transgender women. The vulnerability of this group was not new, but LaLa believed Trump's attitude towards trans people, people of colour and undocumented immigrants only served to empower those who were already transphobic, racist and xenophobic. As she put it: 'It doesn't empower them to say, "Let me shift my mind or how I'm thinking, because he's the President of the United States and he agrees with me!"'

Sadly, I told her, it had been the same in the UK after Brexit: for the first eleven months there was a 23 per cent spike on the previous year in religious and racist hate crimes, and a 147 per cent spike in homophobic hate crimes in the first three months. People who harboured racist and homophobic views had taken the outcome of the vote as an affirmation that those views were supported, and acted on them. Of course, the people affected most by this kind of bigotry were the people who were *both* LGBTQ+ and persons of colour.

'Black women are marginalized in this country, so why would it be any different for black trans women?' LaLa said. 'We are looked at in such a way that is beneath everything that's already going on in a black community: colourism and classism, living in a bad neighbourhood. I mean, you're already combating things that come with living in a bad neighbourhood and now you wanna be black and trans in a bad neighbourhood? It's like, why would you do that to yourself? I got an uncle that says to me, "What's wrong with you? Why would you give up your manhood to be a woman?" I was like: "I never was a man, and if having man privilege is supposed to put me above someone, I don't want it!"' She shook her head. 'There's no education around it, or *any* conversations around it. It's like . . . you just don't do it.'

*

There was a pregnant pause. I had been in LaLa's tiny office for thirty minutes, and I had accidentally welled up twice but stopped myself crying because it would have been too self-indulgent to cry about a problem that didn't affect me. It was a given that I had no frame of reference for experiencing transphobia or racism, and that I would never know that experience, but the conversation was, quite unexpectedly, reminding me of experiences I'd had as a woman but tried to forget, experiences that made me feel powerless: slurs, sexual harassment from strangers on dark streets at night, sexual assault by people I knew.

The irony in all of this was that at home, 3,500 miles from where LaLa and I were sitting, a war was raging between some cisgender women and trans women. Mostly playing out in the pages of the British mainstream media, 'feminist' writers were penning transphobic articles for big newspapers (and they were, somehow, getting published) and self-describing feminists were taking to Twitter to say that trans women were not women, or that they posed a threat to society. The argument often made was that, if we let trans people self-determine their gender, it would allow anyone to use gendered spaces like female toilets or changing rooms, putting cis women at risk of assault. I'd never had any doubt that using trans women as the thin end of the wedge in a conversation about toxic masculinity and rape culture was dangerous; I'd written about it in newspapers, and I'd watched my trans friends dealing with the mental-health fallout of these unwarranted and vile accusations. But now, during my conversation with LaLa, it was really hitting home not just how perverse it was to suggest that the trans people we were talking about, under extreme threat of violence and living in fear, might be a threat to others, but also what an oversight it was. These British 'feminists' were trying to create a divide between cis women and trans women, when really the threats trans people and cis women had historically faced were the same: domestic violence, rape, murder. Every individual's circumstances were different, sure, but we had a common enemy – violence at the hands of the patriarchy. And furthermore, when it came to seeking justice for this violence the law disadvantaged us both.

Call a hate crime a hate crime, I thought, when I was later reading about Kedarie Johnson, the teenager killed in Iowa, and learned that the killers were not charged with a hate crime because state law only included race, religion and sexual orientation as grounds. In the case of Ally Lee Steinfeld, the trans woman killed in Missouri, the county sheriff maintained that the murder was not a hate crime, before adding that all murders are acts of hate. When a cis woman is killed just for being a woman, because her life is not so valuable, that is not classed as a hate crime either. In some countries, there is even a defence that can be made to attempt to explain why you have harmed a woman or an LGBTQ+ person. In Bolivia, for example, there's a crime called *estupro*, which minimizes charges for the rape of girls aged fourteen to eighteen, blaming it on carnal desire caused by seduction or deceit. Until recently, in America, the 'gay panic' or 'trans panic' defence was brought up in court to try to justify why men kill gay people or trans people, often in the context of being deceived. Around the world, crimes against LGBTQ+ people are not prosecuted, because it's illegal or despicable to be LGBTQ+.

When I brought up the fact that justice is rarely skewed in favour of trans people, LaLa told me about a problem she perceived: that the police often prejudge who the aggressor was. This reminded me of the case of Eisha Love and her friend Tiffany Gooden, two trans women who were filling up their car at a petrol station in Chicago, in March 2012, when men began yelling abuse at them. One of the men punched Love, so the women got into the car and tried to drive away, only to be blocked by one of the men's cars while the other tried to prise open the women's driver's door. They tried to turn the car around, and in doing so, injured one of the attackers. Love and Gooden escaped, but when Love later went to the police station to file a report, she was booked for aggravated assault, which was later updated to first-degree attempted murder. She was sent to jail on an attempted-murder charge, at a men's prison, which did not correspond with her lived gender, putting her at great physical and psychological risk. Two months after the attack, Gooden was stabbed to death and her body found in an abandoned building. She was nineteen.

'We have a culture where you can do something to a trans person and there's no recourse,' said LaLa. 'The convictions are rare and the turnaround is high. It's like a granted permission [to attack trans women]. In New York there might be something, but in Arkansas, or Ohio, there's not gonna be a conversation, it's gonna be washed away.

Islan's case was high profile across the country because AVP made it their mission not to let people forget her, but every case is not that lucky.'

And yet, LaLa explained that, for her, conviction was not always the answer.

'Those systems cause us harm. There's a nuance here, of this black man being convicted of something he was not taught *not* to commit. I'm not saying people shouldn't go to jail, I'm not judge nor juror, but I know there has to be another nuanced way. We expect people to know right from wrong but we don't give people the tools they need to understand. That goes for transphobia – systems were created around these biases and then we expect people in the world to understand that that is wrong? Religion is saying me being myself is wrong, political regimes are saying me being myself is wrong, your parents are transphobic, your homeboys are transphobic, so how they gonna have the nuance to understand transphobia is wrong? But then when they get convicted we put them away in the system where they're still not gonna learn a lesson and they're gonna be stuck in it? Because that's the prison industrial complex, it's real. It's no good me throwing more of my people in the prison system, it's about finding alternatives.'

I asked LaLa what this alternative might look like, and she told me a story. When we are born, she said, the expectation is that we will fit into neat categories of boy or girl, male or female, which align with our sex. There is no expectation that because of biology, or DNA, or chance – whatever you want to call it – something might be there in that child or something might shift out of sync with the conceptions of what our gender should be in relation to our biology. Many parents are not prepared for this eventuality; they don't have the ability to understand that the individual they've created has the agency to define themself.

'Some parents might have hopes their child is going to be a basketball player, and force them to play basketball. Then what happens? They're terrible at it!' LaLa analogized. 'So, you throw your child out, and what happens when your child is homeless? They get into risky behaviours, doing all kinds of things, whether it's stealing, or other things life traumas lead them to – sex work, substance abuse, getting killed because they can't afford it . . . it's a cycle of pain within a system that doesn't have anything in place to address those things.'

I knew this cycle of pain to be true for a lot of my trans friends in the UK – some were now sober, because at one point or the other, they had experienced substance abuse problems. Many had experienced homelessness, and almost all of them had been violently attacked. I also knew that trans people in the UK and America, on the whole, earn less than cisgender people, with many trans people trapped in poverty through employment discrimination, further increasing their chances of homelessness.

'My mother loved me. My mother was a pastor so it was hard for her to juggle religious things put in her head. She knew this doesn't seem right that I should have to disown my child cause my child is trans. She couldn't tell me I couldn't be trans, cause that would go against what she taught me as a child, which was to be me. But she also knew that she was releasing me every day as a fifteen-year-old into a world that didn't understand me.'

I just looked at LaLa and she just raised her eyebrows and looked back, and we let it sit for a minute. Then she continued.

'So, if we have conversations in school that might prevent someone in the future from being transphobic, if people in religious platforms stop preaching hate so much, it may help a parent not to throw their child out. Or if we say to parents when they're having their kids, "Yes, this may be a boy or a girl," then maybe that would help them when that moment happens. Like, stop putting gender on a child and let it be a baby. Teachers don't wanna talk about it in schools because parents are like, "You're pushing it on them." You're not pushing it on them, you're just helping a child understand what the world is – there's trans folks in the world, and so many people come here from small cities and they see a trans person and they're freaked out cause that's what they've been taught to hate, to stay away from. Until we have education and culture, how do we shift people's view?'

'What about visibility? Do you think having visible trans people in the media helps? Black trans women like Laverne Cox, or Janet Mock?'

'It is empowering to see. They're making their marks, they're making a platform for some trans person to have some possibility model of what life can be, that trans person who had that dream to be an author or be an actress or actor or whatever. But it's not enough. We have to think about expanding what visibility means. "Go to Hollywood, write a book – you'll be OK!" But people's access to those things is based on race and classism and possibility, and on passing. Some girls don't aspire to pass. They want to be themselves. And everybody is not going to be able to pass – people don't have the resources or the money to pass; surgeries are very expensive. It depends where you live too – there's a waiting list for these affirming surgeries. And surgeries don't define whether you're trans or not, that's for you to define for yourself. So when we see these trans celebrities we expect other trans folks to emulate these things – it sets a precedent.'

'So what do we do?' I said quietly.

'I think the range and the complexities of what's visible and who is visible and who can have a voice, I think that dynamic needs to change. All of us don't want to be an actress or on a magazine. Some of us just want to be a doctor. I know a trans girl who's a firefighter. I know trans people who are parents. Who have had children, or adopted children. Trans folks who are scholars. I knew a trans girl who was like the trans Martha Stewart! She wants to have a cooking show. She cooks down! Some of us just want to be an everyday girl. Some of us just want to be a soccer mom. And now we have all these beautiful trans politicians. This is what we need – we need to expand what we see trans folks are because right now it's one-dimensional. We have to think about expanding visibility so people can think about trans folks as humanized, the people you walk past every single day. Because right now they see us in Hollywood, we're modelling, we're successful book writers, but then you have the other path – where we're dying, or you hear on the news that there was a sex worker sting, or scandals are happening like we're tricking people, celebrity exposure stories. That's what the media focuses on. But we need to show our community as an array of things. We need more contextual stories beyond what's between our legs, and the surgeries and the pain. Yes, there's a lot of pain. But there are a lot of joyful stories too.'

As I left LaLa's office, I thought about something my friend Kai-Isaiah Jamal, a black trans man, a spoken word poet and activist, once wrote that stuck with me. He said one of the problems with transphobia was that, in a lot of people's minds, trans people were more idea than human, an abstract identity. It was easy to understand why this might be; if you were trans and living in fear of the violence that LaLa talked about, you might not be feeling too social. People like LaLa were out there breaking the cycle, but were enough people who were not trans doing their bit?

At one point, when I was talking to LaLa, she told me that the final thing we needed to improve the lives of trans people – on top of justice, education and better visibility – was a stark conversation about alliances within the LGBTQ+ community itself. People wore the word 'ally' like a badge, she said. '"I'm not a racist! I have black friends, I'm an ally!" What does being an ally actually mean? Is it just to say you're an ally? If you see transphobic things happening what are you gonna do? What is your role? If you see someone being attacked are you gonna step in and help or are you gonna get your phone and record for retweets? If you're in your job, in a position of power, what are you doing to dismantle transphobia? Or in your school systems and your neighbourhoods?' she asked, before implicating herself. She told me that she was having to unlearn the racism and white supremacy that was passed down through generations of black women in her family to her. She told me that when she moved to New York, she didn't know what 'non-binary' meant; she had to do her research and learn it. She told me that she had to check her relatively small amount of privilege every single day.

'Privilege is nothing if you're not leveraging it. How do you know you're really privileged if you're not testing the limits of what you're able to do with it?' she asked me. 'Give it to someone else who's gonna do something with it. Every day be better than the system. Show up. Physically. If you're able to have a conversation to shift something, do it. Put your money into things and push policies that will change what's happening. Give. Up. Your. Resources.'

Her words reminded me of something else that Kai said – he said that it's easy to think we are making progress for ourselves as LGBTQ+ people – particularly trans people – because we create safe-spaces and families, like the Harlem ballrooms Kia and I had talked about, or the Anti-Violence Project. However, it's worth remembering that these spaces are only there because we make them for ourselves, not necessarily because we are given them. And that if we stop creating these spaces, these communities, and fighting for their existence, they may cease to be there, giving way to the powers – like Trump – that wish to suppress us.

The way I see it, two things threaten to erase LGBTQ+ visibility and community most – on the one hand there is complacency, and on the other, oppression. But the two are interlinked: one of the reasons we can't become complacent, even if we are living in relative privilege, is because, if my time in New York had taught me anything, it was that acceptance doesn't include all parts of queer culture or all LGBTQ+ people, just those that society deems worthy. And that's in America. There are always, of course, places in the world where our queer siblings live in an even more openly hostile climate, with very little possibility at all.

chapter seven

GAY CAPITAL

'Are you OK?'

'No! I'm exhausted,' said Şerif, laughing. We were on our way to take the metro from Bomonti, a neighbourhood in Istanbul, back to Taksim Square, near where I was staying. He had been translating for me for hours, and my interviewee, Seyhan, had talked quickly. We laughed about how, over the time we had been chatting with Seyhan, she had managed to bring most of my questions back to talking about herself. Then we moved on to her advice – good advice. I was an outsider; I needed to be schooled.

'Look, when we get asked to do interviews with Western journalists, it's like they already have a portrait of Turkey in their mind and then their questions always reflect that,' Şerif said, frustrated. 'This portrait they have, it's an exaggerated, sad version of our lives and that can be offensive. Our lives are not so different from any other LGBTI community in Europe or the US – it's harder to be gender non-conforming, harder to be gay if you're from the countryside or from a religious family or in the military. It's not like we are some exception to the rule . . .'

I told Şerif that it had never been my intention to visit

a country bordering the Middle East and paint a picture of how horrific it was to be LGBTI there, but I did want to hear about how the context – the state's reversion to Islam, the extremely right-wing government in power, the patriarchal culture – shaped my queer Turkish friends' experiences. I told him that, since hearing how difficult life could be for LGBTI people in Serbia and America, I was more aware than ever that discrimination and hate crimes weren't exclusive to one place, religion or culture. And then I told him what I had been going through at home.

After I got back from New York, I moved in with Emily. We lived for a few months in total domestic bliss under the silent burden of the fact that she hadn't told her Christian, three-times-a-week churchgoing parents about my existence, let alone the fact that we lived together. When she plucked up the courage to tell them we were dating, on her twenty-seventh birthday, her mum told her she already knew: she had somehow found my Instagram account.

When Emily relayed this to me, all colour drained from my face. 'But . . . but what about the picture of me outside Berghain at 7 a.m.,' I stuttered. I had a bad habit of making situations that were difficult for other people all about me, but this was practically a free pass.

'I'm sure she hasn't seen that, baby,' Emily responded kindly, when really she must have been thinking, *That's not the point here* and *Why did you put that up anyway, you idiot?*

Her mum cried, she cried, I cried, and then the whole thing sort of got brushed under the carpet. Emily and I went back to our relationship as usual. A relationship which was by now my longest and happiest. Sometimes, she and I talked about it, and occasionally, she and Amrou would bond over their shared experiences with their families, despite Amrou being from a Muslim one and Emily a Christian one.

What this had reminded me of, I explained to Şerif, was that while government regimes like Turkey's existed, everyone's experience was clearly individual. The more places I had visited, the more this had hit home. But still, I wanted to find out what it was like to live in a region where the cultural atmosphere mostly attempted to suppress homosexuality into, well, virtual non-existence.

It was Şerif who'd suggested I interview Seyhan Arman, and that he be my translator since her English was so minimal. We met her in a queer cafe on a Thursday afternoon. While Şerif relayed what she said, Seyhan would interrupt our interview to get up and greet passers-by that she knew, or to take phone calls, or to post photos and videos on her Snapchat. Şerif and I just sat and sipped our tea while she did this, understanding we were in the company of a true diva and must not interfere. Also understanding that, at this rate, the interview would take hours.

Seyhan was a well-known activist for LGBTI rights in Istanbul, and according to Şerif she would help me understand the context of what it was like to be LGBTI there, as someone who was part of the culture and had seen things change over the years. She appeared on Turkish television chat shows to talk about trans rights, did HIV outreach work, and coached the young trans people and their families who reached out to her for advice on social

media. Originally from Adana, she had acted since she was
fifteen, did improvised drag under the name Mademoiselle
Coco, and did TV bit parts and indie films. She embodied
everything that LaLa had told me we needed to see more
of – powerful, successful trans women doing jobs that they
loved. And at the moment, she told me, she was even
starring in her own play, at a theatre not far from where
we were meeting.

She handed me the poster for the play; all bold red
graphics and kitsch scribbly fonts, it looked just like a poster
for one of Spanish director Pedro Almodóvar's films. And
just like Almodóvar's films, Seyhan explained, the script,
soap-opera-like, was designed to make Seyhan's audience
laugh, cry and empathize. A one-woman show about a
transgender woman's fight for self-emancipation in the
1990s and 2000s, with Seyhan delivering theatrical but
campy monologues from the stage in a shoulder-padded
blazer and fishnet tights, it began with a boy on his knees
begging Allah to give him breasts, a vagina and long hair
overnight, and then to send out the news to journalists the
next day so that, once he had become a woman, she could
also become extremely famous. As our trans protagonist
grew up, she ran away from home to the city, became a
sex worker, and experienced discrimination, police brutality
and a lot of the other awful bullshit LaLa had described
to me.

Seyhan told me that the likeness to Almodóvar's posters
was deliberate, but her story was not fiction: it was auto-
biographical, and not just her story but 'thousands of stories.
It's not just the story of a trans person, but the story of a

human being who has love affairs, struggles, whatever a person goes through in life,' she said. 'It's the only mainstream story in Turkey where a trans woman survives and thrives; just when you think her character has been killed, she comes back, and lives to tell the tale.' This too was intentional; 'People have this cliché of trans people having terrible lives and living in horrible conditions,' she explained through Şerif. 'I'm not saying we don't have struggles, but we put our lives together and we make it work. We are strong. Stronger than most people,' she added, flicking back her long, curly and shockingly bright orange hair, which contrasted exquisitely with her magenta puffer jacket.

Seyhan's film work and her play had turned her into a minor celebrity in Turkey, although she warned me that 'Turkish society are hypocrites – people see me on stage and they applaud me, but if some saw me on the street, maybe they would spit on my face.'

In Turkey, as in America, this was a common story. The number of openly trans and gay celebrities in Turkey was surprising. Of these, Bülent Ersoy was probably the most famous, a singer and now a close friend of President Recep Tayyip Erdoğan. Already a household name, Ersoy transitioned publicly from male to female in 1981, and decided to keep the name Bülent despite the fact that it's a popular man's name in Turkey. Some of Ersoy's videos – she made classical Turkish music – had around 10 million hits on YouTube. She was huge, a household name. Then there was Mabel Matiz, a chart-topping gay pop singer, and Zeki Müren, who was basically the Turkish version of Liberace before he died in 1996 (in fact, there was a mural of him

in the cafe where we met Seyhan). But there was a disconnect between this representation and life for everyday
LGBTI people. As one Turkish friend put it: 'It's weird, it's
like the only way that it's truly acceptable to be LGBTI in
Turkey is to be famous.'

Judging by hate-crime statistics, Turkey was the most
dangerous place to be in Europe if you were trans, with
forty-three murders recorded between 2008 and 2016
(although the actual number could be higher). You could
legally change your gender after undergoing gender confirmation surgery from 1988, but with no other legal
protections put in place from then until now, violence and
discrimination were rife. Ines had told me after her time
in Turkey that sex work was a common and dangerous
choice in a climate where finding alternative employment
could be difficult. She was right. 'I wanted to work. I
wanted to do stuff but I couldn't,' said Eylül Cansın, a
twenty-three-year-old trans sex worker who killed herself
in 2015. Another trans sex worker, Warda, was murdered
at home by a client in December 2016. The murderer
disembowelled her and cut off her genitals: horrifying, but
not a one-off incident. In fact, the precariousness of life
for trans people in Turkey was part of the reason that
some members of this community (Seyhan included) took
on a leading role in the Gezi Park anti-government protests
of 2013, to demand a higher standard of protection, a basic
chance in life.

For gay, lesbian, bisexual and queer people, Turkey is
one of the few majority Muslim countries where homosexuality is legal – since as early as 1923 – and it acts as a

safe haven for LGBTI people from across the region. But the climate is still harsh. There are no laws protecting LGBTI people from violence and discrimination. There is less legal protection than in Serbia, even, and since Erdoğan came into power as President in 2014 (before this, he was Prime Minister), the country has been experiencing a strong shift towards conservatism under his neo-Islamist party, the AKP. Not long before my visit, Erdoğan stated that empowering gay people was 'against the values' of the nation, while a handful of LGBTI activists were imprisoned for posting about their rights on social media.

If Pride is the measure of a country's LGBTI climate, in Turkey it painted a fairly accurate picture of how things were changing: 2013 saw around 50,000 people march down Istiklal Avenue, the city's main shopping street, for the biggest ever Pride in the region; in 2015 the event was cancelled altogether. The government justified this by arguing that it clashed with Ramadan. When people in Istanbul headed into the streets anyway, police forced them back into their houses with tear gas and pellet guns. Pride was banned in Istanbul again in 2016 and 2017. From 2017 into 2018, local authorities in the Turkish capital Ankara banned all LGBTI-related events. The country, straddling Europe and the Middle East, was once secular and growing increasingly liberal, but now it was isolating itself geo-politically, becoming more and more conservative, and sending a clear message to LGBTI people that they ought to be afraid.

'We are not as far ahead as other places,' said Seyhan. 'When I go on TV, I have to express myself so the general public will understand. So I say it is the same God who created us all, to popularize the conversation, make it understandable,' she explained. Then she gave an example of someone doing the opposite. When the government banned Pride, they named the holy month of Ramadan as the reason. In Islam there are three holy months, which are also three male names: Rajab, Sha'ban and Ramadan. In a counter-protest to the ban, some LGBTI activists walked down the street with a huge sign that read: 'Ramadan cannot interfere in the relationship of Rajab and Sha'ban', the joke being that Rajab and Sha'ban were in a same-sex relationship. This was deeply offensive, Seyhan said, shaking her head. To progress the conversation around LGBTI rights, it was important to be respectful of the cultural atmosphere, respectful of Islam.

I turned to Şerif, knowing that he was of my generation, not particularly religious, and that he identified as queer, politically speaking. 'Do you agree?'

'I agree,' he said. 'You cannot put people's religious views or sacred beliefs as your target.'

It was fine to talk to LGBTI Turks about all of this, said Seyhan, but I needed to remember that I would never understand the situation fully. There were LGBTI people who agreed with the government's actions; there were religious people who supported Erdoğan's regime, but also many people who were leaving the country and starting their lives elsewhere. There were people who didn't like queer politics, but simply knew what being a trans lesbian was because they were one. And then there were people like Seyhan herself, who, at thirty-nine, would have different queer politics and language to someone of a younger generation. No matter how hard I tried, she warned, I would only be able to speak to a few 'colours of the rainbow'; the same phrase I had read on the DragCon website, only this time I liked it so much that I quickly jotted it down.

The final thing I needed to remember was the disconnect between the general public's impression of LGBTI rights in Turkey and what some LGBTI people believed their rights should be. Seyhan then compared the progress of the LGBTI community to a staircase that had a hundred steps. Some activists were behaving as if we were at the eightieth step, she said, but there were still people in the LGBTI community who had not come to terms with themselves, and who were not even aware that this staircase existed. When it came to marriage equality, for example, the government was completely opposed because it didn't want the idea of the sacred family to be destroyed, she said. It believed same-sex marriage was a 'discussion for the next century', as did most of the heterosexual public, and even a large part of Turkey's LGBTI population. 'I am not opposed to fighting for marriage equality,' Seyhan said, 'but these kinds of fights are higher up the staircase. First, we need to start at the bottom.'

I looked at Şerif again. 'She's right. Here in Turkey we have more urgent priorities,' he said, as Seyhan got up to take another call.

I waited for Ayman outside the Starbucks in Taksim Square. As for what he looked like, all I had to go on was his tiny

WhatsApp picture, which wasn't enough to recognize him when he started coming towards me. He had a shaved head, slits shaved through one of his eyebrows, and he was wearing a black leather jacket. Our greeting was awkward, since he wasn't sure if I was the person he was looking for either; it kind of felt like we were on a blind date. In some ways, we were.

I had read about Ayman Menem online. He was an activist, although I knew he probably wouldn't call himself that; he was also one of the 3.4 million refugees living in Turkey, the country with the world's biggest refugee population, according to the UN Refugee Agency UNHCR. There are no figures on how many of these people are LGBTI, specifically, but it is estimated that Syrians like Ayman make up 90 per cent of the refugees in the country, having fled Bashar al-Assad's regime in their own.

Ayman and I walked to Mis Sokak, known for being the 'anarchist street', where – unlike some other less *haram* districts of Istanbul – you could drink alcohol in pretty much all of the bars. He told me that, like a lot of Arabs in Turkey, he didn't speak Turkish. His English was OK though. Not great, just OK. I assured him not to worry about that: I was terrible at languages. As we walked, he told me about his elderly Armenian neighbours, who invited him round for coffee and talked at him in Armenian. He didn't understand a word, but the old ladies chose not to notice.

We ordered a beer at a metal bar and chatted about Damascus, Ayman's home. He was born and raised there; he said it wasn't the worst part of Syria to be from as a gay person, since it was the capital and the most liberal city. But any gay culture there had remained fairly underground out of necessity, he said, remembering a time in the late 1990s or early 2000s when there were only about seven openly gay people in Damascus. He gestured at our beers and explained that no one would want to have a drink with you out in the open if you were one of these people – as he was. He was a known homosexual and thus a social pariah.

Ayman had come out to his family and friends in his early twenties. His father reacted angrily; his mother cried. They immediately sent him to conversion therapy to avert a crisis. He saw three psychologists in Syria, one of whom inflicted electroshock therapy on him. The doctor would show Ayman pictures of men kissing and zap him. After two sessions, he refused to go back. The last therapist he saw was French, and told Ayman's parents that their son was 'normal' after all. It took about ten years, but eventually, Ayman's parents came to accept his homosexuality – just before he was conscripted, and had to begin the stressful process of hiding his sexuality all over again, this time from his colleagues in the military.

'This is not the Syrian story,' he explained, meaning that he was one of the lucky ones since he was from a leafy part of Damascus and a middle-class, highly educated family who were more progressive than most. 'It is all related to if you are from the centre of the city or from country, if you have money or well-known family . . . all these reasons, they give you power.'

Ayman was living in Damascus in 2011 when the revolution began. As part of the wave of uprisings that happened across the Arab world at that time, young Syrians took to the streets to demand democratic reforms. Ayman would go to protests, sign petitions, write articles. All of his friends were active; they fought peacefully, but the government became more and more violent in quashing public actions until a full-blown civil war broke out. Watching this unfold from inside Syria, Ayman didn't quite see where things were heading. 'I feel it's OK and the regime will go after days or weeks. I keep in this way of thinking until 2013. Every month, I think, "Next month we'll celebrate in Umayyad Square in Damascus." But nothing happened,' he sighed.

The false hope kept him in Damascus for longer than his friends; by the time he left for Beirut in 2013, chemical attacks had started in Syria, and most of his friends had fled to Lebanon, Turkey, Western Europe. 'Not just gay people, all people,' he clarified. 'I do not feel I am gay when I go, I feel I am Syrian refugee. I feel I am alone and there's no work, I do nothing, so I go to continue my PhD in Lebanon.'

Ayman thought he would just go for six months, but the situation in Syria did not improve. Once he had finished his PhD it was late 2015 and Syria was still a war zone, so he decided to come to Istanbul. At this point, we toasted his PhD completion.

'But why did you pick Turkey?' I asked.

'I'd been here in 2005 as a tourist, in summer. A few days. I feel it is really cheap. Beirut is really expensive. I am working online and my life here is better. That's the reason I move from Beirut to Istanbul. But in Beirut I have my friends and my language. Most Turks don't speak Arabic, just those in the south, from old Syrian city.'

'What's changed for you since you moved here?'

'Tea and Talk,' he smiled, visibly lighting up for the first time since we sat down. 'It's changed my whole life.'

Tea and Talk was the reason I'd read about Ayman. It was a support group that met on Sunday afternoons on the Asian side of Turkey, near where most of the Syrian diaspora in the city wound up. It was not just for Syrians, but welcomed all Arabic-speaking LGBTI refugees; there were Moroccans, Kurds, Algerians and Lebanese. It had been going since 2015, although Ayman first went in February 2016. A friend had asked him to be a judge in a competition called Mr Gay Syria, a pageant that arose out of Tea and Talk meetings. He got out his phone to show me the trailer for the Mr Gay Syria documentary, which followed the competition to find a winner, who would then go to Malta to represent Syria in Mr Gay World. When I later watched the film, I jotted down something Ayman said in it: 'I hope that the one that goes to Europe has sex and gets married but I hope that he doesn't forget us. He could start an online page to raise awareness.' The winner never made it to Malta; he couldn't get a visa.

'They screened it in Birmingham,' Ayman said proudly, before explaining that, to fulfil his role of judge, he thought he'd better go and see what Tea and Talk was all about. He ended up going every week, eventually becoming the coordinator, or 'mama', as the group's members call him, which was funny to me because Ayman wasn't at all fem-

inine or flamboyant. If anything, the razor eyebrow slits
had the opposite effect.

Most people would hear about Tea and Talk by word of
mouth. If you wanted to go, you had to request to join the
private Facebook group and Ayman, the admin, would admit
you. You had to be friends with someone in the group to
join, for safety. There were more than 700 members, not all
in Turkey, but around the world – many had left Istanbul
for Europe or Canada or America, said Ayman, more than
120. Sometimes, people travelled across the border from Iran
into Turkey (easier than crossing the Syria–Turkey border)
and came straight to Tea and Talk, as they had nowhere else
to go in Istanbul first. Ayman showed me a picture on his
phone of Katja, a beautiful trans woman in a blonde wig,
explaining that she came over the border illegally into Idlib
before her transition, and once in Istanbul he found her a
place to sleep before she eventually left Turkey for Germany.

Tea and Talk had helped other members with job
searches, language courses, hospital access and Kimlik – a
Turkish identity card that you needed to get work or to
apply for asylum in a third country. Ayman took people
to the police station to help them apply for it, which could
be particularly difficult if you didn't look like your picture
because you were presenting your gender differently.
Ayman even had a spare room in his apartment where
people could stay until they found alternative arrangements. And if he needed something, he said, like a coat to
keep someone warm in winter, he could just post in the
Facebook group or on WhatsApp, and was usually offered
a spare within hours.

About fifty or sixty people would go to Tea and Talk each week; when Ayman started there were no trans people or lesbians, but now there had been many. 'You're comfortable and respected in Tea and Talk – we cannot see in LGBT community in any place masculine with feminine with trans woman all together. It's not possible in Turkey or maybe all of Europe, all these communities, masculine men, feminine men. It's like a family, really.'

'What kinds of things do you do in meetings?'

'We have a theme for the week – healthcare, legal status – or we just play games, or have a party and dance. Sometimes we make *iftar* after fasting, and we put on the Syrian TV to make it feel like home. Nobody comes one Sunday and doesn't come back; all of them come again. It's like therapy, this group,' he said, echoing the words of Amy from Save The Joiners. 'It's two hours, for freedom, safe place. Many of them live here with their families and have a secret life. You should see it – one of them came with a normal look and when he enter through the door I have mirror and he puts make-up and earring. It's like Shakespeare. Like a theatre move, the change.'

I asked Ayman how this differed from life in Syria and he explained that, like him, many of the people in the group had left Syria because they were physically under attack, rather than because they were LGBTI. But in Syria, as a gay man, you would be expected to follow one path: go to work, find a wife, have children. The lowest on the food chain, he said, were specifically 'bottoms'. To be a 'top' *might* be accepted because in the culture, if you were a man you fucked. For gays who got fucked, in Ayman's words, 'it's a nightmare'. Feminine-presenting men in particular could face daily violence, physical or verbal, and it was, anecdotally, much harder to get a job. As a lesbian, you might be accepted more than some gays or your activity would be more likely to go unnoticed, because people wouldn't suspect it. But it was much harder to leave Syria alone. It was unlikely you would go to war or go to study abroad. It was likely that you would have to move with your whole family, or a husband. Most of the lesbians who had come to Tea and Talk had done this; they lived with their families in the Syrian communities of Istanbul, like Fatih, an area Ayman described as like a displaced version of Aleppo. They were in the closet to their families: Syrian law criminalizes homosexuality as 'unnatural sexual intercourse' punishable by three years in prison, and these laws tend to be heavily policed; not just by the government and law enforcement but by the people around you too – families, communities, colleagues. Every year from 2011 to 2016, the International Lesbian, Gay, Bisexual, Trans and Intersex Association has found Syria to be the most dangerous country in the world to be LGBTQ+, based on the number of hate crimes and murders. I asked Ayman how ISIS made a difference, and he said of course they had made things worse, given that after they took hold of parts of Iraq and Syria they began systematically executing LGBTI people. However, if you came from an ISIS-occupied area with your family, you were probably living like a straight man or straight woman. 'To face ISIS you would have to be openly gay or look like you're gay,' he said, adding that this would be extremely unlikely because you probably wouldn't even risk that in your own community.

'How different is it here?' I asked him. It sounded as if Turkey gave most of the people at Tea and Talk a chance to explore parts of their gender expression or sexuality for the first time.

'It's a great chance here,' he said, beaming, as though he was used to being asked this. But then he hesitated. 'Actually, I don't know if it's bad or good. Some of them are killed. We had three members killed, two trans women and one gay in a two-year period in Istanbul. That means there's twenty across Turkey that we don't know.'

It was hard to know because some people were in the closet, of course; others were undocumented migrants with no legal status, and therefore ignored by the police. As I was considering this, Ayman started to tell me about one member of Tea and Talk who had been killed in Istanbul: a gay man. 'We don't know what happened. The killer had Turkish judgment before Turkish court, and they give him ten years in prison, because it's honour reason. It's good reason they kill him.' Muhammed Wisam Sankari, the gay Syrian refugee Ayman was talking about, was beheaded in Istanbul in 2016. He'd told the police he was in danger after being abducted, taken to a forest and raped five months earlier, but that hadn't prevented his death.

The only upside of this horrifying climate of transphobia and homophobia, said Ayman, was that it could help you get asylum somewhere else. 'If you apply to go to third country you should write you are LGBT,' he explained on this point. 'If you just put you are Syrian refugee they don't accept. But you are special case LGBT because your life is dangerous here.' According to the 1951 UN Refugee Convention, which outlined how countries are supposed to protect people fleeing from danger, a refugee is someone who has 'a well-founded fear of being persecuted for reasons of race, religion, nationality, membership of a particular social group, or political opinion', and an EU directive in 2011 specified that persecution for sexual orientation or gender identity is solid grounds for asylum. The problem was, you had to prove you were LGBTQ+, and how could you do that?

'Do you feel like it's getting worse here in Turkey, with the government I mean?'

Ayman shook his head. Despite the murders, to him, Turkey was safer than Syria. 'If you came from Syria you feel here more liberal and comfortable, even now. Not in all Turkey, just in Istanbul,' he qualified. 'Ankara too, maybe, or Izmir. In the south of Turkey it's like Syria. Because we are coming from such a dark place it's just better. We can be half out the closet. We find people with the same problems, the same questions, the same future.'

'What about you? It sounds like you have found your people.'

He smiled, put out his cigarette and got out his phone again. He started showing me a photo slideshow he'd made of the Tea and Talk group – it had an Arabic song playing over it and lots of goofy colour filters. It reminded me of my dad showing me slideshows of his holiday pictures. The photos included lots of group selfies. Some were taken at leaving parties for those about to move on to Europe.

'I know their details. I feel proud when they tell me secrets. I feel like, wow, why? But thank you,' said Ayman, as the faces flashed up on his screen. He shook his head in bewilderment. 'I don't know why we are such a strong community,' he mused. 'Maybe because we haven't support from outside. Maybe because we have the same pain and suffering.'

'Can we go clubbing while we're here?' I had asked Şerif as we left our meeting with Seyhan.

'Of course!' he smiled, in a way that said: *What the hell else are we gonna do?*

Now, a few days later, he was kindly fulfilling his promise. He told me that there were a couple of big clubs for gay men in Istanbul, Tek Yön being the best known. As a woman, I would not be allowed in because I would stand out like a sore thumb, make people feel uncomfortable, and essentially cock-block hundreds of Turkish men at once. Other LGBTI-friendly bars with brilliant names like Jasmin Highheel's, Cheeky Club and Love Dance Point had either closed or fallen out of fashion (which was hard to imagine, with names like that), so instead, Şerif decided to take me to a queer club on Mis Sokak, the street where I had gone for a drink with Ayman.

I didn't know Şerif well. I had met him in London after he took my bedroom in my old house, and we had hung out maybe twice before he moved back to Turkey. As we rode the subway and chatted, he seemed to open up, as if he was starting to see me more as a friend than the journalists he was tired of talking to. He explained that by day, he was a video editor, but by night he moonlighted as a YouTuber, making videos about campy feuds between Turkish celebrities. In his spare time, he volunteered at the LGBTI phone line, because he used to call it for advice when he was a teenager, and wanted to give something back.

Şerif had lived in London for six years as a film student, moving back to Istanbul in 2015, just before the coup d'état attempt in 2016, launched by a military faction to topple the government. When it happened, Şerif was working for a Turkish media company, and although he wasn't in the office at the time, the building was stormed by the soldiers who were trying to seize power from the AKP. The coup ultimately failed, and Erdoğan's grip on the country tightened as he threw a reported 70,000 perceived traitors in jail. A little while after the attempted coup, Şerif quit his job, frustrated with how the publication had caved in to state censorship. Now, he was feeling even more disillusioned with Turkish politics. As a gay man, he had everything he'd had in London: nightlife, a community, two boys on the go at once. But he was deeply concerned about the rise of state-sanctioned homophobia, which was, he said, one of the reasons he'd offered up his time to be my guide, and to get me drunk.

When we arrived at Mis Sokak, the street was packed, which I wasn't expecting, partly because I'd seen in the news that alcohol prices in Turkey had risen sharply under taxes imposed by the AKP, and partly because I wasn't sure that club culture in the city would have recovered after the terror attack on the Reina nightclub down by the water,

where an ISIS gunman killed thirty-nine people on New
Year's Day 2017.

Şerif led me through a dark doorway, and up three
flights of grimy and graffitied stairs vibrating with bass.
We walked into what looked like the living room of a
house, with wooden floors and stripped concrete walls,
and ordered beers from the bar in a side room. The music
was a blend of house and techno with Arabesque music
mixed in. The clientele were gay men, trans women and
lesbians; seemingly it was a small community because
everybody was talking to one another. The room was full
of cigarette smoke, making it hard to see properly. If Jeffrey
were here, he would approve: the bar was secluded, in no
way commercial; it felt non-conformist, non-judgemental
– all a result, perhaps, of the fact that the scene here was
forced underground. We danced, with cigarettes hanging
out of our mouths, always a novelty when you're from a
country where smoking indoors is banned. At one point,
the trans woman who ran the place came up to Şerif and
told him she fancied me, but by the time he had come over
to tell me and pointed her out, which took about forty-five
seconds, she was already making out with someone else.

'Seriously?' I joked to Şerif. 'This whole journey to meet
queer people and the first person to fancy me does so for
less than one minute.'

Privately, I wished Emily was there with me, not stuck
working late nights at her law firm. After our takeaways
and sex-heavy honeymoon period had ended, we had fallen
into a nice habit of going out to gay bars together, and it
was as though I had finally realized you can actually go

gay clubbing with your partner, their friends and your friends and have a good time in the process. What had taken me so long to reach this conclusion, I wasn't sure.

At some point in the early hours, Şerif introduced me to his gay friend Kerim and we sat on the pulsating stairwell that ran through the middle of the building, blocking everyone trying to get to the toilets and talking at speed. A little drunk, and a little more forthright, Şerif seemed more concerned about the situation in Istanbul now. They told me that PrEP, the HIV-prevention drug, had just made its way to Turkey, but it was still hard to get it. They told me that Grindr had been banned by the government in 2013, so now they all used an app called Hornet. They told me that a queer film screening in the district of Beyoglu had recently been cancelled by local authorities, following bans on any LGBTI event at all in the city of Ankara.

'They banned Pride. There are hate crimes. The Islamic media publish homophobic things,' said Kerim.

'The conservative media have chosen us as a target, "perverts are doing this and that",' added Şerif. 'They always print photos, too. Some guys I know went to the Lady Gaga concert in drag, and ever since that summer the same photo has been constantly used by conservative newspapers in every article where they mention perverts.'

'CNN maybe five years ago can be doing news about LGBTI community . . .' Kerim chipped in.

'Before the coup many influential public figures of the LGBTI community could go on TV and talk about the rights we're seeking and what is needed for the community

– but right now we don't exist in the mainstream media, just small online news portals.'

'And you don't exist on the street at Pride now either, just in places like this?' I said.

They nodded. I wanted to know more but I also wanted to dance, so we agreed to meet at Şerif's house the next day.

Şerif lived on the Asian side of the city. To get there from the European side I had to take a ferry across the Bosporus Strait, which cost about £1 and was the kind of thing I'd want to do as a tourist anyway, for the panoramic views of the city, its mosques silhouetted against the sunset.

When I arrived at the apartment, the guys sat round a table smoking out of the living room window. J-Lo videos played on a laptop in the corner of the room and a tiny kitten rolled around on the carpet. Kerim was sitting at the table waiting for me. He was a big guy, but not tall. He wore a white, faded T-shirt with a bunch of flowers on the front and the words 'Late Bloomer'.

Kerim told me he generally identified as gay – he was attracted to men. He was twenty-two years old and an architecture student, originally from the north of Turkey, near the Black Sea. Since he'd moved to Istanbul, he'd started doing drag on the side. I told him, no offence, but I couldn't go anywhere these days without meeting a drag queen. He assured me that he hadn't seen *RuPaul's Drag Race* when he started.

'How did you start then?' I asked.

He turned to Şerif, who would translate. He told him

– us – that when he was in middle school, aged about thirteen to fourteen, his paternal aunt was a state teacher. At the time, it was illegal under Erdoğan's then secular vision of Turkey to wear a headscarf in state buildings (in fact, this was banned from 1923 till 2013), and so she would hide her headscarf under a wig. It was these wigs that Kerim first used to play dress-up, sometimes adding lipstick for an extra-special look.

'What did your dad make of that?' I said.

'He slap me,' he said in broken English. 'After that I didn't show him.'

Şerif explained that Kerim had since picked up drag again, performing in Istanbul at events like 'Istanbul Is Burning', a play on *Paris Is Burning*, and that Kerim had caused quite the stir when he performed in the final, beaten only by a drag queen who had the audacity to set fire to her own outfit while she was wearing it on stage. I gasped to acknowledge the scandal.

'I know. It was so fucking insane – we were scared the stage was gonna burn,' said Şerif.

'Yeah, and after that the stage was so wet I couldn't walk or dance. She fucked my performance up,' added Kerim, as though he were talking about the film *Showgirls*.

'She couldn't win the contest but she made a huge impact,' said Şerif of Kerim, switching pronouns to 'she' to denote that Kerim was in drag.

'Do you perform to English songs or Turkish songs?' I asked.

'I prefer Turkish songs but just one song we were choosing and the other song the jury chooses, so one song was Turkish; the other was "Fergalicious",' he said. 'You know, when you are drag queen they love you on the scene but on the street no. I can make a fuck buddy with this attire, for example,' continued Kerim, gesticulating at his white T-shirt and jeans, 'but in drag no. It's like a no-femme thing.'

This reminded me of what MJ had told me about femme-phobia in drag, and what Seyhan had said about the hypocrisy that trans women face.

'I know it exists everywhere but I feel there is a strong masc culture in Turkey,' I said.

'The same situation exists in all of Europe, going gym and being muscle gay,' said Kerim, agreeing. 'Actually I am drag queen and a bear – it is about being masculine. Being a drag queen and normal gay life are very different for me. Maybe if I'm skinny it can be different but when I'm bear I can't be drag queen with my fuck buddies. It's hard for me. Maybe if I can be normal gay, muscle gay, maybe I can meet with someone like a drag queen.'

'These categories they have for gay men . . . they're ridiculous.' I sympathized but couldn't empathize; I supposed other than 'butch' and 'femme', such strict cat-egories didn't seem to exist for lesbians. I turned to Şerif: 'What are you?'

'When I lived in the UK I thought I was a bear but then I got here and was like, OK, I'm a cub.' We laughed. He called to his non-boyfriend, who was wandering around the flat somewhere. 'You're a twink!'

'He's an otter,' I said.

'You know some things about gay men!' Kerim said, smiling.

'All my friends are gay men, I have to listen to this shit all the time.'

'I have not been in other countries, I've just been in Turkey,' said Kerim, 'but in Turkey the bear culture really is too much. A lot of people like bear and a lot of bear living here.' I loved how, with his sincerity and his wobbly English, it sounded as if he was narrating a nature programme. 'In Europe it's different: they don't like bears as much as Turkey.' Before I got a chance to clarify why this was, Kerim continued: 'But I don't sleep with Turkish guys, I sleep with Middle Eastern guys . . . they like me because I'm blond and blue eyes.'

'They fall in love with Kerim all the time,' Şerif confirmed.

'I have a lot of lovers from Dubai, Beirut, Saudi, Kuwait . . .'

'This reminds me of the period when I was sleeping with an Israeli girl, a Danish girl and a Swedish girl,' I said. 'It was like a UN summit in my pants.'

'Actually, they're coming here for sex tourism. In Istanbul we have Bear Festival.'

'He went,' said Şerif, pre-empting my question. I had already somehow found myself on the Istanbul Bear Festival Instagram account, which was full of pictures of big hairy guys on a boat.

'Of course he went – he *is* the Bear Festival,' I said. Kerim seemed to like this.

'I went with my ex-boyfriend,' said Kerim.

Şerif started laughing. 'You're always married to someone.'

'Yeah, that's what I like! But when he was in the toilet

a lot of Middle Eastern guys came up to me . . . I love it.'

'Why Middle Eastern guys? Is it the novelty of doing something naughty?' I asked.

Kerim also started laughing hysterically. 'Maybe the first time, but now I'm used to it.'

Kerim started to tell me the story of his coming out. He didn't come out to his parents; he was 'outed' by his sister. When he went home from university in the holidays, his sister opened his phone while he was sleeping and saw messages from his boyfriend. A huge fight ensued. Kerim lost. His siblings sent him to see a conversion therapist in Istanbul, just as Ayman's parents had.

'We talked about my family. How, when I was child my father was old . . . my first big sister is thirty-eight now and has three children. My father retired, they opened some shops, and my sister was managing that. My father was not working; he was drinking raki every night and actually I didn't see him, just Sunday morning and next Sunday morning, until I was sixteen. My therapist told me, "You are gay because you didn't see your father and you saw your sister taking money for your family. You don't know how you can be a man because you don't have a male role model." Then he told me, "You're gay because you're fat and your friends didn't take you to play football, so you were playing with girls." Then he told me, "You are gay because you were jealous of boys and it changed and then you were loving boys." Then he told me I'm jerking off too much.'

'Wow.' We all laughed.

'He told me I'm a narcissist,' Kerim continued, pleased to be entertaining everyone.

'Aren't all drag queens?' I replied.

'And the next time he told me I'm a hysteric,' Kerim chuckled.

'This guy needs a new textbook,' tutted Şerif, stubbing out his cigarette.

Kerim 'broke up' with the therapist after three months, promising his siblings he could fix himself. On the one hand, he said, the therapy was helpful, because for a while the therapist told Kerim's family that he would take care of it; they should leave him alone and not talk to him about his homosexuality. On the other hand, the therapist's questions caused Kerim a lot of mental anguish. Plus, while he was going through it, his sisters told his parents he was gay, and for a whole summer he felt pressured to act as if he was straight, in a concerted effort to become so.

'How is it now?' I asked.

'My sisters told my parents, "He is going to gay clubs – if he doesn't have money he will not be gay!"' He laughed. 'So three years later still they will not give me money. Three years later they're calling me saying, "Do you have a girl-friend?" At first it was hard but now I don't feel anything towards them, my parents. My sisters say, "I know you can't change but to be gay it is too much wrong in our Islam, so please don't do that. You don't have to marry a girl or make a child with girl. Just don't have sex with males. Don't say you are gay in public. If you share that then people will say something about our family."'

'Because it's a sin,' Şerif chimed in, although I had understood this.

Kerim then explained that, just as things were getting a tiny bit better with his parents, they found out he was a drag queen, which made everything a whole load worse. Some kids he'd been to school with had found pictures of him in drag on social media; they set up a WhatsApp group to share them and gossip about it. Someone showed someone else, who showed Kerim's sister, who showed his uncle, who showed his parents. They didn't even confront him at first, he said; they just fought about it among themselves. Until a week earlier, when he'd got the phone call. He seemed visibly upset for the first time in our interview while telling me this.

'It takes time, you know. It's a process of attrition,' I said.

'I think in time they will change. Maybe they will, maybe they will not,' said Kerim hopelessly.

'Were your parents very religious?' I asked.

'Yeah, too much. Really. Every day that I talk to my mum she tells me to read the Quran.'

'And were you religious as a kid?'

'Actually I was, but when I was thirteen I read letter to my counsellor at school saying I'm not Muslim, I'm an atheist, and he invited my parents to the school. They were annoyed so they sent me to Quran school for the summer.'

'If you have religious parents, traditionally you will go to Quran school during summer break,' explained Şerif for context, 'but before that they used to send him to boating or swimming courses, so it was a change.'

'I went there and fucked with boys,' said Kerim casually.

'I stayed one and a half months. It's like seven floors and three floors in the basement, and the third floor in the basement they have a hammam – you should go in the morning at 6 a.m. when you wake up and then you go to pray blah blah, but we were escaping praying and going to hammam and having sex. The first day there were two people; the last day ten.'

I was shocked by this information. 'What, full sex?'

'Yeah, weren't you just jerking each other off?' said Şerif, who had obviously heard the story before.

'No, some jerking off, others oral sex, one full sex too,' said Kerim proudly.

'Were you thirteen?' I asked.

'No, no, I was older. This was my second Quran course,' said Kerim. 'The first summer at Quran school we were touching each other with clothes on. The second time I went we did a lot of sex. It was good!'

'Wow, I wish the convent school I went to was more like that,' I said.

'He was studying at an Islamic school for middle school, and the imam's son was at the same school and they were fooling around for seven years,' Şerif said.

'Yeah, some days he is still writing me: "Where are you?"'

'Is he out?' I asked.

'No! And I don't write him back now because he's not my type.'

'Well, I suppose now you're in Istanbul you have more choice.'

'Yeah – too much!' said Kerim. 'You can go to Tek Yön, this gay bar. When I go there first time I think, wow! I couldn't believe how many guys in Istanbul. This is too much! Too much.'

'Well, you don't have to fuck them all at once,' I replied.

Before I left Şerif's apartment I had to wash my face because I had had a huge allergy attack from the kitten. I splashed my eyes and looked into the mirror. They were bloodshot. Şerif and Kerim came to the door of the bathroom to ask if I was OK. I thanked them and asked when I'd see them next. They told me about a gay party the next day, and a drag event at the weekend, and asked if I wanted to come.

'There are so many drag events here!' I said, my eyes burning.

'You know, it is very common for the rich conservative people in Turkey to go to dinners where drag queens are performing,' said Şerif.

'Ironically, in a way, I feel like this is the gayest country I've ever been to,' I said.

Kerim said something in Turkish. 'What did he say?' I asked Şerif.

'He said when the government falls we will be the gay capital of the world!'

I laughed for what felt like the hundredth time since I'd got there, said goodbye and left. I walked back to the ferry thinking about how much these guys reminded me of my friends back home. You could swap out the situation, the political climate, the level of rights, but when it came down to it, there was usually a shared sense of humour, and almost always a mutual sense of understanding. What I loved about them was that I felt they were – as Jeffrey had made me see it – doing gay, rather than simply being gay. Their sexual identity was a big part of who they were, they craved queer spaces, and, well, then there was the sex . . . and the talking about it, too.

At first, it had made me feel uncomfortable when Kerim described straight people as 'normal' but then I began to realize that he was saying it without contempt, without shame. He was simply stating the facts, and the fact was, in Turkey, under Islam, to be straight was 'normal', and to be anything other than this came with great challenges. It made me wonder about Turkey's potential, about what would happen if the government did fall. It made me wonder how many LGBTI people had discovered themselves after leaving Syria. If half of 18–24-year-olds in Britain said they were something other than straight, and 48 per cent of Gen Z in America, how many LGBTI people were hiding in Turkey? In other parts of the Middle East? In the world? How many more of us were waiting to come out, once we felt that we actually could?

chapter eight

A QUEER UTOPIA?

They say you never really 'come out' because it's a continuous process. Every time you find yourself in a new situation, with new people who assume that straight or cisgender is the default setting, you have to go through the rigmarole of coming out again. Each occasion comes with a new, unspoken requirement to push against the 'norm'. For some people, whose bodies are perceived as queer or genderqueer, there's a risk attached: you might not have control over your ability to come out, or over other people's reactions. For others, whose bodies are not, there can be a quiet pressure to say something. To 'own up'.

It was in Turkey that I had most starkly been reminded of this. It was the place that I had visited where there was the least scope to deviate from what was thought of as acceptable within the heteronormative or patriarchal culture, and the friends I had met and the stories they had told me reminded me of the weight that is placed on the coming out process, the schism between life 'in the closet' and outside it. Members of Tea and Talk had been rejected by their families for being LGBTQ+ and travelled to

Istanbul, where they hoped they could live more openly.
And yet, many of them were still closeted when they got
there, forced to hide the fact that they were gay or transgender for fear of contempt, violence, or even death.

Talking to Ayman had made me think about my own
coming out story for the first time in a while. Mostly, about
how good I had it, comparatively. I came out youngish, at
nineteen. After having feelings for the girl at college, it was
becoming more apparent to me that a same-sex relationship
was something I was going to explore. I moved back to
London and basically fell in love with the first out lesbian
I met (which isn't to diminish how great she was – I was
just really, really keen). In the beginning, we hooked up in
secret, in one another's bedrooms, and acted like friends
in public. A few weeks later, we were making out in a
toilet cubicle at a nightclub and looked up to see a couple
of our friends peering over the door. We had been caught,
but their reactions were much kinder than I had expected
– which was maybe what emboldened me to take my new
girlfriend home to my mum's house. There, I introduced
her as my 'friend', but it took my mum less than twenty-
four hours to work out we were more than that. Her
reaction was probably the most relaxed she's ever been
about anything (although she has, ironically, insisted on
calling my girlfriends my 'friends' for the decade since).
Eventually, I told my dad that I wasn't straight, and he
took a little longer to come to terms with my sexuality.
To be honest, I don't think he fully understood it until I
got a girlfriend that he fancied too.

Coming out, for me, was like ripping off a plaster:

painful, but after a while the sting began to fade. And in all my privilege, I didn't always have to tell everyone about my sexuality or how I felt about my gender. I could move through the world like a straight person, relatively accepted by my friends and family, free from violence. And yet, for some reason – perhaps because of this privilege – I gradually chose to tell more and more people about this part of my identity: bisexual, lesbian, fluid, whatever I was (and it changed almost daily at that time). As I approached my twenties, I felt compelled to make it a big part of my life, writing about it for a living, or consuming queer art and films and books. I surrounded myself with gay boys, trans people and other queer women. I searched for a community, and because I lived in London, it was there to be discovered.

My acceleration from 0–60, from not-gay to super-gay, didn't go unnoticed by the people around me. As well as confusing the boys I'd slept with in my teenage years, my decision to immerse myself in queer culture confused a lot of the girls I started to go out with. To them, my behaviour was odd; why did I need to pathologize my sexual identity when no one else was seeing me in that light? Weren't we in a time and place where I could live as an LGBTQ+ person without it having to mark me out as different? Or, as my mum would later put it: 'Why don't you write about something else? You sound like a broken record.'

Some of the people in my life interpreted it as an absence I was trying to fill with a kind of wider political purpose: that as a white, middle-class female whose homosexuality hadn't caused me any major problems, I just wanted a marginal identity group to belong to, a classic by-product of the age of identity politics. Others wondered if it spoke to an insecurity about being gay, that a sense of community somehow legitimized my sexuality. Or was it a self-defence mechanism: a kind of 'I'll call myself gay before you can'? Maybe it was a bit of all these things. But now that I thought about it again after Turkey, I suddenly found I had a much more straightforward answer: my journey had reminded me that I'm in love with it, all of it. The challenging, the questioning, the universal truths that make me feel that we're all bigger than our own queer experience, interconnected somehow. My journey had thrown the differences into sharp contrast – like those between Ayman's coming out story and my own – but it had also given me the opportunity to think about what we have in common as queer people, what our shared goals are, what we are collectively striving towards. And on this we seemed to be able to agree: we wanted to be rid of shame and stigma, we wanted our rights enshrined in the law to protect us, and the freedom to express ourselves as we wish. But most crucially of all, perhaps, it seemed to me that fighting for all of these things was, in and of itself, what made us queer.

This idea is not new; it's been there since the very beginning in queer studies, the notion of queerness as something to enact or work towards, rather than an achievable end point or a fixed category. The academic Eve Kosofsky Sedgwick described queerness as 'the open mesh of possibilities'. The academic Judith Butler argued that we produce queerness as we go along, acting it into being. And another,

José Esteban Muñoz, even developed it into a utopian vision of the future: 'Queerness is not here yet,' he wrote. 'Queerness is an ideality. Put another way, we are not yet queer.' Muñoz described it as 'the warm illumination of a horizon imbued with potentiality', and equated it with looking through an open window. By looking out of the window, we're supposed to be dreaming of something better – a world where no one is oppressed along the lines of gender, sexuality, race or ability, a world beyond binaries, beyond the idea that we're either male or female, straight or gay, monogamous or polyamorous. A place to be free. A utopia.

After Turkey, I also found myself thinking about where to end my journey. I knew utopia wasn't a real place, but I thought I might as well try and get close. I wanted to go somewhere progressive, somewhere that set the bar high.

For a while, I thought about going back to Iceland. Maybe in the process, it would give me some more closure. Emily even told me that, if that was what I wanted to do, I should do it, that she'd support me – even come with, if I wanted her to. But I concluded that I just couldn't face it. I hoped I'd meet Salka again some day, and I hoped she was happy, but when we talked, for every minute we spent on the phone it became more apparent that what had happened was best left as a happy story with a sad ending. I missed her, and maybe she missed me, but there was nothing we could do about it – bar forging some painful, long-distance friendship – and I didn't need to return to Iceland and exacerbate my nostalgic tendencies.

Instead, I chose to visit somewhere else with a good standard of LGBTQ+ rights, somewhere forward-thinking, somewhere that people were living their life outside of the binary. I chose to go to Sweden because I wanted to climb those higher steps of Seyhan's staircase, to see what it was like up there.

'Sweden is a chicken-shit country.'

'Oh,' I said, slightly disappointed. 'What do you mean by "chicken shit" exactly?'

I was sitting with Timimie Märak, poly, non-binary and queer, a spoken word poet and LGBTQ+ activist. Timimie was also Sami – Sami people being the indigenous population of northern Sweden.

'Sweden wants to look good to other countries but Sweden is a joke,' Timimie continued. 'We who are moving about in Sweden, we have so many privileges, we do, but it is chicken shit.' Timimie railed on: 'They say we haven't had war in two hundred years, but they are selling arms to other countries. They say we are open with sexuality because we have cis white gay males running Pride, then people who are against same-sex marriage and abortion are walking in the Pride parade. They say we are open borders but you still shit upon the Samis. I can't remember the term in English . . . what do you call it when you are changing to what your friends are doing?'

'Fickle? A fair-weather friend?'

'Yes. Sweden is like that.'

Timimie and I were sitting in an anarchist cafe called Kafé 44 in Sodermalm, one of the central islands that make up Stockholm. The cafe was covered in graffiti, animal rights posters and ACAB – 'all cops are bastards' – stickers. Timimie ate a vegan burger while holding forth in a huge, red (fake) fur coat, spread out across the sofa like a cat. At one point, I enquired about the tattoo on their face, a small line drawing, almond-shaped, just beneath the eye. Timimie proudly explained that it was a vagina, and although not immediately obvious, once this had been pointed out I couldn't unsee it.

Timimie was a friend of my ex-girlfriend, Madde (yes, another one), who was one of the reasons I had decided to come to Sweden. Not only because I could stay at Madde's house, but also because her lifestyle had gone a long way in shaping my view of what life for queer people in Sweden could look like. To put it plainly: nothing made me feel as vanilla as hearing about Madde's sex life, which comprised polyamorous relationships and a dedicated immersion in the Stockholm kink scene. Madde, for the moment, self-described as a 'relationship anarchist', which for her meant that she didn't subscribe to preconceived rules about relationships or monogamy, just making it up as she went along instead. As for her interest in fetishes, she once sent me a picture of an S&M torture chair that looked like something out of the *Saw* films. And a few weeks before I visited, she told me she had attended a BDSM-themed adult baptism, in a church, where everyone wore kink gear.

Sweden was somewhere that I had always perceived to be on the front line of a sex and gender revolution, but it wasn't just Madde and her friends that gave me this impression. Sweden was famously an early adopter of LGBTQ+ rights, with same-sex sexual activity legalized in 1944 and the age of consent (fifteen) made equal in 1972. Sweden was also the first country in the world, in 1972, to allow transgender people to change their legal gender after gender confirmation surgery – all relatively ahead of the curve in comparison to other countries.

Since the 1960s, Sweden has had the word *hen*, a gender-neutral pronoun that you can use when you don't want to assume someone's gender, which is now widely used in the media, socially, and in legal documents. It has become a way to make language not just less sexist, but also less violent towards trans people. To say 'I'm a hen' is to say 'today I don't have a gender'. And then there is the law that has been in place since 1998 to ban teachers from promoting gender stereotypes in kindergartens: no 'boys do this' or 'girls do that', as I was taught at my Catholic convent school, something I had discovered while shooting a documentary about raising kids gender neutral in Sweden a few years earlier. In one of the kindergartens I had visited, Egalia, there was actually no mention of the words 'boy' or 'girl' at all, just 'children' or 'friends'.

In these schools, I watched as they read the kids stories about two male giraffes trying to have a baby together, and two princesses falling in love, years of avoidable gay shame flashing before my eyes. The producers of the documentary had me climbing trees with five-year-olds asking how they identified (something I wasn't wholly comfortable with) but the kids themselves seemed disinterested in labels. When I asked them what they wanted to be when they grew up there was no worry about gendered professions; when I asked them about games there were no conceptions that boys were better at anything than girls. These Swedish institutions were actively pushing against binary under-standings of gender from a young age; the idea being that, if you could raise kids to view gender as fluid or varied, and sexualities as myriad, then maybe you'd have a less sexist and more queer-friendly society.

However, according to Timimie, the gender revolution in Sweden hadn't quite happened yet. Yes, there were a lot of out non-binary people, and there was a lot of visibility around this on the Internet. There were figures like Freja Lindberg, a well-known non-binary trans activist with tens of thousands of Instagram followers, or Timimie, who had their own loyal following. There were a handful of gender-neutral schools like the ones I had seen. And there were gender-neutral toilets in certain galleries and public buildings. But there were few general statistics about how many people were trans or non-binary in Sweden, little understanding of these issues amongst the general popu-lace, and in Timimie's mind, there were only a few hangouts for trans and non-binary people. Perhaps this was the most important point – that these spaces were needed because life for trans and non-binary people was not neces-sarily safe. Timimie even gave me an example: the previous year, they'd run into an ex in a club and got chatting. Timimie told the ex that they were now using gender-neutral pronouns. The conversation grew more heated, until their ex started shouting transphobic abuse, and then attacked Timimie physically. There were several witnesses and the act was caught on camera (cleverly, Swedish bouncers wear security cameras). When the case went to court, the perpetrator was prosecuted, but it was tried as a case where a man punched a woman he had dated for not wanting to have sex with him. 'That's one of the most common statistics today in Sweden, that men who are drunk and want to have sex punch women,' said Timimie, referring to Sweden's domestic violence rates – yet another reason it was not quite utopia. 'But it was not because I'm a woman and it was not because I didn't want to have sex – it was because I'm trans. And there were like seven people who can say it's because I am trans. I won the case in court but in the papers it says the wrong pronouns for me and the way it was prosecuted means that the statistics are still wrong.'

'Right. Because you can't . . . *prove* that you're trans . . .?' I said. Timimie identified as non-binary, so hadn't legally changed their gender because there wasn't yet a third option (although in November 2017, the Swedish government announced that they're considering it).

'Exactly. You don't get killed for being LGBTQ+ in Sweden . . . at least not by the police, but until recently there's no law to say it's a hate crime to punch a trans or non-binary person in the face.'

As Timimie spoke about this angrily, it occurred to me that their case was a lot like those I had discussed with LaLa, in that a lack of recognition of someone's gender, or a disavowal of how they chose to identify, led to their invisibility in the eyes of the law. In some of the most supposedly progressive countries in the world, you still can't legally define your gender yourself unless you've had surgery or gone through a long bureaucratic legal process, and there is no official legal category for non-binary people. This was why Sweden once ranked highly on the list of the world's most LGBTQ+ friendly countries, but has since dropped to tenth place. Sweden, like Britain and the Netherlands, was falling behind in the rankings for LGBTQ+ rights because no matter how progressive you are, there's always somewhere new to keep pushing.

'In the UK some schools are introducing gender-neutral toilets and uniforms, as are institutions, and there is a bill up for debate that would allow people to self-determine their legal gender . . . where are you at with that here?' I asked Timimie.

'What Sweden needs is people being open to form a new movement. The conversations you are talking about – gender-neutral schools and toilets – it's happening very slowly. It's not the politicians pushing for this, it's the activists and the artists doing this.'

'Do you think Sweden has become complacent?'

'A lot of people here are white and live friction-free . . . If you are a white kid in Stockholm, people before them have paved the way for them to come out as non-binary. I'm not saying it's easy, I'm just saying it couldn't happen without all the other stuff before it: Gay Liberation, women's rights, trans rights. In Sweden thirty years ago there were huge demonstrations for equal rights and homosexual rights, and the homosexual men got it better, and then they just disappeared from the front lines and the struggles and left behind all of the queer people, all of the women, all of the non-binary people, all of them.'

'Right,' I said. I gathered that while Timimie probably wasn't solely referring to themself in this last group, they were at least in part. This was, after all, why I had wanted to meet them.

I didn't know a great deal about Sami people, but I knew a bit. Sami territories stretch across to Finland and Norway. A reindeer-herding civilization, their culture is thousands of years old, and they generally lead a secluded life in the snow under the Northern Lights, where temperatures can drop to minus forty-five degrees and brutally cold winters can last as long as eight months. Timimie told me that we can think of Samis as a bit like the European version of Native Americans; there are huge cultural differences, of course, but the struggles that they face are similar, namely colonization from outsiders and the knock-on effects of climate change on their ecosystem. I had anticipated that Timimie would be a little biased about the progressiveness of Sweden, given that the government had a long history of using Sami people and their land to its advantage; mining it, building power plants, polluting waters by using them as waste dumps and then claiming that the Samis were in the way. For more than a hundred years, Sweden had displaced Samis to access iron, coal and oil. Samis, said Timimie, often came out looking like the bad guys; if they protested, then they were denying Swedes power and jobs.

I guessed there weren't many Sami people who were non-binary, and Timimie seemed to confirm this when they later told me that they knew maybe six or seven others (and being the most well-known LGBTQ+ Sami person there was, I thought that they were probably well placed to estimate). What Jeffrey had said was true – we are all minorities of one – but equally, there wasn't much precedence for an identity like Timimie's.

Their story, they told me, started with their mother, who moved down from Sapmi, the area in which Sami people live, when she was fourteen years old. In Jokkmokk, the Sami village where Timimie's family were from, there were around three thousand people, and Timimie's grandfather was the priest, meaning that their mother couldn't get much privacy. She moved to Stockholm in search of the anonymity of a bigger community, and so Timimie was born and raised in the city, mostly, but also in Sapmi. Being of indigenous culture and ethnicity in a big, modern, progressive city like Stockholm came with complications, especially since Samis were often maligned or subjected to racism. There was a pressure for young Sami kids to assimilate into the colonizers' society – to start speaking Swedish. But whenever Timimie went back to Sapmi, it would be the other way around; they had to minimize their queerness. In the reindeer society 'gay is not OK', said Timimie, describing it as a harsh, cis-male, patriarchal society where sexism and transphobia were the norm. While a lot of Swedish queer people decided to step away from their family if their family did not accept them, 'As a Sami kid you can't really do that,' said Timimie, 'because you are your family.' The whole society was built on familial ties. 'Falling between cultures, being taught how to be a Swede but never being Swedish enough, and never being a stereotypical Sami, being queer, being non-binary, being poly, also working with art, it annoys people there a lot. There's a way of being a stereotypical Sami, and when you're not matching that role people get annoyed. But here in Stockholm, being Sami has always been seen as being bad.'

'So it's a sort of lose-lose situation?'

'Yes. You always feel like one or the other has to be more important. Do I want to be Sami and less queer and always be in a fight about that? Or do I want to be queer and always have to explain my Sami part or slowly let it fade away a bit? That can seriously give me anxiety attacks.'

Timimie came out as queer first, then, later, as non-binary. They told me they had always wanted to be a boy, or something like a boy. As a teenager they oscillated between dressing up as a man and loving burlesque: 'All of my life I have felt like I'm doing drag, no matter the way I dress.'

Timimie started to identify as genderqueer in 2015. They joined a performance group at a theatre, and as part of the process of creating the performance they decided to 'decolonize the room and break it down to an almost molecular level'.

'What does that mean, to decolonize a room?' I asked.

Timimie explained that it meant deconstructing the 'norms of the space', be that the language used, or presumptions about other people's backgrounds. Instead, they went around and shared their pronouns regularly, and people could talk in whatever language they felt comfortable with where possible. It wasn't assumed that anyone had money, or wanted to go out drinking after rehearsal, for instance. And they talked about how they could actively drive toxic masculinity out of the space. 'It might sound like I have it more figured out now but this was a process of six months where we tried to create this toxic-masculinity-free room. It was things I've been thinking since I was eleven when I first heard about *SCUM Manifesto*.'

'What kinds of things were you thinking about?' I asked.

'I'd been working in so, so many environments where men take up space. I was and I am a loudmouth and I take up a lot of space and I say what I feel, but for me, massive changes started to happen within me at that time and I began to open my mouth about what was moving inside of me. I started to notice people in my family making jokes and I would say, "That's not funny." I started to see that my biological family was not even a safe space. I was dating another non-binary person at the time, which I realized was not a good relationship at all, and then I met this other person who was a trans guy and we started to talk a lot about this stuff and he was the first one to say my actual name.'

'You mean "Timimie"? Is that a chosen name?'

'Yes, that's a chosen name. He was first to say it and it's weird because even my big sister had been asking me like, "OK, so you're dating a guy who is trans, what is he like naked?" I said: "You can't ask that, that's weird. You're dating a cis man and it's not fair to ask if he's big or not. It's actually quite rude, but if you want to weigh that up for this that's actually an easier conversation because that

is a cis male person. I wouldn't want anyone to ask what
are your tits like when you aren't dressed. It's just rude."
I tried to talk to my mother about it but she said, "You
have to understand that people are wondering," and I was
like, "No, you don't! What would you do if my dad had
conversations about your pussy with his friends?"'

'Wow. What did she say to that?'

'Well, she has a way of being like, "Well, OK, right . . ."
She's very good at acting like she's offended; then she can
come back six months later and been studying everything . . .'

'That's good?'

'Yeah. But it's also a very Sami way, I think: "I don't want
you to rub it in my face that I don't know about this." We
had a conversation about the guy I was dating and how
when he came out as trans to his mum she was like, "I don't
want to have lost my daughter! You'll always be a 'her' to
me!" And he was really upset. I was talking to my mother
about how it's hard for the one giving birth to see a child
and be like, "This is a girl, this is my daughter and your
name is . . ." And twenty years later, someone goes, "Yeah,
OK, no." But what I don't understand is the rage and the
need to push your sorrow onto someone who is already
having a really difficult time coming out as themselves.'

I thought about the rage and the hatred and the lack of
understanding I'd heard about from LaLa. I thought of all
the strangers that go around meddling in other people's
genders; the self-appointed gender police. 'Why do people
get so upset?' I said, thinking out loud. 'About something
that's not even affecting them?'

'Nobody wants to be the stupid one, the one to get it wrong. If you do something to me and I come and be like, "I don't like that," you can be like, "Shit, I messed up, I made this person uncomfortable." But you don't want to be the bad guy. Everybody wants to be the good ally or the underdog . . .'

Timimie seemed to be saying that people were embarrassed, or defensive. I didn't agree; I felt that people just really hated change, or hated seeing something in other people that they weren't free enough to express themselves. But before I could say this, Timimie carried on.

'So anyway, I was talking to my mum about it and she was like, "I would feel weird if my kids were like, I want to be this or want to be that," and I suddenly realized that my whole life she had never realized something about me . . . that I can be a both or a nothing, that sometimes it changes, that sometimes I feel absolutely man and sometimes I don't know. So I said to her, "What about me? That is neither?"' Timimie let this sink in.

'Then what happened?'

'Then we had a long argument about it. She was flipping chairs over and being like, "I have not been giving birth to a *them*," and my whole body was like somebody put claws inside of me.'

'Hmm,' I said. 'It's interesting you say that cause a lot of people think being non-binary is a political stance or, you know, just people trying to be difficult, while you're saying that it's emotional, that it's deeply connected to how you feel . . .'

'*Yes*,' Timimie said, continuing even faster, 'and after

that we didn't speak for like one and a half years, and that messed me up, that privately I didn't have a family to speak to, that I couldn't call my mum up, but also from a Sami perspective where you are your family, having to pretend that everything is fine to the rest of Sapmi, trying to hold yourself together and at the same time do the struggle of, "OK, this is me, I'm trans, I need this." People go, "OK, what does your family think about this?" And I'm like, "I will never be able to talk about this in Sapmi without putting my family name in filth!"'

'I think my parents would find it hard to grasp,' I said, wanting Timimie to feel better.

'Yes, and I think it's the same thing as discussing not having borders at all, or veganism . . . it demands so much of a person. Saying we have gender roles but there's no such thing as gender, saying we shouldn't exploit animals or anyone's body to eat, saying there's no borders because everybody should be able to go and live anywhere: it fucks up people's heads in a way that coming out as homosexual did just ten or twenty years ago. It's not easier to be gay, it's just worse to be more than gay.'

'And to be poly, too, I guess . . .'

'I've tried to be in monogamous situations since I was sixteen and it never worked, not because I am not able to be faithful – although I think that's a weird term because it sounds so religious – but all of the time I was in monogamous relationships people have been cheating and then devastated that I'm not devastated. I'm like, "If being a blacksmith makes you happy, travelling the world or reading books makes you happy, I don't mind as long

as you want to be here and share some time with me."
But if you call me up and say, "I want to be a librarian
and never have time to see you ever," then I would be
sad. It's the lies that get me, not the being with someone
else.'

'Does being non-binary relate to your sexual identity as
poly and queer?'

Timimie finally stopped and thought for a second. 'If
I'm open as a non-binary Sami trans poly weird little shit,
maybe my sister's little kid will grow up and be whoever
they want to be. And be able to sunbathe without a shirt,
without it being a thing. And not have to come out. And
not have to be on the barricades fighting for their everyday
life.'

'You use the terms "trans" and "non-binary" interchange-
ably. How come?'

'I think because, for me personally, I identify with both,
and since I want people to understand what I am saying I
think maybe they will identify with it if I use both words.
I don't want there to be a gap between the two because
both are just people. We will find similarities in our differences.'

'So what are the similarities between trans and non-
binary?'

This time Timimie did not need to pause for thought.
'Seeing beyond what is given to us.'

We left Kafé 44 and walked through the snow to Madde's
apartment, Timimie kindly carrying my bags despite my
insistence otherwise. They told me more about Sapmi,

about the winters, about the traditional dress, about the wooden houses. Back at Madde's house, she and I lay in bed together – I had not specified the sleeping arrangement to Emily, but it didn't feel like a big deal – and talked about my meeting with Timimie. We talked about how they linked the colonization of Sami culture to the colonization of queer culture. How the corporatization of Pride was like going onto Sami land and mining their resources. We wondered aloud whether anything was sacred. Whether, if we ever even got a queer utopia, we'd just ruin it anyway.

Madde suggested one last person for me to meet while I was in Stockholm, so the next day I got on the metro towards where they lived. All I knew was that their name was Zafire, and they had a kid that they raised with two other people. Despite not really knowing any queer parents in my private life or in my professional life until Patty, I had written before about the difficulties same-sex parents face: how expensive the process of conceiving can be, dealing with the assumption from the rest of the world that you're friends and not a couple, and the heart-breaking biological fact that, no matter how in love with your same-sex partner you are, you cannot physically conceive a child together. I had written about individuals who had asked a sibling to donate sperm or eggs to their partner in order to create a baby that was related to them biologically, as Patty and Christina had done. I had written about parents trying to raise their kids gender neutral, be it with unisex clothes and toys or a gender-neutral name and pronouns. But I had never met anybody raising their kids in a queer, genderless, three-parent commune before.

I got off the subway near Zafire's house and found them waiting for me in the station. I realized, as they stood up to greet me wearing incredible red tartan punk trousers, with wavy blue hair and a septum piercing, that my brain immediately tried to place their gender somewhere within the binary. Or maybe it had already done this before I came to meet them, and now it was correcting itself. I wondered how long it would take to decondition myself from doing this entirely, to decolonize the room in my brain. Whether it was even possible.

We made our way to their apartment together, the snow thicker under foot now that we were outside the centre of Stockholm. We chatted – the usual pre-interview preamble. Zafire told me they identified as queer and either anti-gender or non-binary – meaning that they didn't have a gender, or identify with any gender. Pronoun-wise, they used 'Zafire'. 'It's a great name. I'm happy if you can use that as a pronoun,' they said, telling me that otherwise I could use 'they' in English and *hen* in Swedish. For them, *hen* was a way not only to de-gender the language but also to create a de-gendered position as a person. They believed that it had opened up 'non-binary' as a term in Sweden: 'Language is incredibly powerful. When I came out, a little bit more than twenty years ago, I first came out as gay because I didn't know about trans or non-binary.'

'I hear this a lot, that people first come out as gay, then trans or non-binary,' I said, thinking of Paris, and then of

Amrou, respectively, 'and as the language improves, people find even more accurate ways to self-describe.'

We let ourselves into their building, a giant block of apartments in an even more giant complex. They were made of a metallic light blue material and seemed to dissolve into the sky. Zafire told me about their career as an artist and a sex educator. Though they were based in Stockholm they worked all over Sweden and internationally, teaching teenagers and grown-ups with disabilities, or the professionals who worked with them, how to approach intimacy, creating possibilities for people to go on a date, have sex, flirt, or have a relationship. Zafire even made a TV show on the topic that aired on Swedish national television in 2013, hosted by Zafire and students with learning difficulties. The work was all user-led, so for the TV show, for example, they solicited hundreds of questions from students and tried to answer as many as possible: How do you know if someone wants to have sex? Where do I find friends? What do you do on the first date? After the show, they created a free app that could be used by people with special learning needs to access information – they conveyed this information in multiple languages; spoken word, images, photos, films, role plays, anything that could embody the knowledge somehow or make it more accessible than someone just explaining it verbally.

'The other thing I'm doing is more trans-centred sex education, not just "trans inclusive",' said Zafire, pouring me a cup of coffee. 'Sex education is usually very focused on men and women, and in Sweden traditionally very gender separate, and I think this is just strengthening the binary system and reproducing gender roles and sexist stereotypes. So instead of focusing on men and women and trying to be trans inclusive, I would centre on trans and the similarities between everybody, because our bodies are super similar, regardless of what our genitals look like, and whether we obtain them through hormones or surgery, or if it's something we were born with.'

'You could say we're all similar, or you could say each individual is so different, what's the point of splitting everything in two,' I said, thinking of how I had tried to gender Zafire, and why that was always the first thing our brain sought to do.

'Sure. There's a bigger difference sometimes within the same sex. And when you look at the anatomy of how the body works, they look different but they function in a similar way when they are stimulated or aroused. So I'm also developing sex education that focuses on the similarities and does not use a gendered language. We've had mandatory sex education here since the 1950s and yet special schools got their first material that was targeting teenagers and students with disabilities just a few years ago. That was from my TV show. So before then students didn't get sex education, or they got sex education that wasn't accessible because it was some other material not specifically for them, or just created by the teachers at the school, something they thought was suitable. Which is better than nothing but doesn't guarantee a quality.'

'My school didn't teach us about same-sex relationships, but it would have been invaluable if they had,' I said. 'Where did your passion come from? How did you end up in this job?'

'I'm very interested in accessibility as a way to make the world better. I think sexual rights is such an important part of human rights. I work in special schools because I think it's incredibly nasty that a large group of people in Sweden are kept like children even when they grow up and are like grown-ups in so many areas of their lives. The system tries to give them independence and the right to choose for themselves, but when it comes to relationships there is so little service. But it's not me there going, "Hmm, maybe this target group is asking these questions, and maybe this could be a good answer." I haven't guessed anything. I've worked together with them to get the right approach. They're the experts, I'm just someone who can facilitate.'

'And personally – is there anything in your own life?'

'And me . . . like a lot of people who are queer or trans, I've never had sex education that was meant for me or people like me. All the sex education I've learned . . . or how I've learned how to integrate sex into my life, that's something I had to learn by myself. But of course, later on when I found my queer and trans community, it's something we had to learn together.'

'At CRS?'

'Exactly,' said Zafire.

One of the things I had come to discuss with Zafire was the Centre for Radical Sexuality. I'd heard a little from Madde, but asked Zafire to tell me its story. It was a place in Stockholm (a secret location only known to its guests) that Zafire started with their partners Cal and Mina in 2016. They described it as a centre for queer and trans and

non-binary people who want to explore what radical sexuality could be. Occasionally they allowed some straight or
cis people to attend, although that wasn't really who it was
aimed at. The centre was about openness, so they were
open to the idea that only being separatist may not be
radical. Basically, everything was up for discussion.

The work they did in the centre sat at the intersection
between 'sexuality, trans, BDSM and spirituality', Zafire
explained. 'So we try to explore the spiritual side of sex
and the spiritual side of BDSM and the potential that BDSM
could bring to us as queer and trans people. It's a delicious
mix of things. It's a play space, it's a space for workshops
and trying things, and we focus on practice rather than
theory.'

This was the important part, Zafire explained, and the
part that linked back to their other work as a sex educator
for differently abled people. There was a gap in Sweden,
they believed, between theory and practice. 'Sweden has
a reputation of being super gender equal, for example,'
they said. 'Yes, the legislation makes it equal, but when
it comes to the practice of what it looks like we have
the same shitty patriarchy that's everywhere anyway. We
also have one of the most progressive anti-discrimination
laws in the world, but that doesn't mean we don't have
discrimination. To have something in theory and to have
it in practice are not the same thing.' On this point, they
echoed Timimie's sentiment: 'And yet Sweden has a self-
image of being like, "Oh, we're free from racism, from
sexism, it's the world's most equal country," and yeah,

on paper we have laws protecting people, but if they're not used or respected . . .'

The way that the centre approached this gap, then, was not just to talk about sex but to practise it too. They ran workshops on topics like consent, negotiations or impact play, and encouraged people to try these things out through exercises. When I asked for an example of consent, Zafire explained the theory: that it's important to negotiate and make sure that if you have sex with someone, everybody wants to.

'A theory that, unfortunately, a lot of people don't observe,' I said.

'Yeah, like if this should be a given, how come so many women and trans and non-binary people have faced sexual violence? It's not practised. So we ask: "How can we practise it?"'

Zafire explained how an exercise would safely and gently explore where people's limits lay, what their boundaries were, and how you could read someone else's boundaries. Zafire did the same thing in their schools for people with learning difficulties: 'Like, how close can I stand to someone else before it gets too close? That boundary is constantly moving and it depends who it is – if I like them they can stand closer; if I don't know them we need more distance. It's incredibly basic, but one thing is to talk about it and the other is to practise it.'

'Why is this relevant for queer people though?' I asked.

'Queer and trans people have had to define sex for ourselves or use different types of rules or role plays and images to embody sexual energy or desire or horniness. How do I negotiate those boundaries when things might not be super clear to someone else about how I'm feeling or how I want to be touched or what I want people to think when they touch a certain body part? So it's a kind of somatic sex education that we do in the centre.'

'And for my mum, who probably thinks BDSM is the last taboo, why is BDSM relevant?'

'Well, if it is the last taboo we should work with that!' Zafire laughed. 'BDSM can be so many things. It doesn't have to be someone giving someone else pain – although that is a delicious part of BDSM. What is often the most fundamental thing is consent and negotiation, and I think that is the element we can bring into so many other parts of our lives. We can learn tools for communication from BDSM. It's a way to disarm power structures and to heal from all the crazy traumas we get from patriarchy. You can play a scene you've experienced before but the roles are negotiated and the space is safe; you can re-enact something that has possibly been painful or violent and be in charge and secure. For me, BDSM is very therapeutic and those tools it's given me have helped me so much in other parts of my life, in terms of clarity.'

'Can you give me an example?'

'Well, in the family here I think it's easier to communicate about something, or with friends, or at work or whatever, if I'm just able to articulate a need for something. And of course to be able to read other people's boundaries. I'm not saying I would negotiate my whole life and all the people that I meet – it's not a constant negotiation – but I do get really aware of boundaries and how to respect them. You get more sensitive, which is handy for a relationship with anyone.'

'How would one be able to go to a workshop?' I asked. Was I fishing for an invite? Zafire was, admittedly, selling it to me.

'We have a Facebook page and people can approach us on Facebook, but we have to know people and people recommend others that come to us. It's a small place and it's important for us to make it as safe as possible, so it's better to let it grow organically than to advertise it widely.'

'How many people come to CRS?'

'If we use our own space we're usually between ten and fifteen people, but we sometimes do things in other spaces that can take more people. For big events of thirty or thirty-five, we try to find another space.'

'What would that be?'

'Then it would be more like once a year, a big play party where we would invite all the people that joined us during the year. But personally my big interest in the usual space is the intersection between BDSM and spirituality.'

Madde had told me about this, and I had also read about it on the Facebook page, but as a not-very-spiritual and slightly cynical person I had failed to understand it. 'Go on,' I said.

'I do a lot of things on sex magic and on different kinds of sexual meditations. I do a guided meditation called the Queer Breath of the Universe, which is connecting to our ancestry and the queer courage and the queer breath that is made in previous generations and previous species before humans.'

I must have looked puzzled because Zafire put on a patient face and carried on explaining: 'If everybody would have done the same thing all the time evolution wouldn't have happened. So species that do differently could be considered radically queer or non-binary or fluid or questioning. We are the ones who make evolution possible. If beings would have been normative, binary, nothing would have happened.'

'Shit,' I said, Zafire having induced an epiphany.

'Humans wouldn't exist,' continued Zafire casually. 'That shifts the perspective totally, that means we should celebrate that we are trans, non-binary and queer. Because we are creating the future. And if binary gender starts to dissolve, all of us who are already living outside the binary, our experience is incredibly valuable because we have so many tools already. It's like people who live without money, or try to – when capitalism falls, the experience of surviving your life without monetary transactions is extremely valuable. I think it's similar with non-binary people: our experience will be valid for the future of humanity.'

'Can you see that happening . . . gender falling?'

Zafire deliberated for moment. 'Yes, but maybe not in my lifetime. Things are happening. When I guide this meditation and go back to the beginning of time and connect with queer energy that made evolution possible, we also look forward to the future and breathe with the queer existences that will be there in the future. So of course it will happen because I can feel it, even if I might not experience it.'

'I feel like I'd cry if I did your meditation.'

'That's OK,' they smiled. 'Everybody does. I cry too.'

Zafire went to make us more coffee and I looked around their apartment. It was brightly coloured, with flock wallpaper in greens and purples and oranges. Outside, it was starting to snow. What I admired about Madde's friends, I thought, was that they were a community of people who were actively trying to erode the very boundaries that I felt trapped by after my break-up with Salka: heteronormativity and queerness, decorum and freedom, success and failure. In many ways, when I talked to Madde, while I didn't necessarily want to go to a BDSM baptism myself, I felt I wanted to embrace the ideals of the people who did. Which is to say that I always felt I was hearing about a group of people who were living by their desires rather than shaping their desires into arbitrary boxes society had handed them. They were creating new structures that worked for how they felt, not the other way around.

This, as far as I could gather, was what Zafire was doing with their family, and I wanted to know more. 'I would love to know who lives here, how you met them,' I said when Zafire came back.

'I live with three other people: a child that's five years old, called Rio, and then Rio's other two parents, Mina and Cal,' Zafire smiled, visibly lighting up. They told me that Mina was partnered with both them and Cal, and that they had other partners outside this constellation. Mina and Zafire had been partners for maybe seven years, and Mina and Cal had been partners for about fifteen years. They decided to move in together in 2011 and began thinking about having a child, which was something Zafire had wanted for a long time. 'The other two had too, but they'd been partners for a long time, and weren't sure they wanted to be two parents. They weren't sure that they believed in that idea, and they were afraid that that would affect their relationship too much to be just the two of them.'

Because Zafire had experienced trying to create a family and also a family with multiple parents before, they could initiate a discussion on power dynamics, and who should be the legal parents and who should be the biological parents. In Sweden, only two parents can be legally acknowledged. So they discussed openly who had the most power, who could read the other people better, who had the most advantages when it came to their needs and wants and recognition and experience. They decided that, because the person who carried the child would automatically become the legal parent, they would divide it so that one got the other legal position and the other got the biological position; that way, they were all linked to each other and it would be harder for someone to run away with Rio or shut someone else out. 'This is how the legal system would protect us,' Zafire explained, 'but since we don't have a full legal protection we needed to create those hooks on each other ourselves. It's worked incredibly well; all three of us are sex educators, work with communication and finding solutions to things, so we have a very functional family based on evening out the power structures within the family. And a very rational agreement.'

'So how do you divide the responsibility?'

'Since the very beginning we divided the responsibility into three, so Rio was not breastfed, which was a choice that Rio made because Rio didn't want to eat from the breast, so we had a pump and everybody could feed Rio. We also divided up the responsibility so that we would be responsible for one night each, so the other two could sleep a full night without being disturbed, or maybe they would wake up but they could just go back to sleep. We share a household, we are a family together, but we still divide the time between the three of us and other people in the extended family, people who have their own rela- tionship with Rio. We're all here, but we have responsibility every third weekend each, and one or two or three nights a week where Rio would turn to us for wanting or needing something, or there might be slightly different rules, for example, the rules of the person who is in charge, which makes for much fewer conflicts between us.'

'Is it a gender-free household?'

'As much as possible. We use gender-free pronouns for Rio. Whatever Rio wants to define as they can define as that, they can be a shark or a rabbit or a dog. I'm not saying that's the same thing as being trans, but just to make sure that Rio gets acknowledged and respected, it makes them more courageous and more clear. Since about a year and a half, they've picked a non-binary identity, for now. They've said that, "Yes, I want to be a *hen*, not a boy, not a girl." I feel like this is really the choice they've made and they're free to change that whenever. We are all non-binary and *hen* so it's easy because we all have the same pronouns, and "parent", for example, is easy because it's a gender-neutral word already.'

'If Rio chose a binary gender identity how would you feel?'

'Fine, as long as it's their choice. I'm amazed that Rio is so unaffected by gender. I didn't really know that this was possible. In the beginning, when they started to speak, they used "she" for everyone. Now they use *hen*. But it's really important to have a gender pronoun if you're a binary trans person, for example – it's incredibly important to be recognized as the gender you have. This is what made us talk to Rio about gender in the first place, correcting Rio if they say "she" to a trans man, for example. If it was a cis man I don't think it matters as much but it's less nice to say "she" to a trans man.'

I inhaled as I took in everything Zafire was telling me. In that moment I thought about my mum again, and how insane she would find it all – or had found it all, when she'd watched the documentary I made when I was last in Sweden. Admittedly, there were moments when it felt as if the parents in that film were being more forceful about instilling gender neutrality on their children, the kids not ready to break free from gender norms when in their outside lives they were still exposed to them. When the rest of the world is fixed on binary ideas about gender, it can be hard trying to push past this, to be the first, and you could argue that an adult is better equipped to bear the burden of that than a child. But you could also argue that people shouldn't go around telling kids, or anyone for that matter, what colour clothes they can wear, or how they should express themselves, or what name they should use. This was what Zafire's family set-up tried to avoid, but I understood how people could find it challenging, such as – according to Zafire – some of Rio's grandparents.

When I raised this with Zafire, they pointed out that it didn't make total sense because, actually, a lot of parents don't subscribe to gender roles; a lot of people have extra-marital relationships, and a lot of families don't look like your traditional family.

'Restructured families are maybe more common than a nuclear family that sticks together. In Sweden nearly half of marriages end up in divorce, so they would be families that don't look the same as they looked when they were created. It's more common to have a bonus sibling, live with one parent one week and another the next. But the advantage we have being queer and trans and creating our own structures is that we are more prepared for things that nuclear families aren't – they're often not prepared for the restructuring of family life at all . . . if you create a new family with someone then that partner would not have legal rights to the kids unless they are related to them or adopt them, which can make family life difficult on the legal side. And if you fit into the binary monogamous nuclear family constellation there's so many things you haven't negotiated or talked about: How would you deal with conflict or a potential break-up? How can you secure your relationship to the kids? It's not something you talk about because you have a mould already that you're supposed to fit into. Our family is so strong and healthy because we negotiated it rationally, non-romantically, around feminist values and a queer and gender-neutral upbringing. I'm not saying our family will last forever – who knows? – but it's a very safe foundation. And the special thing about us is we planned this from the very beginning, we created this from scratch, and I don't know many families who have done that.'

'I guess you're right. At one point, with step-parents, I had four parents; my parents broke up after I was born and they recoupled with other people. There was animosity between parents at different times, and my stepdad left and I never saw him again after twelve years of living with him, and I think some of my parents are progressive but my mother would baulk at the idea of this three-parent family without realizing I came from a four-parent family, only here everyone gets along. So many families aren't nuclear families any more but they're not doing it in a caring way or a communal way or a queer way . . .' I trailed off, unexpectedly emotional.

Zafire nodded gently. 'I think so many of those families can benefit from realizing how much advantage queer families can have when it comes to negotiations and rational solutions and creating safety outside of boxes we don't fit into. I think we should honour and celebrate queer life and non-binary existence.'

Zafire's attitude – like Meredith's – was that the rest of the world had something to learn from queer people. Zafire believed in the theory and demonstrated in practice that we could queer the institution. And that didn't mean every-one had to live in a queer commune, it meant taking tradition and doing it your own way.

'Final question: What to you is utopia? Would you say you guys are doing your best to create it?' I said.

'I don't think I would call it utopia because it's here, I live it. It's not a dream so I wouldn't call it utopia. We have a queer, gender-free, safe environment that we are parents in. It's nothing that we might have in the future. We have a space where we can explore what is radical in sex, and talk about how we can transform ourselves and our envi-ronment and our future. Even if it's three or five or twenty people. It's possible to do that here and now. The whole world doesn't have to become a queer utopia before we can start.'

I left Zafire's apartment, and trudged through the snow back to the metro station. I rode the train silently to Central Station. I bought myself a hot dog in Pressbyrån, the Swedish alternative to 7-Eleven, and sat on a bench inside the station.

Emily called me on FaceTime Audio.

'How was it?'

I told her about Zafire and Rio and the queer sex magic workshop.

'Do you think I should go?' I said. 'It's in three weeks. Would that be weird?'

'Well, you can go if you want but I don't think you'll like it. You're not very spiritual and you always describe sex parties as organized fun.'

She was right. 'You're right,' I said, thinking about how

there wasn't much point taking up space at things where you weren't going to contribute anything anyway.

'So are Cal and Zafire in a sexual or romantic relationship, or are they each just in one with Mina?' she asked.

'Oh, I forgot to specifically ask,' I said. Emily would always ask me a really obvious question right after an interview that I forgot to ask during the interview. 'I don't suppose it matters,' I said, quite chuffed with how liberal I sounded.

'Did you like the three-parent family thing?' she asked.

'I did. And I think, if we decide to have a baby, we should have three or four parents, because then we have more free childcare and could go on holiday more often.'

'Agreed. I'll start asking around,' she said.

Then I told her what Zafire had said about utopia, how you didn't have to wait for it, that you could build it yourself. As I spoke, it dawned on me that this was what we were best at as queer people, this world-making, and that everyone I'd met had – in their own way – created their own utopia in the now; for Patty, it was her family; for Jeffrey, it was in a nightclub basement; for Hans, it was his Pride Walk; for Kia, the ballroom; and for Ayman and his friends, it was the four walls of Tea and Talk. To me, the fact that there were so many versions of utopia probably spoke to the moment we were in – a moment we had fought for ourselves – when life for many LGBTQ+ people was starting to have a new potential: the potential to look like whatever you wanted it to.

I had recognized this moment at the beginning of my journey, and I had wondered if it was as good as it was cracked up to be, whether this unprecedented acceptance of LGBTQ+ people and everything that came with it – from same-sex marriage to drag TV shows to 'queer' Instagram filters and stickers – was necessarily a progressive thing. After everywhere I had been, it was clear that there was no easy answer to this question: to some people, our assimilation into straight culture was just another form of oppression or cultural dominance; to others it was the long-awaited prize for years of political fighting.

In truth, I saw both sides of the argument, but I knew, more firmly than ever before, that acceptance would homogenize us. What I had seen was more options, more multiplicity, more ways of being. Our myriad genders and sexualities were nothing new, of course, but now, instead of denying their existence, we were finally giving them words, allowing them to be, educating about them, and as a consequence, we no longer lived in such a binary, hetero-normative world. We were evolving out of one, and as Zafire would have it, queer people were leading the charge.

But what would come next? What would become of the places further down on Seyhan's staircase, or the fights happening outside the mainstream, the new frontiers, the smaller minorities, where fewer people were at the protests or the Prides? How would we react when progress didn't always move in a straight line? What would we collectively decide to do about it?

These questions seemed as important as whether assimilation was good or bad for us. Because if the outcome of improved LGBTQ+ rights was that not all of us had to be fighting any more, I had also witnessed the catch; and it was that our work would never be done. That we could have our freedom and our rights and equality on paper, but we would still carry shame, trauma and internalized hatred, as long as we were still taught that there are right and wrong ways to be, or that some LGBTQ+ people are more worthy of acceptance than others.

As far as I was concerned, equality hadn't arrived until it arrived for everyone.

On the flight home from Stockholm – a much more pleasant easyJet flight – I considered where I'd been personally at the start of my journey, how I didn't feel queer and I didn't feel *not queer*; why I had been able to come out to the world comfortably, but it didn't necessarily follow that I was comfortable with myself; why my lifestyle, my politics and my desires were caught within a binary. I suppose I had felt confused about what the LGBTQ+ people before me had been fighting for: our right to be the same as everyone else, or to be different. Now, I realized, it was both, it was the ability to choose.

Relationship-wise, I had ended up in one that wasn't a million miles away from the relationships that Madde and her friends had – self-constructed, on their own terms. Emily and I had committed to each other, and despite the family difficulties, we had built our own family, with its own language, formulation and ever-shifting parameters. We negotiated everything, constantly: children, monogamy, being together. It felt like there was no power imbalance, no immovable set of rules. Her trust, the fact that she never grilled me about what I was doing, meant that it didn't feel as if there were any strict boundaries to step over. No matter how heteronormative the choices we made in the future might be, something about that felt quite radical.

But ultimately, being in a relationship wasn't the point; whether or not it worked out, I no longer viewed the rest of my life as two paths set before me. I had seen enough to know that there wasn't one version of success or failure. Throughout my journey I had experienced a weight – a literal weight – lifting, as I came to understand that we don't have to be one thing or the other, but can be many things at once.

ACKNOWLEDGEMENTS

Thank you to my agent, friend and life coach, Emma Paterson, and my editor Kris Doyle at Picador, as well as everyone else at Picador who lent their expertise, particularly Grace Harrison. Thanks to Emily, Natasha Bloor and Bryony White for being my first readers, and so generous with your time.

To Sarah Raphael, Kate Ward, Christene Barberich and Gillian Orr at *Refinery29* for your support and mentorship. To the editors at *Vice* who taught me so much when I started, and later, Nosheen Iqbal at the *Guardian*, Hanna Hanra at *i-D*, Sam Wolfson at *Vice* and Alice Casely-Hayford at *Vogue* for the work that allowed me to support myself while writing this. Plus my colleagues at *Dazed* and *Dazed Beauty* who have been very encouraging and understanding.

I'd like to thank everyone who let me sleep on their sofa or in their spare room after Iceland – Tessa, Kirsty, Ella, Kate and big sis Hannah Philp – and when I was writing and researching this book: mad aunts Debbie and Joanne, and Alix, Lottie, Madde and Patrick – I owe you.

Also, a huge thanks to my unofficial fixers; Masa Milutinovic and Jovana Netković from *Vice Serbia*, and

Cathy Renna in New York. In Turkey, Louise Callaghan (I'd never tell you to your face but I'm in awe of you), as well as the incredibly kind and brilliant Ekim Açun.

To Gays Aloud for teaching me how to be gay: Zara Toppin, Zoe Marden, Samuel Douek, Bryony Stone, Hannah Hopkins, Luke Ferris, Fiontan Moran and Rafaela De Ascanio Hughes. Then, of course, to my loves Tom Rasmussen and Amrou Al-Kadhi. I'm so proud of both of you (and highly recommend your books to anyone reading this). And to the divine goddess Paris Lees, for always giving great advice, whether or not I asked for it!

It also feels important here to thank Professor John Howard, who first taught me what queer studies was and who has remained a dear friend, Amin Ghaziani for your kindness and for informing the way that I think about things, and Michael Warner, Sarah Schulman and Jack Halberstam for your work, which has been a massive influence.

I'd like to thank Claire, Lyss, Fiona, Lottie, Jenna, Nat, Sara, Poppy and Trew for your support over the years, and Sasha, Penny and Alice. Plus, of course, my family: my father Steve Abraham, my mother Martine, my stepmother Tessa, and my brother and sister, the lovely Harry and Stella.

And finally, I'd like to thank everyone in the book for sharing their stories.

The original 'Lady Marmalade' was written in 1974 by duo Bob Crewe and Kenny Nolan. The lyrics quoted on page 146 are from the 2001 cover version, recorded for the soundtrack of Baz Luhrmann's *Moulin Rouge!*, by Christina Aguilera, Lil' Kim, Mýa, and Pink, and produced by Missy Elliott and writing partner Rockwilder. The lyrics from 'Vogue' quoted on page 230 were written by Madonna Ciccone and Shep Pettibone.

Some small sections of this book appear courtesy of *Refinery29 UK* and *Vice UK*, where they were first published; my thanks to them both.